IBM® LinkWay™

Hypermedia for the PC

Richard Harrington
Bill Fancher
Peter Black

John Wiley & Sons, Inc.

New York Chichester Brisbane Toronto Singapore

Editor: Therese A. Zak
Managing Editor: Frank Grazioli
Design, Editing, and Production: Impressions Publishing Services, Inc.

Library of Congress Caraloging-in-Publication Data

Harrington, Richard, 1965-
IBM LinkWay : hypermedia for the PC / Richard Harrington, Bill Fancher, Peter Black.
p. cm.
Includes bibliographical references.
ISBN 0-471-51298-2
1. Hypertext systems. 2. IBM LinkWay (Computer program) 3. IBM Personal Computer—Programming. I. Fancher, Bill. II. Black, Peter, 1951- . III. Title.
QA76.76.H94H37 1990
005.75—dc20 89-28874
CIP

Printed in the United States of America

90 91 10 9 8 7 6 5 4 3 2 1

CONTENTS

PREFACE

IBM LinkWay is a software package available from IBM. You can purchase the full IBM LinkWay authoring package. A runtime version of IBM LinkWay is available for free by calling 1-800-627-0920. You cannot create IBM LinkWay applications with the runtime package, but all applications will work with it.

Acknowledgments

Our thanks to IBM, especially Tony Peacock, for providing equipment and support for this project and to Larry Kheriaty for providing a project to write about.

We also would like to thank our families for their understanding of our love affair with the computer keyboard.

Trademark Acknowledgments

INTRODUCTION

There is a vast and dramatic change about to take place in the computer industry: multimedia. It has nothing to do with the spreadsheets, word processors, and databases that have built the foundation of the microcomputer industry.

It is the next step—the advance that integrates text, video, and sound, plus the magic ingredient of hypermedia—and yields something totally new and unexpected.

IBM clearly wants to be at the leading edge of this new wave. International Business Machines has announced new hardware that brings sound and video into the PC® and PS/2® worlds. They have developed or licensed an array of powerful multimedia software products, which will be their weapons in the forthcoming battle of the computing titans.

LinkWay is certainly one of the most significant of those products. It is hypermedia for the masses. It's fast, reasonably simple, and works on just about any IBM PC or clone. It costs very little, and IBM has set a policy of charging anybody who wants to create and publish a product under LinkWay absolutely nothing.

We do our best to explain LinkWay to you in this book. We have developed quite a bit of experience by creating several products with Apple® Computer's Hypercard®, including our own Time Table of Science and Innovation, The National Directory on CD-ROM, and the Microsoft Office on CD-ROM.

The book aims to provide a healthy perspective on LinkWay and where it fits in the world. We lay out how to use LinkWay—first for the beginner, then for the more adventurous and technically sophisticated souls—in a fashion we hope will prove a useful addition to IBM's own documentation. Finally, we include Appendix F, which provides detailed comments on the correspondence of Apple's Hypercard and LinkWay features.

The key element of the book isn't what we write or how we write it; it is the choice of subject matter. LinkWay is a special piece of software. It doesn't really fall into a generally accepted classification for software—

it's not a spreadsheet, database, word processor, graphics program, or even a programming language. LinkWay is a way for normal people to get some measure of control over their IBM PCs and use the computers as devices for delivering information in a way that approximates how humans think and process that information. LinkWay tames the information-overload beast.

That feature is important, because people today face such mountains of information in daily living and there are so many computers that could help them scale those mountains. Not just standard PCs can be used, but newer desktop machines such as IBM PS/2s, the portables, and even laptops. The whole western world is chock full of MS-DOS® machines. They are the core of microcomputerdom, the installed base.

MS-DOS machines are all relatively unpleasant to look at, with their vague system prompts and hard-to-remember command lines. LinkWay, running on a normal MS-DOS machine, offers an impressive contrast. LinkWay commands a bright interface that gives you, most importantly, the freedom to exercise your computer the way you exercise your mind.

Up to now, such pleasant climes were the domain of the Macintosh® with its desktop metaphors, and its Hypercard software. The ungainly old PC—the kind millions of businesses and schools and homes were stuck with—seemed incapable of catching up.

That's not to say that the newer PCs don't hold promise, with their 80286/80386 microprocessors, VGAs, and Microchannels™. They are faster, and better looking, and more capacious in memory. And Microsoft—the company who visited MS-DOS upon us all—has all kinds of fancy plans in the works, with Windows, OS/2™ and Presentation Manager.

It all seems a bit exotic and distant, however, to the poor user sitting at a desk with a regular PC and a finite bank balance. All the fancy new bells and whistles cost quite a bit and run excruciatingly slowly on a normal PC—if they work at all.

Right in the midst of this rather dreary prospect appears LinkWay—an IBM software product! It's fast and compact enough to work on a normal PC, and the graphics can work on a seemingly obsolescent old CGA adapter (though they are dandy on EGA/VGA). Best of all, LinkWay demands only 384K of internal memory at minimum—something even the most retrograde of PC owners are likely to have.

Put simply, LinkWay will probably run on your computer. You don't have to buy new equipment or pay for a heart transplant on the old dog.

You don't even have to buy a new monitor, unless you are saddled with the old monochrome adapter card.

LinkWay does not require you to add extended memory; the standard 640K suffices. You do not need a hard disk drive, although for all the normal reasons of convenience and speed it surely is great. One item is required, however: a Mouse. LinkWay is a "point and click" sort of software that requires a device with which to point and click. Fortunately, of all the goodies you may be driven to buy as add-ons for a personal computer, the mouse is among the cheapest and most useful.

Most importantly, LinkWay does not require you to be what you are not—a computer programming expert, not that a little nerdiness won't help now and then. The point is this: You don't have to be that way. Any commoner can sit down and put together a dandy application with LinkWay—something that hangs together and can do something useful, maybe even something grand.

Your applications will accomplish their tasks with a sharp graphic look, perhaps even a bit of color and style. LinkWay offers just the kinds of features that make your creating, storing, and retrieving information so easy to accomplish with LinkWay's more famous predecessor, Hypercard.

Some people call LinkWay a database construction set, which is a close description, but a bit vague. Others call it a user-friendly, object-oriented, multimedia programming environment. This label includes entirely too many hyphens! Hypercard is simply a fun way to fiddle with a computer, and in particular to manipulate the graphics and sound. Equally important, it is a way to interconnect ideas without having to observe the discipline of linear A then B then C exposition.

Perhaps the most notable feature about LinkWay is its buttons. You can put a little graphic thingie on the screen—it doesn't have to look exactly like a button, but in practice often does—and give it a task to do when pressed. For example, your button can mean, "Select me to display a map of all the bookstores in West Los Angeles." Then you can add another, "Select me and I'll show you all the greasy spoons in West L.A."

You might even combine various buttons to show you all the places where you can mix a cheeseburger and a good book without much walking. That would require that you draw the maps on the computer screen, but LinkWay has the tools for that.

In essence, to pull up information you just point and click, and things work together. LinkWay provides computer programming for normal folks. LinkWay enables you to write complex technical programs like those you've seen from hackers. What's important is this: you don't *have* to when you want to accomplish something useful.

The fun of Hypercard has migrated to the PC. It's time to get out the window cleaner and remove the inkstains from the keyboard and the thumbprints from the screen. There is life in the old beast yet, and that life comes from LinkWay.

Whether you are creating curricula for school, a dynamic desktop presentation for the boss, or simply for the pure heady pleasure of taming that PC, LinkWay is the answer to the unspoken prayers of hundreds of thousands of PC owners and users.

System Requirements

To run LinkWay, you must have at least a PC or compatible with 384K of memory, preferably 512K or 640K. IBM LinkWay is usable with one disk drive. However, two drives or a fixed/hard disk is much better for operating the software and storing data. If your computer is part of a local area network (LAN), contains a write once read many (WORM) drive, or uses a CD-ROM drive, you probably should have 640K of memory for LinkWay, because each of these configurations requires drivers that use memory of their own.IBM LinkWay works on PS/2 models, PCjr™, PC, PC XT™, PC AT®, and PC/XT/AT compatibles.

You can use any IBM graphics display.

You must have one of the following: IBM PS/2 Mouse, Mouse Systems' PCjr mouse, Microsoft® Mouse, or a compatible mouse.

Optionally, you can use the following hardware:

- Any LAN supported by the IBM Classroom LAN Administration System Version 1.10 or later, which runs on Advanced NetWare™ 2.0a or later
- Any IBM graphics printer
- IBM PS/2 Speech Adapter
- IBM PC Music Feature

You must have the appropriate version of DOS for your computer.

How to Use This Book

As condescending as the title sounds, do read this section. Every publication struggles between clarity and brevity. It is hard enough to explain an example without having to explain that you are giving an example. Is that clear? Well, how about this:

This is an example. This is a comment about the example.

In many such examples presented in this book, the text on the left is the example. The text on the right is an explanation.

A lot of the terms used to describe objects in the IBM LinkWay software can also be used to describe your computer hardware. There are physical mouse buttons, keyboard buttons, computer buttons, and software buttons inside of IBM LinkWay. The context should tell what type of object is being talked about.

The following abbreviations represent the keys on your keyboard:

ESC The escape key, usually near the top left corner of the keyboard.

SHIFT, CTRL, ALT These are known as *modifier keys.* They modify the actions of another key pressed at the same time. The SHIFT key behaves like the shift key on your typewriter. Press it and another key to get the character shown on the top half of the key. The abbreviation CTRL represents control. Control keys historically controlled the behavior of printers, but their responsibilities are assigned by the program you are currently using. The abbreviation ALT stands for alternate. There weren't enough CTRL keys to go around, so the ALT key was added. Some programs use the CTRL and ALT keys together to modify another key.

ENTER, RETURN All keyboards provide at least one of these keys. Most will have two. This book refers to both as the ENTER key, because their behavior is identical.

Function keys Some keyboards have 12 of these; all keyboards have at least 10. They may be along the top of the keyboard or to one side. The abbreviation for each key is the letter F followed by the key's number. For example, function key 1 is shown as F1 on your keyboard.

INSERT or INS On some keyboards the zero (0) key on the calculator-style keypad may behave like the INSERT key. The NUM LOCK key controls its behavior.

DELETE or DEL On some keyboards the period (.) key on the calculator-style keypad may behave like the DELETE key. The NUM LOCK key controls its behavior.

NUM LOCK Most keyboards have a calculator-style keypad on the right side. Most of the keys have two labels—a number on top and an arrow or command below. The keypad has two modes, controlled by the NUM LOCK key. When the NUM LOCK key is on, usually the key remains depressed or a light comes on, the top label is active, and the keypad behaves like a calculator keypad. When the NUM LOCK is off the labels below become active.

We hope you have fun learning the possibilities of hypermedia with LinkWay.

CHAPTER 1

Using IBM LinkWay

IBM LinkWay is an event-driven, object-oriented, hypermedia programming system with a graphical user interface.

Now that you've stopped reading, I'll tell you what that really is.

IBM LinkWay is a program for presenting information. You can use it in either of two ways: to run applications created by other people or to create your own applications. Application information is presented by means of pictures, text, and sound. How the information is displayed is really up to the person who creates the application; the possibilities are endless.

First, you need to know some terminology. The IBM LinkWay *program* enables IBM LinkWay *applications* to run. The program does not change. It is used to create and run applications. Or to put it another way, an application uses the program to communicate with you. An application provides a *personality* that the program must follow when talking to you. This means that most features of applications are very similar because they all use the same program.

But they are different and distinct applications created by different people and therefore there always are differences in the way applications work.

IBM LinkWay is event driven. You are the event, the *driving force.* When you do make an entry, IBM LinkWay reacts. It is like driving a car; you choose where you want to drive.

The Basics

A small device, the mouse, is attached to your computer by a cord, its *tail.* You use this to drive IBM LinkWay and to navigate around screens. There are a couple of buttons on top of the mouse, usually two or three. The left and right buttons perform the same actions in IBM LinkWay. To use the mouse, place your hand over its top, covering the buttons with your fingers. The tail should come out of the end of the mouse furthest from you and should be underneath your fingers, not your palm.

When you move the mouse while using IBM LinkWay, a small arrow, the mouse cursor, moves across your computer's screen. The direction you move the mouse controls the direction the mouse cursor moves. Figure 1.1 shows the mouse cursor arrow.

If you run out of space on your desk to move the mouse, lift it off of your desk and put it down where there is room. The mouse does not know where it is. It only knows how far it has moved in a given direction. If you are trying to get the mouse cursor to the far left side of the screen and your keyboard is in the way of any further mouse movement left, pick up the mouse and move it to the right, then put it down and continue the movement left.

FIGURE 1.1 *The Mouse Cursor*

The physical techniques of using the mouse may take a little time to learn. Always remember to keep the tail of the mouse facing away from you. If the mouse is facing the wrong way, the mouse cursor will move in the wrong direction.

One tip: Keep your desktop clean. The innards of the mouse tend to get dirty if you aren't careful. I'm not saying that you have to continually clean and polish your desk. Just keep that area where your mouse lives clean.

The mouse cursor symbol moves across your computer's screen, over any pictures or words. The display remains unchanged by the cursor until you press the mouse button. It is as if the mouse is drawn on a piece of glass mounted over the background.

Some areas of the screen are active. They react when you press the mouse button while the mouse cursor is inside them. Usually, but not always, these areas contain a small picture called an *icon.* An icon is a symbol or representation of an action. The icon is a logo telling you what it does.

You *select* an active area by moving the mouse cursor over it and clicking the mouse button.

Usually, selecting an active object causes an immediate visible reaction. If pressing the mouse button does not cause a reaction, chances are the mouse cursor is not in an active area. The pictures on your screen may or may not be related to active areas. In fact, an active area can be invisible.

One type of active area is called a *button* because you press it to make something happen. Well, you don't actually press it; you move the mouse cursor over it and press the mouse button. Thus, the physical button mounted on the top of the mouse activates a conceptual button on the screen of your computer. You can try pressing the button on the screen, but all you will do is smudge the glass.

The first display you see when you start IBM LinkWay is the Main menu, which is shown in Figure 1.2. A *menu* is a list of choices. The Main menu has six buttons, one for each choice.

The first five buttons are the rectangles surrounding the phrases Sample Desktop Tools, Sample Teacher Tools, My Own Folders,

Development Help, and Exit IBM LinkWay. The sixth is the small eight-sided shape with the word HELP in its center.

Selecting the bottom button, labeled Exit IBM LinkWay, you can exit IBM LinkWay.

Selecting the HELP button on the right side of the page displays a *text pop-up.* As the name implies, this block of text appears when the button is selected. In this case the text pop-up contains general instructions on using IBM LinkWay. The size of the text pop-up is relatively small compared to the amount of text it can hold. To see the rest of the text, select the small triangular-shaped arrows on the right edge of the box. The arrow on the bottom will move the text up.

FIGURE 1.2 *IBM LinkWay Main Menu*

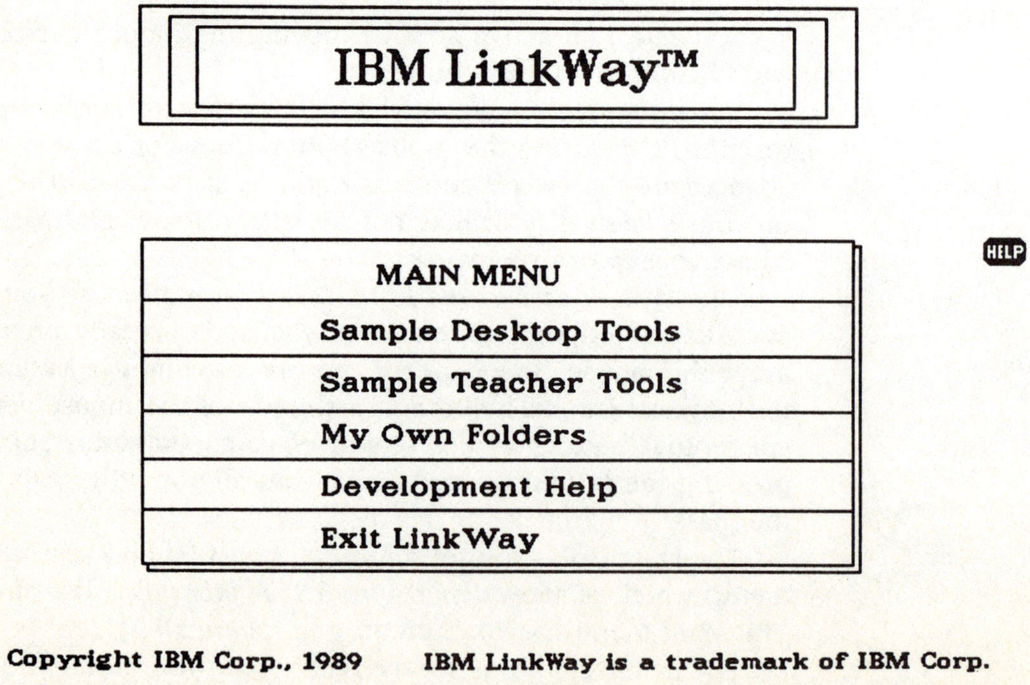

IBM LinkWay™

HELP

MAIN MENU

Sample Desktop Tools

Sample Teacher Tools

My Own Folders

Development Help

Exit LinkWay

Copyright IBM Corp., 1989 IBM LinkWay is a trademark of IBM Corp.

It's time for some more complicated jargon: text pop-ups are *modal.* They have two modes—on and off. A text pop-up continues to display until you tell it to go away. There are two ways to close a text pop-up. The first method is to select the small circle, called the *close circle,* in the top left corner of the text pop-up box. The second way is to press the mouse button while the cursor is anywhere outside of the box. There is a slight difference between the two methods. If you use the second, and there is a button underneath the mouse cursor, pressing the mouse button will close the text pop-up and then select the button.

There are many other modal objects. They may serve different purposes, but they all close the same way.

The Not-Quite Basics

You have already seen just about everything you need to know about using IBM LinkWay. You move the mouse cursor over an object and press the mouse button to make the object react. Now it is time to learn about some of the other objects.

The metaphor for how IBM LinkWay operates is that of a folder full of pages. It's a folder rather than a book because the pages can be more heterogeneous than homogeneous. You can insert a bunch of unrelated things in a folder, but you cannot change a bound book. All IBM LinkWay pages share common traits simply because they are IBM LinkWay pages. But their appearance and behavior are as varied as the people creating the pages.

When you use IBM LinkWay, you are viewing a page. Each page may have a radically different appearance, but they all work the same way. Think of a page as a piece of paper with objects drawn on it. However, unlike a passive piece of paper, the objects on an IBM LinkWay page are active.

Pages are kept in folders. Pages cannot exist outside of folders. In functional terms, each folder is a DOS file with a DOS file name. Outside of IBM LinkWay you can use normal DOS commands to copy and rename folders. The personality of a folder is based on the personalities of the pages.

The name of a folder is the same as the name of the file it is stored in. IBM LinkWay supports four of the many IBM graphics modes. Each folder is designed for a specific graphics mode. You'll see later how to convert a folder to a new graphics mode.

Keep in mind that some of these objects are modal. They have a beginning, middle, and end, just like a story. The beginning is the point where you select the object, such as pressing the mouse button to open the HELP text pop-up button. The middle corresponds to the time when you are reading the text pop-up or answering questions. You can scroll through the text pop-up to see all of the text. But you cannot do anything outside the pop-up. When you are finished, you can close the pop-up and move on. Some objects are even simpler. They open up and require a simple response like pressing a keyboard key or the mouse button and then they go away. If you select an unfamiliar object and it displays some information, you know that it wants you to react in some way. The simplest reaction is to close the object. Some objects require a series of inter-related actions and reactions. But the process can still be interrupted by closing the object.

Let us reiterate some jargon (the word *reiterate* is the perfect example of jargon, because the word *iterate* means the same thing).

You select an object by moving the mouse cursor over it and pressing the mouse button. An active object reacts when you select it. The quickest way to find active objects is by selecting them.

Some objects are modal; they open when you select them and they remain open until you close them. These objects generally display something on the screen and wait for you to respond. Some close immediately after you respond, but most require you to explicitly close them. While a modal object is open your choices are restricted to the opened object. You cannot do anything outside the object until it is closed. A text pop-up is opened or closed. When it is closed, you cannot see its text. When the text pop-up is opened you may look at the text. However, you cannot select any other buttons.

You have a choice about closing most objects. You can press the mouse button while the mouse cursor is outside of the object, or you can select the small circle in the upper left corner of the rectangle. If you use the first method and the mouse cursor is over another object, it will be selected. On a crowded page you might have to select the close circle to prevent other objects from being selected.

The standard *computerese* term for an object that communicates with you is a *dialog box*. A *dialog* is a discussion or conversation between two parties. A dialog box usually asks you for information you type at the keyboard or it asks you to select something with the mouse. In IBM LinkWay there is usually a title at the top of the dialog box just below the close circle. Below the title there may be one or more choices (as shown in Figure 1.3). Moving the mouse cursor over the choice and pressing the mouse button selects that choice. Sometimes the choice changes appearance when you select it or when the mouse cursor moves over it.

Above the simple choices there may be a place to type some text. This area is called a *field,* and it is set off from the rest of the

FIGURE 1.3 *The Open Folder Dialogue Box with a Selection Entered in Its Field*

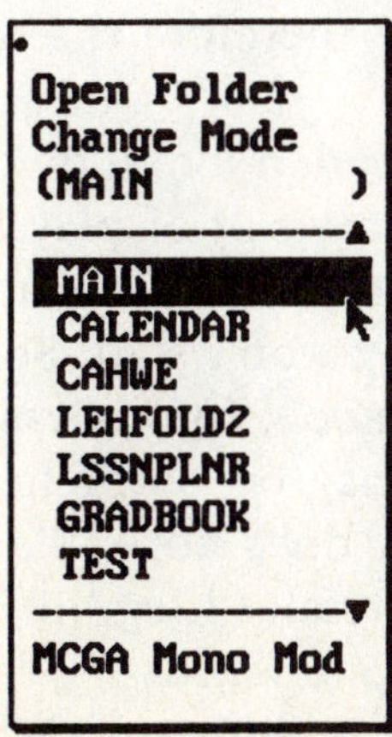

dialog box by two parentheses, (), with an empty space between them. In the figure, the word MAIN appears in the field on the third line.

Dialogue box fields are modals within modals. You could say that they have three modes. When you select the field, you switch to text entry mode, and a text cursor appears. If the field is empty, the text cursor appears at the beginning of the field. Otherwise, the text cursor appears where the mouse cursor was. Any characters you type are added to the field until the field is filled. You can use the left and right arrow keys to move the cursor. When you press the RETURN key you move back to the dialog box mode. You will still have to close the dialog box. This way if you make a mistake you have a chance to correct it.

This is a very general introduction to dialog boxes. There are many different types of them but they do work in similar manners.

Some Technical Details

A *graphics mode* is a standard that describes the hardware needed to use it. IBM LinkWay supports the four major IBM PC graphics modes: CGA, EGA+VGA, MCGA Mono, and MCGA 256. The MCGA modes were introduced with the PS/2 computers and if you don't have certain models of PS/2 your computer may not support them. The CGA mode is the oldest and therefore the most likely mode that your computer will support.

Two pieces of hardware are needed for video displays: the card inside your computer and the monitor or display. Your display and the display card must support at least one of the four graphics modes. If it doesn't, IBM LinkWay won't start. Some adapters and displays support more than one mode. In this case the mode with the most colors is used. There may be problems if your adapter supports modes that your display does not. This is obviously the case when the display becomes totally illegible. If this happens, see the troubleshooting tips in Appendix I.

The three major attributes of a graphics mode are its horizontal resolution, vertical resolution, and number of colors visible simul-

TABLE 1.1 *Graphics Display Modes*

Mode	Horizontal Resolution	Vertical Resolution	Number of Colors
CGA	320	200	4
MCGA 256	320	200	256
EGA+VGA	640	350	16
MCGA Mono	640	480	2

taneously. A picture is composed of a rectangular grid of colored dots. Each dot is called a *pixel* or *pel,* which is an abbreviation for picture element. The horizontal resolution is the number of pixels on each horizontal line of the grid. The vertical resolution is the number of pixels on each vertical line. Table 1.1 compares the attributes for the four supported modes.

The MCGA 256-color mode is capable of showing 256,000 colors, but it can display only 256 at a time.

Each folder is designed for a specific graphics mode.

Every folder has a *base page,* which is used as the background for all pages in the folder. The base page provides continuity to all pages in a folder. It also saves memory by reusing data.

CHAPTER 2

Starting IBM LinkWay

Before you start IBM LinkWay, you must install it using the instructions provided with the software. This chapter assumes that you have correctly installed the software and are ready to start IBM LinkWay for the first time.

There are three ways to start IBM LinkWay, depending on the number and type of disk drives in your system.

One Diskette Drive

If you have a single floppy diskette system with no hard disk, use the following startup procedure.

1. Place the IBM LinkWay Program Diskette in drive A and turn your computer on.
2. Enter the date and time if you are prompted for them.

3. Type **GO1**, and you should see the IBM LinkWay Main menu display.

Two Diskette Drives

If your computer has two floppy diskette drives and no hard disk, use the following startup procedure.

1. Use your normal startup procedure to turn on your computer.
2. Place the LinkWay Program Diskette in drive A and the Development Files Diskette in drive B.
3. Type **GO2** and you should see the IBM LinkWay Main menu display.

A Fixed or Hard Disk Drive

If your system has at least one hard disk, use the following startup procedure.

1. Start your computer as normal.
2. Change directories to your working directory.
3. Type **MOUSE** and press **ENTER**, then type **LINKWAY** and press **ENTER**. You should see the IBM LinkWay Main menu appear.

The MOUSE.COM program file must be in the current directory or in a directory mentioned in the path. You can also execute the command from the AUTOEXEC.BAT file. See your DOS manual for more information on batch files, the AUTOEXEC.BAT file, and setting the path. Some manufacturers give their mouse driver programs different names than MOUSE.COM. See the program's documentation for the exact name.

When you start IBM LinkWay, the folder MAIN is automatically opened. If you want to start with another folder, just type its name after the LINKWAY command.

Note: There is always the chance that new versions of IBM LinkWay will have a different startup procedure. If the instructions that came with your copy of IBM LinkWay differ from those listed here, please follow those in your manual.

CHAPTER 3

The Components of IBM LinkWay

IBM LinkWay has many ways of communicating with you, ranging from asking you simple yes-or-no questions to prompting you to make longer entries on the keyboard. This chapter introduces the various means you use to interact with LinkWay.

Buttons

Figure 3.1 illustrates some of the many types of button icons in LinkWay. Selecting a button causes an action. Each type of button performs a different action. Buttons also have many appearances, and some buttons are even invisible.

There are three general button appearances: signs, icons, and pictures. A *sign* is a word or phrase in a box. When a button is created, you can assign it a name that appears in the sign. An *icon* is a small picture, approximately two characters square. A *picture* can be any size. Actually, a picture button is really an invisible button placed over a picture. It's called a picture button because it appears as if the button were part of the picture.

As mentioned before, you select a button to perform an action. To select an object, simply move the mouse cursor over the object and press the mouse button.

Fields

Fields are a way of showing textual information. When you enter information into a database program, you type text or numbers into fields. There are two flavors of fields: locked and unlocked. You cannot change the contents of a locked field; therefore, they are used purely for presenting information. Values in unlocked fields are changeable. The fields shown in the left-hand column of Figure 3.2 are locked. The fields in the right-hand column are unlocked. In IBM LinkWay, the contents of a field are saved when the program quits. If you type something into a field and then exit the program, the text is still there when you come back (this doesn't work if you unplug the computer with your file open; you must exit the program).

FIGURE 3.1 *Button Icons*

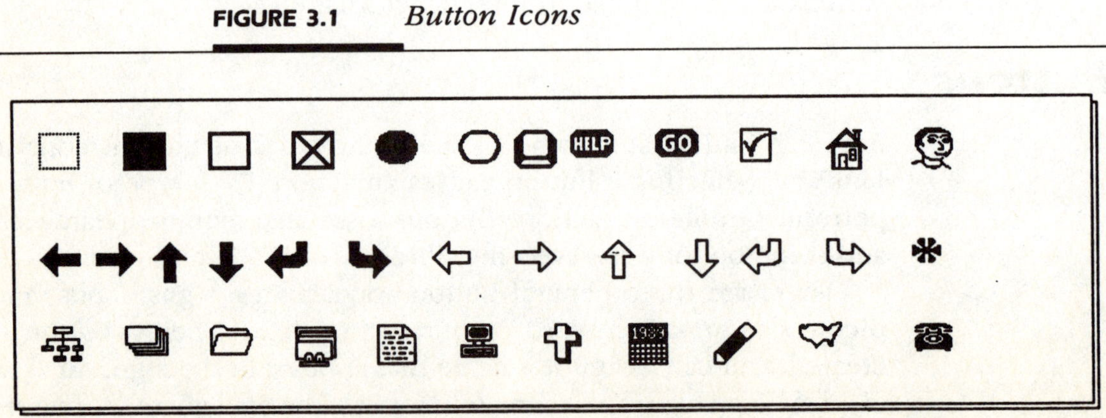

A locked field displays one or more lines of text. When you create the field, you specify its color, size, and font.

On LinkWay's Main menu are five locked fields, as shown in Figure 1.2. The first contains the words `IBM LinkWay`. Because each field can only display one font at a time, the letters `TM` are in a second, separate field. The third field displays `Main Menu`. The fourth field contains the names of the five choices, `Sample Desktop Tools`, `Sample Teacher Tools`, `My Own Folders`, `Development Help`, and `Exit LinkWay`. The fifth field is at the bottom and contains the copyright notice. As you can see, these fields are different colors and sizes. Characters have different styles or appearances. A collection of characters in the same typestyle is called a *font*. The trademark symbol is a different field so that it can be a smaller font. You cannot have characters of different fonts in a single field.

FIGURE 3.2 *Field Names and Values*

Principal	160000
Interest Rate	11
Term (in years)	30
Monthly Payment	1523.72

Select this button to calculate the payments for the current principal, interest, and term.

Select this button to calculate the term for the current principal, term, and payment.

An unlocked field is similar to a locked field, except that you may edit its contents. The field text cursor is a thin vertical bar somewhat taller than the text in the field. Pressing the mouse button while the mouse cursor is inside a field inserts the field cursor between the two letters closest to the mouse cursor. The line containing the field cursor is the current line.

When you type a character, it replaces the character after the cursor. The only way to insert a character is by using the INSERT key, described in a moment.

The arrow keys move the cursor in the directions indicated. The BACKSPACE key is the same as the left arrow; it moves the cursor one character to the left.

The following keys have special meanings within fields. Remember that the letter F before a number denotes the function key of that number:

F10 Insert a new line before the current line.

F9 Delete the current line.

INSERT Insert a space after the field cursor. The field cursor does not move.

DELETE Delete the character after the field cursor. You cannot use this key to concatenate two lines of text.

F2 Exit

ESC Exit

You can change a locked field to an unlocked field, and vice versa. You'll learn how to do this later in Chapter 6.

Fields have both a maximum size and a maximum number of characters. The size is not strictly related to the number of characters. As you type, if some characters disappear at the right edge of the field or you can't quite reach the right edge, you know that the size does not match the number of characters.

Text Pop-Ups

A text pop-up, shown in Figure 3.3, is actually one of the many types of buttons. It is an outlined rectangle of text drawn over the current page. Initially the *text cursor,* a filled rectangle the same size as a character cell, is at the top left corner of the rectangle. The top right and bottom right corners have triangular-shaped arrows. Selecting one of these arrows with the mouse causes the text cursor to move in the direction of the arrow. If you are selecting the down arrow and the text cursor reaches the bottom of the rectangle, all of the text in the text pop-up moves up one line and the next line is displayed. The up arrow works the same way, except that you cannot scroll beyond the very first line of the text pop-up. The text cursor may also be moved by pressing the arrow keys on the computer keyboard or pressing the mouse button while the mouse cursor is inside of the text pop-up.

The text pop-up remains displayed until you close it in one of two ways: selecting the small circle in the top left corner of the rectangle or pressing the mouse button while the mouse cursor is outside of the rectangle. The page's appearance is restored when the text pop-up is closed.

The following keys perform special actions when you use text pop-ups:

F10 Insert a new line before the text cursor if the cursor is at the beginning of the current line. If you are in the middle of a line, F10 moves the rest of the current line down to the next line.

F9 If your cursor is at the beginning of a line, F9 deletes the whole line. If you are at the end of the line, F9 appends the

FIGURE 3.3 *Sample of a Text Pop-Up*

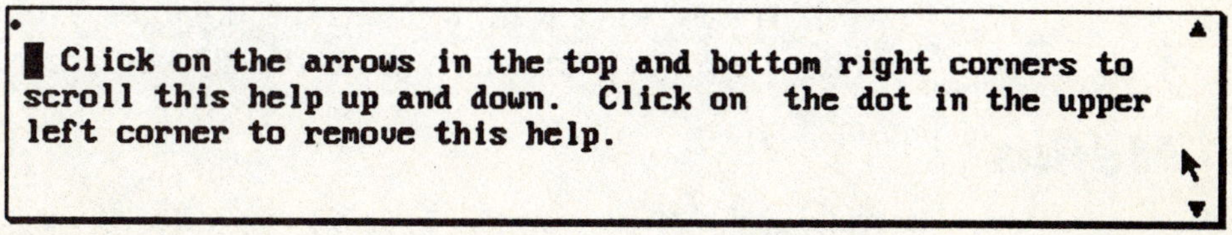

```
█Click on the arrows in the top and bottom right corners to
scroll this help up and down.  Click on  the dot in the upper
left corner to remove this help.
```

next line to the current one. The key has no effect if your cursor is in the middle of a line.

INSERT Pressing this key toggles the insert/replace state. If you are using insert mode and you press the INSERT key, you will switch to replace mode, and vice versa. When you use replace mode, any character you type replaces the character under the text cursor, and the cursor moves to the next character. In insert mode, any character you type is inserted before the text cursor.

F2 Exit

ESC Exit

Documents

Documents are like extended text pop-ups. When you select a document button, the current page disappears and another screen appears. Selecting a document button automatically loads the text editor called LWEDIT. With this program you edit text stored in ASCII files. The ASCII format is the most common format for storing textual data that is imported or exported between programs. You can also use the LWEDIT program outside of IBM LinkWay for editing text files.

See Chapter 4 for more information about the LWEDIT program.There are three steps to remember about using the LWEDIT program:

- Press **F1** to display some help.
- Press **F2** to save the current file.
- Press **F3** to exit LWEDIT and return to IBM LinkWay.

If you made changes to the file and haven't saved them when you try to exit LWEDIT, you see a warning that you will lose unsaved work. If you don't want to keep the changes, continue. Otherwise, press the **F2** key and then press the **F3** key again.

Menus

Occasionally you will be asked to choose an answer to a question in a menu, such as the one shown in Figure 3.4. A box appears on the screen with one or more lines of text. When the mouse cursor passes over a line of text, the text lights up or changes appearance. To choose that answer, press the mouse button. Pressing the mouse button while it is outside the box selects nothing and closes the menu.

Input Boxes

Input boxes such as the sample in Figure 3.5 enable you to type some information from the keyboard. A rectangle containing the input message appears on the screen. In the upper left corner is a close circle you select to close the input box. The middle line is an explanation or question. The bottom line contains two parentheses separated by spaces with a text cursor in the first space. Answer the question and press the **ENTER** key when you are finished. If you press the **ESC** key, whatever you have typed is ignored, and whatever process was happening is stopped.

FIGURE 3.4 *A Simple Menu*

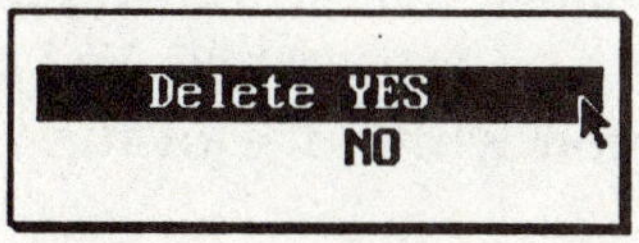

Delete YES
NO

FIGURE 3.5 *Sample of an Input Box*

New Folder Name
(myfolder)

Using the Menu Bar

You were introduced to the menu bar earlier. As Figure 3.6 shows, it is a rectangle one character in height across the top of the screen. It is always accessible, although it may not be visible. As the word *menu* implies, it is a list of choices. First the Main menu choices of the menu bar are described in general, then they and their sub-menu options are covered in full.

The menu bar is divided into five sections, each with a title. Because of differences in the IBM graphics modes, the sizes of the menu bar and its sections change. In the MCGA 256 color and CGA modes, the five sections take up the entire bar. In the EGA and MCGA Mono modes, the bar takes up approximately two-thirds of the bar line, starting at the left edge.

Move the mouse to the top left corner of the screen and press the mouse button. You have just selected a *pull-down menu,* so named because it appears to be pulled down from the menu bar. The title of this pull-down menu is Folder. If the menu bar is currently visible, you can see the title. Otherwise, it is represented by an empty square.

The menu is composed of several rows of text displayed below the title. If you move the mouse cursor down the menu, each row will "light up," change color or appearance. You choose an option by pressing the mouse button while one of the rows of text is lit up.

As an example, if you move the mouse to the bottom of the pull-down so the phrase `Exit LinkWay` is lit up, then press the mouse button, you will exit LinkWay.

FIGURE 3.6 *The Menu Bar*

```
Folder     Page      Object     Go to      Option
```

You can close the menu without choosing anything by moving the mouse cursor outside of the title box to some other place on the menu bar or by pressing the mouse button while the mouse cursor is outside of the pull-down area. You will know the menu is closed because it disappears.

The titles of the five pull-down menus are: Folder, Page, Object, Go to, and Option.

The Folder pull-down options listed in Figure 3.7 control the LinkWay program and the current folder. With this menu you can switch to another folder, create a new folder, save the current folder, or exit LinkWay. These options control the most general operation of the LinkWay program. That is why they are located in the first menu on the left, where they are the most easily accessible.

The Page pull-down controls the current page. As you saw earlier, folders are a collection of pages. The options in the Page menu either create a new page or change the current page. While you use LinkWay you always view a single page, the *current page*. By extension, only one folder can be open at a time. Returning to the earlier analogy of a folder containing pieces of paper, the choices in this menu affect entire pages but not the pages' contents.

The third pull-down menu is entitled Object. Just as pages are the building blocks of folders, objects are the building blocks of pages.

It's time for some more terminology/jargon. The LinkWay metaphor is based on a hierarchy of objects. What is a hierarchy? Well,

FIGURE 3.7 *The Folder Pull-Down Menu*

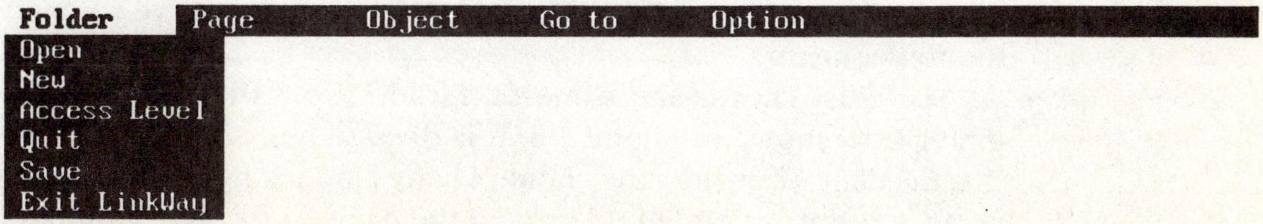

```
Folder   Page       Object     Go to      Option
Open
New
Access Level
Quit
Save
Exit LinkWay
```

think of a group of departments within a company that builds airplanes. At the bottom of the hierarchy are the departments that make objects like rivets, nuts, and bolts. The next level of the hierarchy uses these objects to build engines, landing gear, and devices capable of converting edible food to airline food. These intermediate parts are then assembled to create the entire plane. The bigger parts are made out of smaller parts. The biggest parts in LinkWay are the folders, which are made out of pages, which are assembled from objects.

The nuts and bolts of a LinkWay application are created from the Object pull-down menu.

The Go to pull-down controls movement from page to page. These choices change the current page to a new page.

Finally, the Option pull-down controls attributes of the current folder. Any option that doesn't fit in the other menus is located here.

To make the menu bar visible, select the choice Menu Bar from the rightmost pull-down menu, Option. You see the five areas of the Main menu labeled. The Menu Bar option, then, toggles the display of the menu bar: Selecting this option when the menu bar is visible will make it invisible.

The Folder Pull-Down Menu

Open

The instant you select the Open option, any changes made to the current folder are saved and it is closed immediately. If you mistakenly choose this option, you are out of luck. You have to open the folder again.

You must choose the name of a folder from the Open Folder dialog box, shown in Figure 3.8. It is divided into six parts: a close dot, the dialog box title, the choice Change Mode, the current folder name, a list of available folders, and the name of the current mode. Only the folders in the current mode are listed.

The current folder name is displayed between parentheses. When you first open the dialog box, the name is empty. You can enter a folder name by pressing the mouse button while the mouse cursor is between the parentheses and typing the name. Or you can select a name with the mouse from the list below the parentheses. Above and below the list of folder names are two lines with arrows at the right edge. When you select one of these arrows, the list of names moves in the opposite direction of the arrows. That is, if you select the down arrow the list moves up, and if you select the up arrow, the list moves down.

Selecting the choice Change Mode displays another type of dialog box. The first line is the title Change Mode; it is inactive. The lines below are your choices, the four graphics modes. Selecting one of these displays a greater-than symbol, >, at the left edge of the box. To choose that option, press the mouse button while the mouse cursor is outside of the box and the Open Folder dialog box reappears in the new graphics mode.

FIGURE 3.8 *The Open Folder Dialog Box Showing the Name CALENDAR*

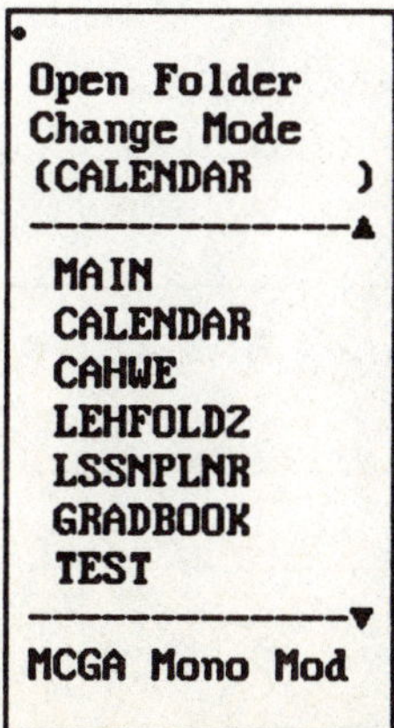

If you chose a display mode that your display adapter cannot use, the mode reverts to the mode with the largest number of colors that it can use. If you haven't selected a choice, pressing the mouse button outside of the box will give you a blank screen. This means that there is no current folder; only the Folder and Option pull-down menus will be active. Selecting other pull-down menus will display a message box that says `No folder currently open`.

After you have selected a folder name and graphics mode, select the circle in the top left corner of the Open Folder dialog box or press the mouse button while the mouse cursor is outside of the box. This step opens the new folder.

When a folder is created, you have the option of creating a button on the base page with the name AUTOEXEC. Every time the folder is opened, the button is executed as if it had been selected with the mouse.

New

Selecting New in the Folder menu creates a new folder for which you type a name, as in Figure 3.9. This is an empty folder created in the current display mode. Later you will learn about pages and objects; at this point creating folders will become useful.

Access Level

Every folder has an access level, which represents the file rights you have inside the current folder to read, update, insert, delete, or

FIGURE 3.9 *The New Folder Dialog Box with a Name Shown in Parentheses*

```
New Folder Name
(myfolder)
```

format. The levels are ranked downward from most restrictive to least, each level adding privileges, as Figure 3.10 shows. You may give folders passwords that prevent the access level from being changed.

The Read option is the lowest, most restrictive level. You may look at and use a folder in this mode, but you may not change anything, including text fields.

Update is the next option. At this level, you may enter or change text in unlocked fields.

At the Insert option level, new pages may be created.

The Delete option's access level permits you to delete pages.

Using the Format option's level, you can create, edit, and delete any LinkWay page or object in the folder. Until you are ready to create your own folders, it is best not to change the access level. If you accidentally set the access level to format, new actions start to happen on your screen. Selecting an object draws a dotted box around it. Pressing the mouse button twice activates it as usual. Until you know the possibilities and limits of the format access level, reset the access level to delete.

When you select Access Level you are asked for a password if the current access level is below format. Figure 3.11 shows the prompt you see to type your password. If there is no current password, just press the **ENTER** key or click the mouse outside of the dialog box. Otherwise, you must type the exact password in.

FIGURE 3.10 *Changing the Access Level*

```
Access Level
   Read
   Update
   Insert
   Delete
>  Format
```

After you have selected a new access level, you will be asked for a new password if the level is below format. Figure 3.12 shows this prompt. Just press **ENTER** or click the mouse to leave the password blank.

Quit

Select the Quit option to exit the current folder without saving any changes you have made. This option displays a menu (shown in Figure 3.13) with two choices: Quit without saving folder YES and NO. When the mouse cursor moves over each choice, it lights up. Press the mouse button to select your choice. If you select YES, any changes since the last save (described next) to the current folder are not saved, and the program ends. If you select NO, you are returned to the current folder.

FIGURE 3.11 *Typing in an Existing Password*

```
Type password
to continue.
(█          )
```

FIGURE 3.12 *Typing in a New Password*

```
New password.
Remember it!
(█          )
```

Save

Select the Save option to store changes to the current folder to your disk. You are prompted to enter the name of the folder, as Figure 3.14 shows. The default name is displayed between two parentheses on the third line of the dialog box. Select this line to enter a new name from the keyboard. Select Cancel to exit this process without saving the file. Press the mouse button while the mouse cursor is outside of the box to save the folder with the selected name.

Exit LinkWay

The Exit option is used to exit both the folder and IBM LinkWay. Selecting Exit saves changes to the current folder and exits the program. Choose the option if you have made changes you wish to keep. Use the Quit option if you do not wish to save any changes.

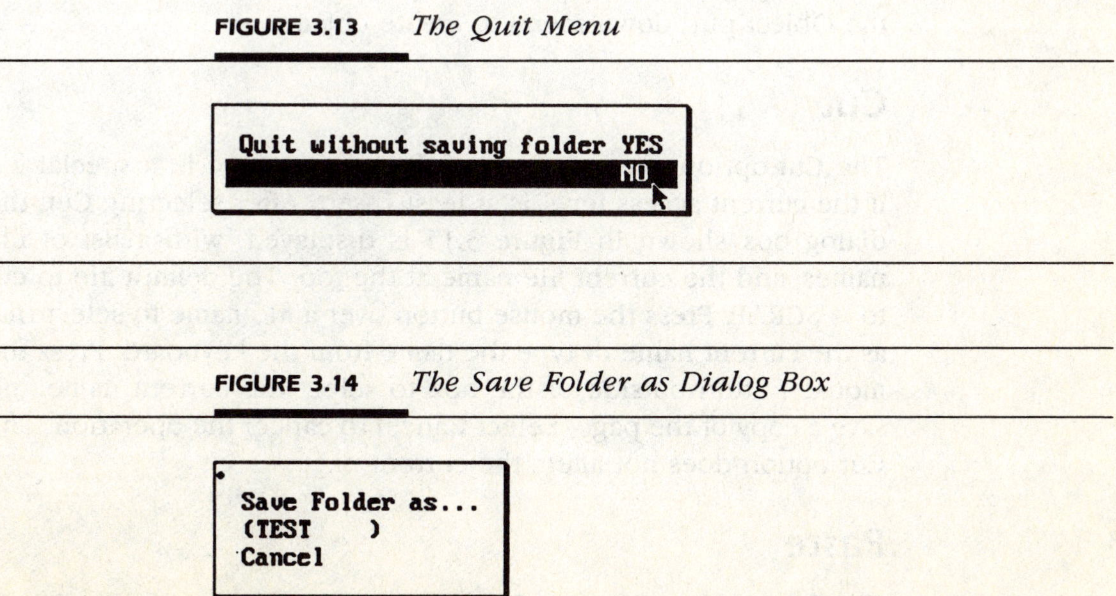

FIGURE 3.13 *The Quit Menu*

FIGURE 3.14 *The Save Folder as Dialog Box*

The Page Pull-Down Menu

The Page pull-down menu contains options for manipulating individual pages. The current access level determines which options work. Choosing an invalid option has only one effect—issuing a warning message.

Print

To print a page, you must have an IBM Proprinter™ or Epson®-compatible printer. Choosing this option calls the program LWPRINT, which prints the current page without the menu bar. See the discussion of LWPRINT in Chapter 4 for more information.

New

If the current access level is insert or above, you can use the New option to insert a new page after the current page. Only objects on the base page will be visible here. No new objects are created. Use the Object pull-down menu to create objects.

Cut

The Cut option places a copy of the current page in a special file if the current access level is at least Insert. After selecting Cut, the dialog box shown in Figure 3.15 is displayed, with a list of file names, and the current file name at the top. The default file to cut to is SCRAP. Press the mouse button over a file name to select that as the current name or type the name from the keyboard. Press the mouse button outside of the box to select the current name and save a copy of the page. Select Cancel to cancel the operation. The Cut option does not affect the current page.

Paste

The Paste option, shown in Figure 3.16, inserts a copy of a previously cut page after the current page. Select the page you wish to paste

FIGURE 3.15 *The Cut Page Dialog Box*

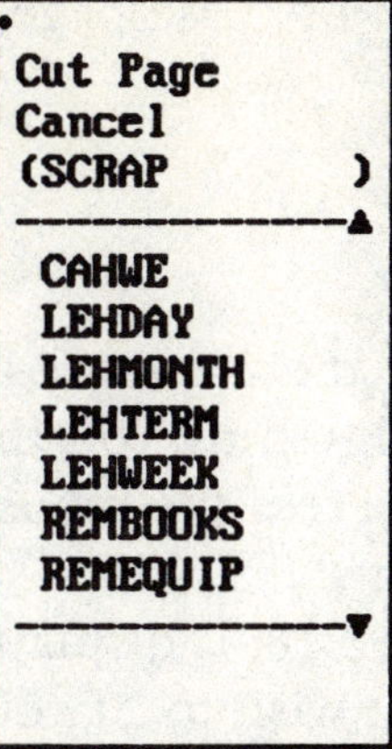

FIGURE 3.16 *The Paste Page Dialog Box*

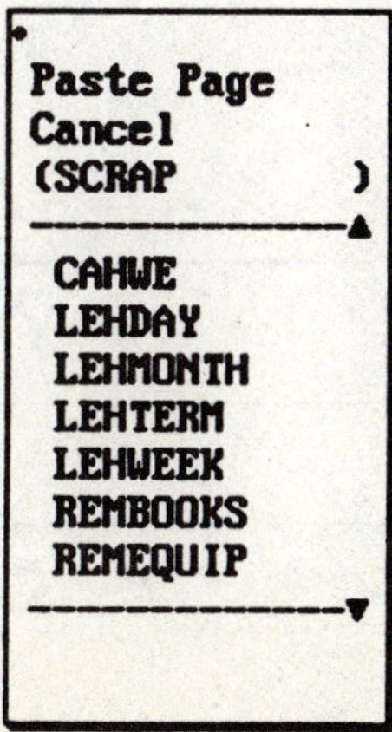

the page to from the menu of file names or enter the file name from the keyboard. Then press the mouse button while the mouse cursor is outside of the box. A new page will be inserted after the current page. It contains all the objects on the base page, plus the objects on the previously cut page.

Delete

Use the Delete option to remove the current page. The warning shown in Figure 3.17 is displayed, telling you that all objects on the current page will be deleted. Press the mouse button to continue.

A short menu, shown in Figure 3.18, is displayed. Select YES to delete the page, NO if you do not wish to. If you select YES, the selected page is removed, and the previous page will be displayed. This operation is irrevocable. Once you complete the delete you

FIGURE 3.17 *The Delete Page Dialog Box*

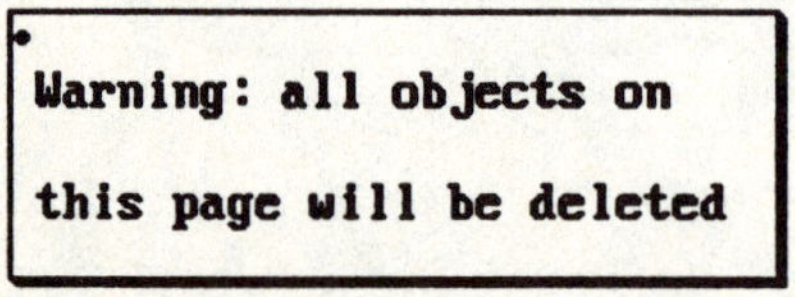

```
Warning: all objects on
this page will be deleted
```

FIGURE 3.18 *The Delete Page Menu*

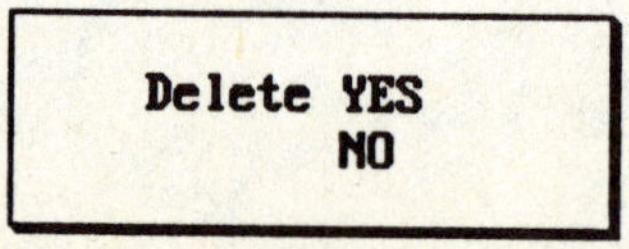

```
Delete YES
       NO
```

cannot recover the deleted page using LinkWay. Your access level must be at least delete to perform a deletion.

Box/Line

To use the Box/Line option, you must have the format access level. When you choose the option, a small square, drawn in the current foreground color, replaces the arrow cursor. When you press the mouse button, the top left corner of a rectangle is placed there, and now moving the mouse permits you to set the size of the rectangle. The cursor may not move to the left of or above the top left corner of the rectangle.

Each rectangle is drawn in XOR mode. This is a mathematical logic term meaning that each pixel drawn is a combination of the previous pixel color and the foreground color. Two lines or boxes of the same color in the same position will negate each other. Lines or boxes of different colors are displayed as another color at their intersection.

Each line or box is added to the end of a sequential list. The Undraw option erases the last line or box in the list. You may select Undraw until all lines and boxes are erased. You cannot erase a line/box in the middle of the list, so try not to change your mind!

The Object Pull-Down Menu

There are three basic LinkWay objects: buttons, pictures, and fields. The Object pull-down menu is used to change and create the three basic objects. This brief discussion serves as an introduction to these objects; detailed information is in Chapter 6.

Select the New option to create a new object.

The other options are Move, Move+Size, Edit, Cut, Paste, and Delete. These are covered later.

The Go to Pull-Down Menu

As you have read, a folder is a collection of pages. Pages are stored sequentially in the folder; each one has a sequence number. The sequence number is the page's location in the folder. The first page has the sequence number 1, the second page is number 2. Every folder has a page called the *base page,* which is a special page. Whatever is on the base page is shared with all the pages in the folder. Backgrounds that do not change inside a folder are stored there. The base page has sequence number 0.

Every page also has a unique ID number assigned to it when it is created. The position of a page within a folder may change, changing its sequence number, but its ID number never changes.

Both the ID and sequence numbers are in the range 0 to 65,535.

Figure 3.19 shows the Go to pull-down menu, which has the following options.

Base Page

Selecting this option takes you to the base page in the current folder.

First Page

The First Page option displays the first page after the base page.

FIGURE 3.19 *The Go to Pull-Down Menu*

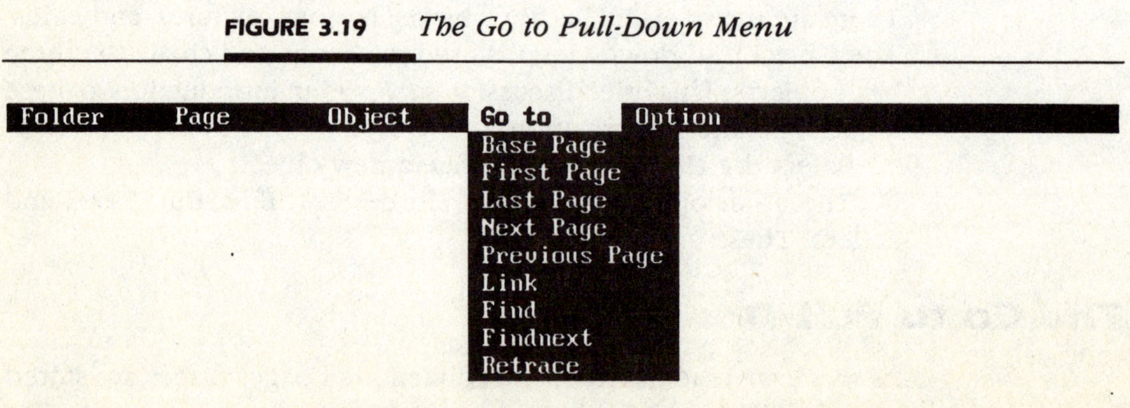

Last Page

The Last Page option displays the last page in the folder.

Next Page

Next Page displays the next page in the folder. If the current page is the last page, this option takes you to the first page, not the base page.

Previous Page

The Previous Page option displays the previous page. If you are at the first page, this option takes you to the last page, not the base page.

Link

Use the Link option to link to a page in the current folder or in a different folder. This option displays a dialog box with two data fields, shown in Figure 3.20.

If the page you are moving to is in the same folder, leave the Folder field empty.

The first field is a pair of parentheses with the label Folder to its left. Select this line to place a text cursor at the beginning of the field. Enter the name of the folder you wish to go to. Press

FIGURE 3.20 *The Link Dialog Box*

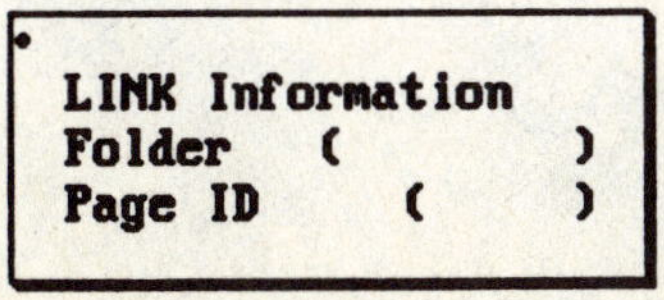

```
LINK Information
Folder   (        )
Page ID     (     )
```

ENTER when you are finished, and the cursor will move to the second field. This is the ID number of the page within the folder that you wish to go to. Input the number and press **ENTER** again. Then press the mouse button while the button is outside of the dialog box, and the new page will be displayed.

Using Link to move to another folder is not the same as using Open in the Folder menu. It does not execute the AUTOEXEC button on the base page.

Find

Use the Find option to search for a text string in the current folder or a different folder. Selecting this option displays a dialog box, shown in Figure 3.21, that contains three dialog fields labeled Folder, Field, and SEARCH String. Each label is followed by a pair of parentheses separated by spaces. Press the mouse button while the mouse cursor is anywhere on the line containing the parentheses to enter the data.

Pages can contain objects called *fields.* For clarity, they will be called page fields here. Dialog boxes also have fields, called dialog fields.

If you enter a search string, all of the page fields in the remaining pages in the current folder are searched for the string of characters.

FIGURE 3.21 *The Find Dialog Box*

```
FIND Information
Folder      (        )
Field       (        )
SEARCH String
(                )
```

The page where the string is found becomes the current page. If the string isn't found, a message box tells you so.

If you enter a name in the dialog field labeled Field, only the page fields with the specified name are searched. Say you are on page 3 in a folder containing 7 pages. If you enter the name *address* in the dialog field labeled Field and the word *avenue* in the dialog field labeled SEARCH String, all of the page fields called address on the pages 4 through 7 are searched for the string *avenue.*

If you enter a name in the dialog field labeled Folder, that folder is opened and searched instead of the current folder.

If you leave all three fields empty, the last Find command is executed again, starting at the current page.

Findnext

Selecting the Findnext option repeats the previous Find command starting at the next page.

Retrace

LinkWay keeps a list of the last 10 pages you have seen. When you select the Retrace option, the previous, topmost page in the list is displayed. You can only move back through the list, you cannot move forward. Every time you select Retrace you take the topmost page out of the list. You cannot move past the end of the list. Selecting this option when you are at the end of the list only redraws the current page.

Remember that when a new folder is opened, the first page displayed is the base page. But you usually do not see it. The AUTOEXEC button found on most base pages usually transfers control to another page immediately. If you are using the Retrace command you see every page that was opened—even those pages that you didn't see before.

The Option Pull-Down Menu

You were briefly introduced to the Option menu when you turned on the menu bar. You use this menu to change your LinkWay environment, such as the background and foreground colors and the display of the menu bar. The pull-down menu is shown in Figure 3.22.

DOS Cmd

This option opens a DOS shell and displays a DOS prompt. LinkWay uses a great deal of memory, and this memory becomes unavailable to the DOS shell. From within LinkWay you can only run programs that fit into the current free memory.

When you are finished running the other program, type the command **EXIT** at the DOS prompt to return to LinkWay.

Set Mode

This choice changes the current graphics mode. Choose one of the four graphics modes shown in Figure 3.23 or press the mouse button while the cursor is outside the dialog box to remain in the current mode. When you choose a new mode, the current folder is closed and the default folder in the new mode is opened. If you specified a folder name when you started LinkWay, that is the default name. Otherwise, MAIN is the default folder name. The default folder can also be changed with the MODE script command.

FIGURE 3.22 *The Option Pull-Down Menu*

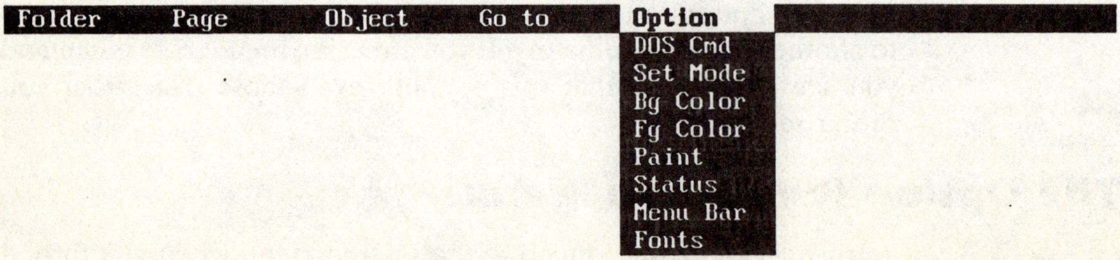

```
Folder     Page     Object     Go to     Option
                                         DOS Cmd
                                         Set Mode
                                         Bg Color
                                         Fg Color
                                         Paint
                                         Status
                                         Menu Bar
                                         Fonts
```

If you choose a mode that your graphics adapter cannot use, the highest resolution mode that the adapter can use is substituted. If you choose a mode that your graphics adapter can use but your display cannot, your display becomes totally illegible. If this happens, you may have to reset your machine. According to some display manufacturers, using invalid display modes may damage the monitor, so do not leave the adapter in modes the display cannot use. See Appendix B for more information about starting LinkWay in other graphics modes.

Bg Color

You can set the background color of every page in the current folder by selecting Bg Color from the Option menu. Each time you select YES from the dialog box shown in Figure 3.24, a new background color is shown. Press the mouse button outside of the box or select NO to choose the current color. There are eight possible choices. MCGA 256 color mode pictures use a *palette,* which is a subset of the range of colors for that graphics adapter. Each picture may have a different palette. If you use the Bg Color option, any pictures currently being displayed have their palette reset to the default palette, changing the colors in the picture.

FIGURE 3.23 *The Set Display Mode Dialog Box*

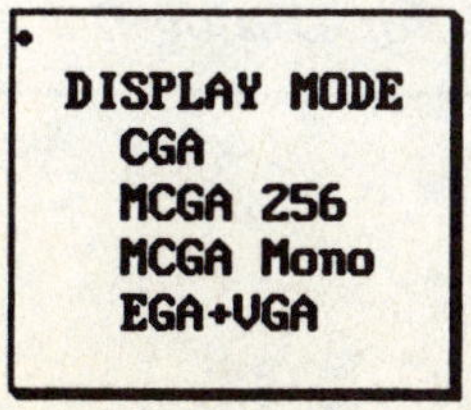

```
DISPLAY MODE
  CGA
  MCGA 256
  MCGA Mono
  EGA+VGA
```

Fg Color

In the Page pull-down menu is an option called Box/Line, which enables you to draw lines and boxes on the screen. The Fg Color in the Option menu enables you to set the color for all subsequent Box/Line operations. This does not affect any lines or boxes already drawn.

Paint

Pictures may be created by a program called LWPAINT. Selecting the Paint option from the Option menu puts LinkWay on hold while LWPAINT is executed. Pictures may be created in any graphics mode your graphics adapter is capable of using. See Chapter 4 for more details about LWPAINT.

Status

Each page has an ID number and a sequence number. Selecting the Status option toggles the display of the current folder name, the current sequence number in parentheses, and the current ID number in the lower left corner of the screen. If the status line is visible, as it is in the lower left corner of Figure 3.25 and you select the Status option, the line becomes invisible, and vice versa. The status line is extremely helpful to display while you create folders and pages.

FIGURE 3.24 *The Background Color Dialog Box*

```
New Background YES
               NO
```

Menu Bar

The Menu Bar option toggles the display of the menu bar. Even when the menu bar is not visible, it is still active, and you can still select menu items.

Fonts

A font is a collection of characters of the same typestyle and size. LinkWay pages may contain text of up to four fonts. The Font option enables you to set which fonts will be assigned to the small and large sizes, as Figure 3.26 shows. Select the font name, then press the mouse button outside the dialog box for both choices. You may

FIGURE 3.25 *Selecting the Status Choice of the Option Menu to Display the Status Line*

TEST(4) Id=4

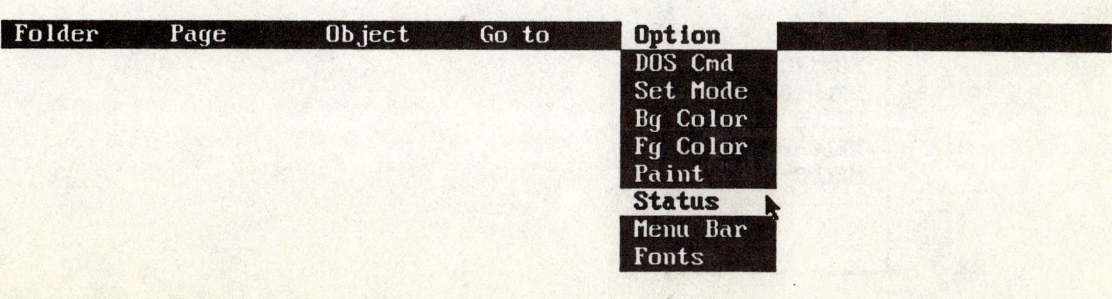

also type in the name of a font, press **ENTER**, then press the mouse button outside of the dialog box.

Using IBM LinkWay

IBM LinkWay applications are not like conventional programs. A program is a sequence of actions that a user interacts with and guides occasionally. In contrast, you control just about everything that an IBM LinkWay application does. Pages are just waiting for you to tell them what to do. A page can represent a single concept, such as the name and address stored in an address book. A page can also serve as a table of contents to a group of applications, like the IBM LinkWay Main menu.

The Main Menu

After you have started IBM LinkWay, you see the Main menu. There are six buttons from which to choose:

FIGURE 3.26 *The Font Dialog Box*

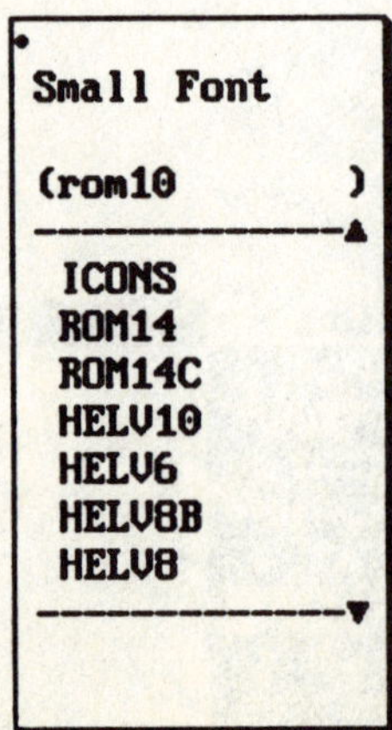

Sample Desktop Tools

Selecting this will display another page with two choices: Calendar and To Do List. Figure 3.27 shows the display.

The Calendar mimics a wall calendar. You can type in reminders for dates in an 18-month period. Your display must support the MCGA Mono mode.

The To Do List is similar to that piece of paper you post on your refrigerator—it lists tasks that you haven't done. Your display must support the MCGA 256 color mode to use this feature.

Sample Teacher Tools

The Sample Teacher Tools section shown in Figure 3.28 has five options:

FIGURE 3.27 *The Sample Desktop Tools Page*

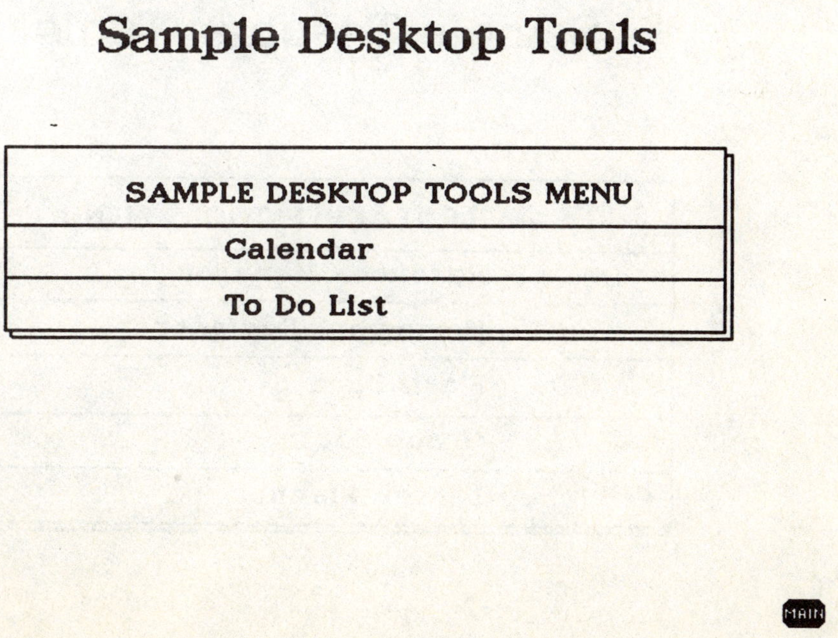

Resource Manager A tool for keeping track of resources such as books and equipment.

Homework Designer A tool for storing and printing questions.

Flash Card A sample application of individualized math, spelling, and language practice.

Grade Book A tool for keeping track of grades in a series of subjects.

Lesson Planner A feature similar to a calendar but oriented toward planning class lessons.

My Own Folders

A button near the top of the page is labeled MyFolder; it is shown in Figure 3.29. Later you will go through the process of creating a folder, and this button is described fully in that discussion.

FIGURE 3.28 *The Sample Teacher Tools Page*

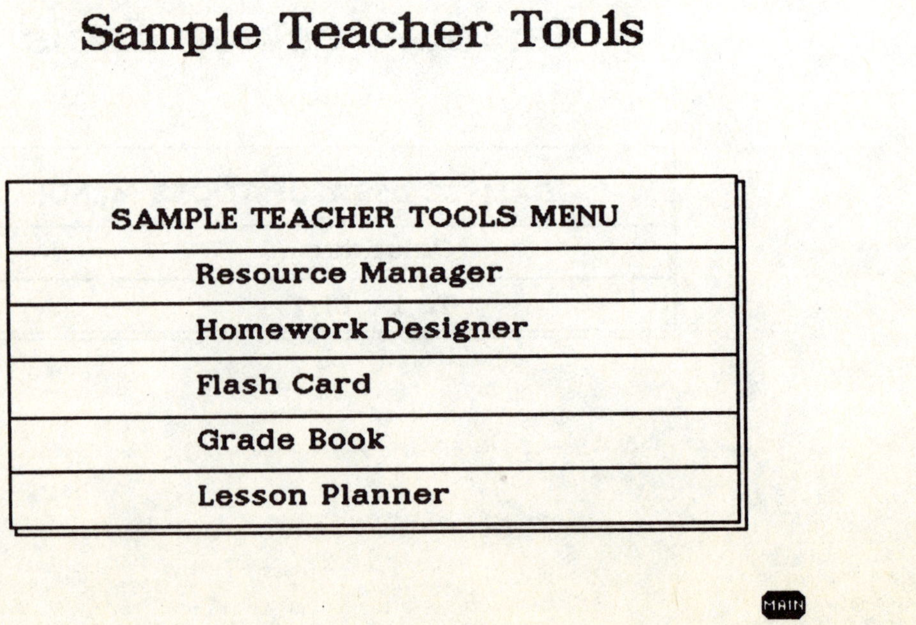

Development Help

Check all of these choices, as listed in Figure 3.30. They show you a variety of the development tools available to programmers.

Exit LinkWay

When you wish to exit IBM LinkWay, select this object. Any changes you have made will be saved.

A Quick Tour

Now you're ready to take a quick tour through one of the applications distributed through IBM LinkWay.

FIGURE 3.29 *The My Own Folders Page*

My Own Folders

MyFolder

MyFolder description

MAIN

Start the IBM LinkWay program as described earlier. You should see the Main menu.

Select the second button on the screen, which is Sample Teacher Tools, by moving the mouse cursor anywhere in the box surrounding the label and pressing the mouse button.

A new page with the label Sample Teacher Tools at the top of the screen appears. Refer again to Figure 3.28.

What's that line of text at the top of the screen, you ask? That is the menu bar, as shown in Figure 3.31. The menu bar can be turned invisible, which explains why you haven't seen it before. The menu bar features are covered in more detail later in this chapter.

FIGURE 3.30 *The Development Help Page*

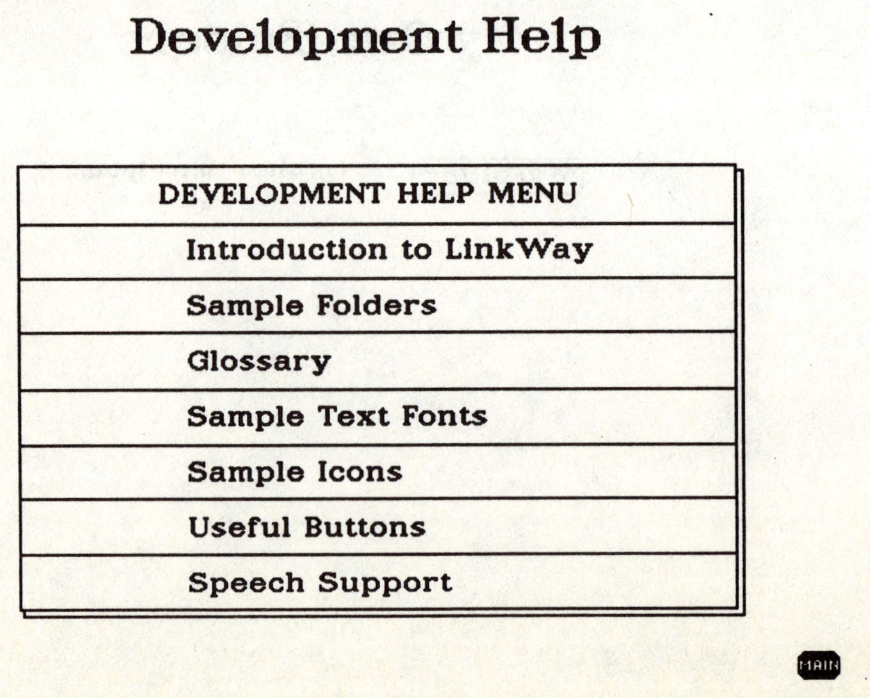

On the bottom right side of the screen is an octagonal icon with the word `MAIN` in its middle. Selecting this button takes you right back to the Main menu—thus its name.

The two locked fields on this page are Sample Teacher Tools and SAMPLE TEACHER TOOLS MENU. Pressing the mouse button while the mouse cursor is over these objects has no effect.

Below these fields are five active buttons. Now you want to use the third, Flash Card. Move the mouse cursor to any place in the rectangle surrounding the words `Flash Card` and press the mouse button. The buttons are invisible. Five locked fields below the buttons give them their appearance. Because the buttons are on top of the fields, you cannot interact with the fields. The fields appear to be buttons because the buttons themselves are invisible.

This page looks different from the previous two pages. However, the page is composed of the same elements. Figure 3.32 shows the title at the top, `Flash Card Samples`. It is a locked field.

Below the title are three choices, Arithmetic, Spelling, and Language. This time the choices are surrounded by invisible rectangles that begin on the left with the check marks and extend a bit to the right of the text. Selecting any part of this rectangle selects that action.

There are also two familiar buttons at the bottom of the screen, MAIN and HELP.

On this tour you will practice spelling techniques, so select the check mark to the left of `Spelling`.

The background remains the same, but several new elements appear, as shown in Figure 3.33. In the middle of the screen you see a picture of a cat. To the right of the picture are three choices. Below them are some simple instructions.

FIGURE 3.31 *The Menu Bar*

```
Folder     Page      Object     Go to     Option
```

The bottom of the screen has three buttons: the familiar MAIN and HELP buttons and a button whose icon is a check mark. Selecting the check mark button returns you to the Flash Card Samples page.

This is a very simple application. It has two types of pages, the one in Figure 3.33 and the page you see when you select the correct answer by moving the mouse cursor over the word and pressing the mouse button.

The page in Figure 3.34 is similar to the previous page, except that the three choices have been replaced by one empty rectangle, and another button has appeared. The empty rectangle is an unlocked field. A thin vertical line is visible on your screen at the beginning of the field. This is the text cursor.

The first feature to notice is that pressing the mouse button anywhere outside of the unlocked field only displays the word CAT

FIGURE 3.32 *The Flash Card Samples Page*

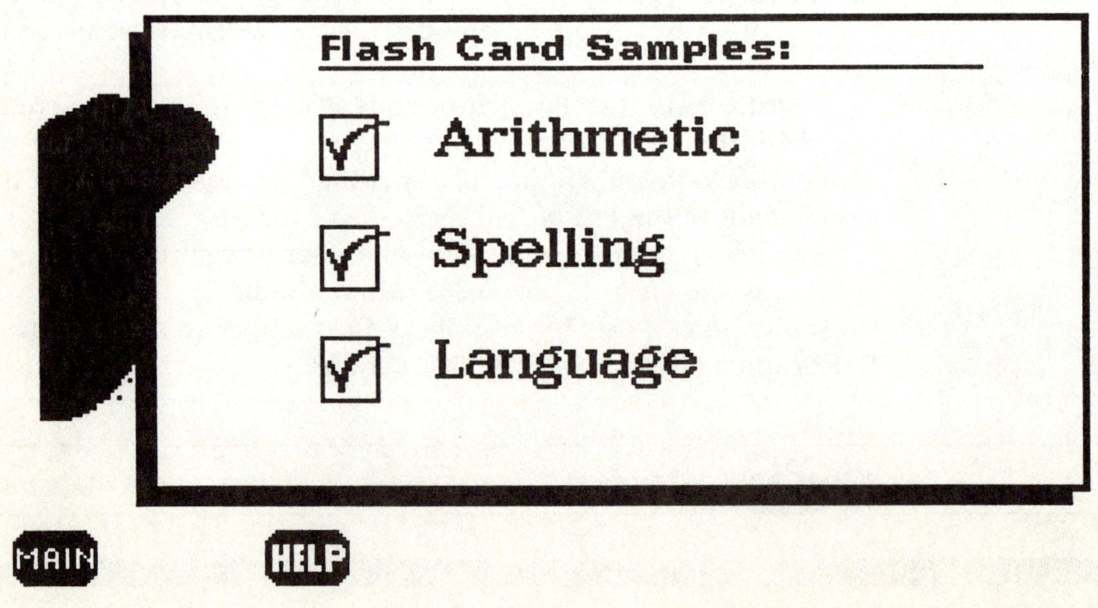

below the field for a second. You cannot select any buttons or even the menu bar. You have two choices: type the correct answer and press the **ENTER** key or press the **ESC** key.

If you press ESC, the quiz is ended and the buttons at the bottom of the screen become active again.

The only choice for people who don't like quitting is typing in the correct answer. Notice that the text cursor moves to the right to make space for the new characters. If you make a mistake, use the DELETE key to erase the character just before the text cursor. The BACKSPACE key only moves the text cursor; it does not change characters. You can also use the left and right arrow keys to move the text cursor.

When you have entered the correct answer press **ENTER** to continue.

FIGURE 3.33 *The First Page of the Spelling Test*

Take a few moments now to explore the IBM LinkWay applications. If you've gotten this far, you know just about everything you need to know about using IBM LinkWay.

Time to Dive In

You cannot learn how to swim from shore; you must jump into the water. The following LinkWay swimming lesson isn't going to create a full-fledged application; it just tours the available features.

Start the LinkWay program as you normally do. If you are just experimenting, try going to the LinkWay directory and typing **LinkWay**. If your computer's default is the MCGA 256 mode, you see the Main menu in color.

FIGURE 3.34 *The Second Page of the Spelling Test*

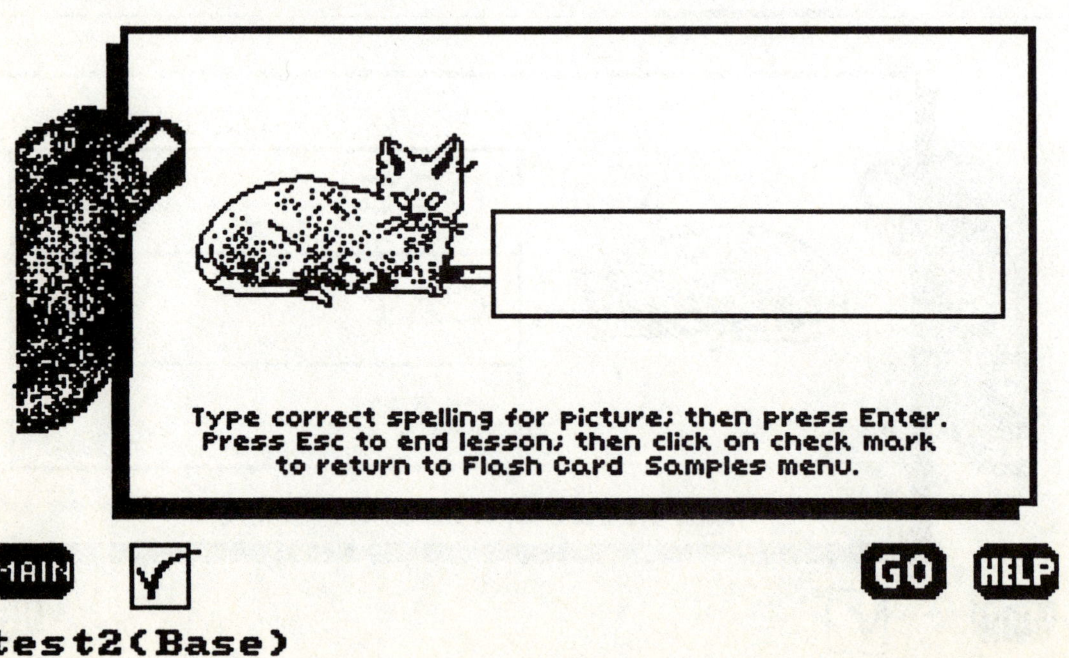

Move the mouse up to the top left corner of the screen and press the mouse button. The Folder pull-down menu should appear.

Move the mouse down until the word New lights up and then press the mouse button again. This process is shown in Figure 3.35.

Next you see a dialog box like that in Figure 3.36 with the title `New Folder Name` displayed.

The instant you selected New the current folder was closed. There should be no folders open now. If you close this dialog box without entering a name, you remain in LinkWay but your choices are restricted. If you change your mind and want to return to the previous folder, you must select Open from the Folder pull-down menu and open the folder named MAIN.

Now, because you do want to create a new folder, type its name in. Because this is just an experiment, give the folder the name **TEST**. Normally you would give it a more descriptive name. The

FIGURE 3.35 *Creating a New Folder*

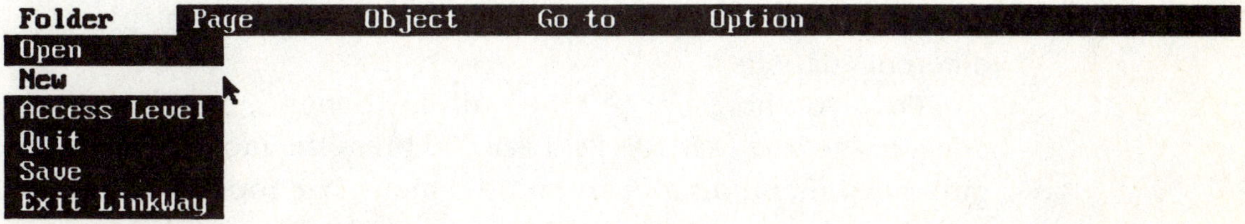

```
Folder    Page        Object      Go to       Option
Open
New
Access Level
Quit
Save
Exit LinkWay
```

FIGURE 3.36 *The New Folder Name Dialog Box*

```
New Folder Name
(TEST    )
```

text cursor—the rectangle at the beginning of the text field—is already visible, so just start typing.

When you have typed the folder name, press **ENTER**. There is a small chance that a folder with that name has already been created. If it has, a warning box appears that says `Folder already exists`. If this happens, select New again and type in a different name. Just keep in mind that when this lesson mentions the TEST folder, yours may have a different name.

Congratulations, you have created your first folder!

Before you start populating this folder, take a look at some features.

First, if the menu bar isn't visible, make it visible. You want to find the Option pull-down menu. This may be a bit tricky, so keep trying. Move the mouse cursor to the top right corner of the screen and press the mouse button. If nothing happens, move the cursor a bit to the left and try again. Keep doing this until a pull-down menu appears. The first line of the pull-down should say DOS Cmd. If it doesn't, you have gone too far to the left; move back to the right and try again. Because of differences among the four IBM graphics modes, the pull-down menus are in different places for different adapters.

When you have opened the pull-down menu, move the mouse down to the line that says `Menu Bar` and press the mouse button. The pull-down menu disappears and the menu bar appears. Remember that the menu bar is always there, even when you can't see it.

From now on, to select something from a pull-down menu, this lesson simply instructs you to select the choice from the proper menu. It doesn't go through the whole process of moving the mouse to the menu bar and pulling down a menu first.

In the bottom left corner of the screen there should be a line of text that says `TEST(Base)`. This is the status line. Like the menu bar, this line may be visible or invisible. Selecting Status from the Option menu toggles, or switches between visible and invisible, the appearance of the status line. You see the status line in the bottom left corner of Figure 3.37.

The part of the status line before the parentheses is the name of the current folder. The part inside the parentheses is the number of the current page. What? You say that the word Base is not a number. Well, perhaps it isn't. The first page of a folder is special. It is the base page, because it serves as the basis for all of the pages in the folder. Any element formatted on the base page is formatted that way on every page in the folder. Because of this feature, you can give all of the pages a similar appearance. If every page is different, then don't put anything on the base page.

Now type the words **Quick Tour** at the top of the page. Select New from the Object menu to display the Object Type dialog box

FIGURE 3.37 *Displaying the Status Line*

```
Folder     Page     Object     Go to     Option





TEST(Base)
```

shown in Figure 3.38. There are three choices: Button, Picture, and Field. You are making a field, so move the mouse over the word Field and press the mouse button. An arrow should appear to the left of the word. Close the dialog box by selecting the close circle or by pressing the mouse button while the mouse cursor is anywhere outside of the dialog box.

When you create a field, you specify a rectangle where the text will be displayed. As soon as you close the Object Type dialog box the mouse cursor changes to a series of dots in a small rectangular pattern, shown in Figure 3.39. This cursor selects the first corner of the field rectangle. Move it to the place where you want the text to start and press the mouse button. For this application, move it to the top left corner.

When you press the mouse button, the first corner is anchored at that position. Now you can choose the diagonally opposite corner.

FIGURE 3.38 *The Object Type Dialog Box*

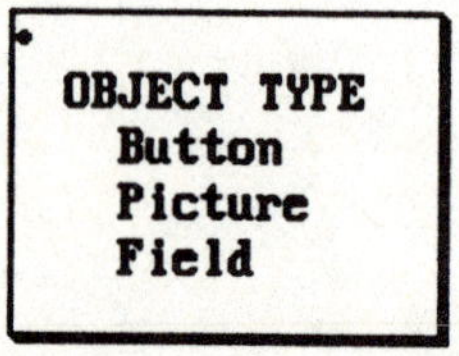

FIGURE 3.39 *Choosing the Size of a Field*

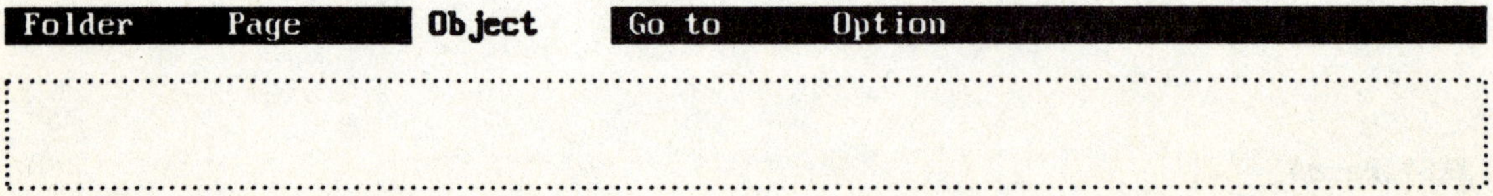

As you move the mouse, a rectangle follows its movements. The first corner doesn't move; the second corner follows the location of the mouse. The rectangle moves in small jumps, the size of one of the characters in the menu bar. In fact, the smallest rectangle you can make is the size of one character.

Make the rectangle about three characters high and about the width of the screen, then press the mouse button.

The rectangle now disappears, and a dialog box with several lines of letters appears, as Figure 3.40 shows. The dialog box is divided into four lines. Each line displays the letters `ABC abc` in different sizes. Choose the top line, the one with the biggest characters.

Another dialog box now appears. Its title is `Field Information`, and Figure 3.41 shows how it looks. You don't need to change any of this information, so just close the dialog box.

If you have a monochrome display, the process of creating a field is complete. If not, you must select the color of the text. Each of the three color modes has a different palette of colors: CGA mode has 4, EGA+VGA has 16, and MCGA 256 displays 256 colors simultaneously and has the potential of 16 million! If you are using the CGA mode, choose a color from one of the three squares displayed in the Color dialog box. The EGA mode has 16 squares, and the MCGA 256 mode has 256 squares.

FIGURE 3.40 *The Font Dialog Box*

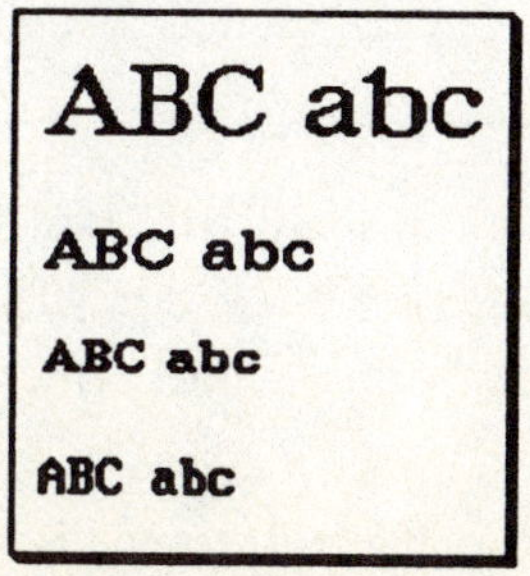

ABC abc

ABC abc

ABC abc

ABC abc

To choose a color, move the mouse cursor over a colored square and press the mouse button. All of the text in the field is the same color. Until you change the color, all of the text in that field will always be drawn in that color.

You have now created an empty, unlocked field on the base page. To fill the field, move the mouse cursor over it and press the mouse button twice in succession until a vertical line appears in the field. This is the field text cursor. Notice that the mouse cursor is still shown on the screen. However, all of the action happens where the text cursor is.

Type the words **Quick Tour** so they appear as in Figure 3.42. If you make a mistake, use the arrow keys on the keyboard to move

FIGURE 3.41 *The Field Information Dialog Box*

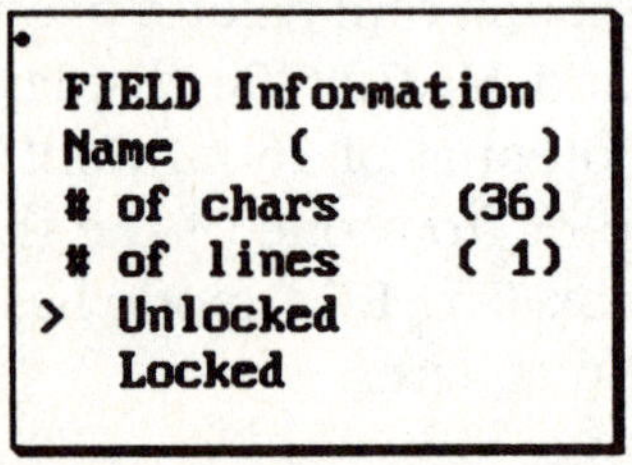

```
FIELD Information
Name       (       )
# of chars      (36)
# of lines      ( 1)
> Unlocked
  Locked
```

FIGURE 3.42 *Your Base Page*

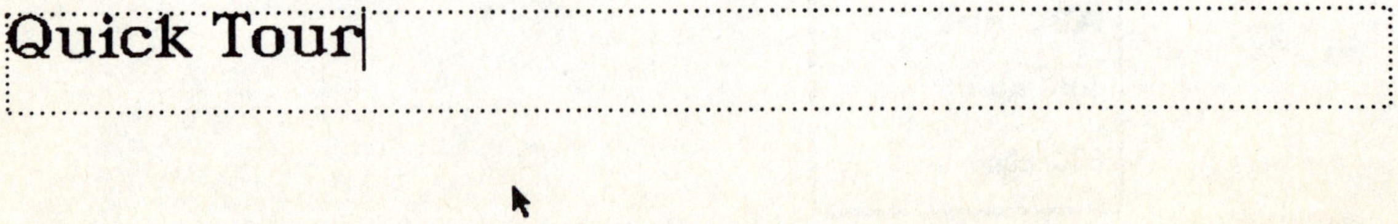

```
Quick Tour
```

the text cursor, the DELETE key to delete characters, and the INSERT key to insert a space before the text cursor. These keys don't behave like they do in most word processors. If you want to insert something, you press the INSERT key once for each character you are inserting.

When you are done, press the mouse button while the mouse cursor is outside of the field. If the mouse cursor is inside of the field, the text cursor moves to the position closest to the mouse cursor.

You are also going to create a button on the base page. Select New from the Object menu and select Button from the Object Type dialog box. The cursor turns into a small dotted rectangle just like it did when you created the field. This time, place the rectangle in the bottom right corner. The size of the rectangle doesn't really matter; make it about two characters square.

When you have defined the size of the button the Button Type dialog box, shown in Figure 3.43, appears. Select the first choice, Go, then close the dialog box.

When the Button Name dialog box shown in Figure 3.44 appears, close it immediately, because you don't need to give this button a name.

Whew! There are only two more decisions to make.

FIGURE 3.43 *The Button Type Dialog Box*

```
BUTTON Type
 Go
 Link
 Find
 Text Pop-Up
 Picture Pop-Up
 Script
 Document
```

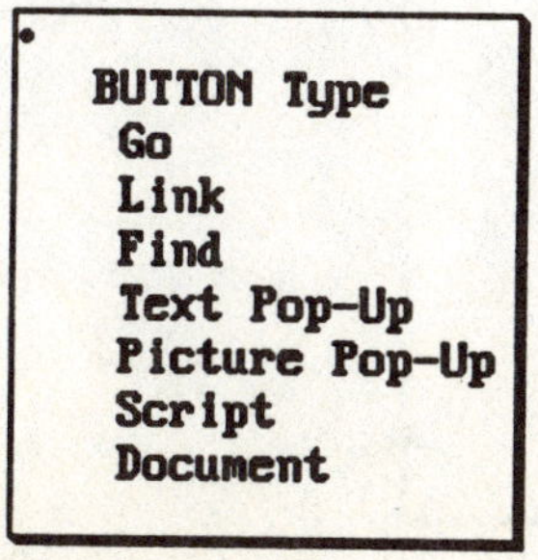

First, you choose the icon to be displayed for the button. Remember that an icon is a small picture. In fact, icons are about two characters square, the size you made the button rectangle. Don't worry, though, if you didn't make the rectangle the correct size. If you are using an icon, as in this lesson, the size of the rectangle doesn't matter. Only the first corner of the rectangle that you defined is vital.

You may not find the Button Icon dialog box shown in Figure 3.45 very clear at first. It presents a simple conceptual problem. The top part of the box is a list of icons to choose from. The bottom is a series of dialog buttons. If you select the blank shadowed rectangle in the middle row of the dialog box, the button is displayed as a *sign*. This means that the name of the button is shown in the

FIGURE 3.44 *The Button Name Dialog Box*

BUTTON Name
(   )

FIGURE 3.45 *The Button Icon Dialog Box*

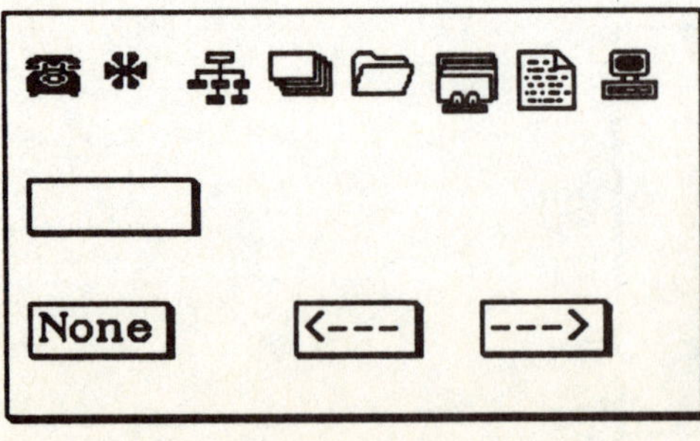

middle of a shadowed box. If you select the dialog button in the left bottom of the box labeled None, the button you are creating becomes invisible. The last two buttons, the ones with the labels <--- and --->, change the list of icons on the top row. When you select one of these buttons, the list of icons in the top half of the dialog box changes. If you keep selecting the button, the list of icons will cycle through all of the available choices and start again.

Now step back a bit. You are creating a button that will be displayed on a page. You are using buttons inside of this dialog box to create the new button. There are two types of buttons here—those in the dialog box and those that will be displayed on the page.

The purpose of the button you are creating for the page is to move to the next page in the folder. It's not really a standard or convention, but right arrow icons are generally used to represent this action. If you looked at the list of icons earlier in Figure 3.1, you saw many different styles and sizes of arrows. Choose a right arrow icon by moving the mouse cursor over the icon and pressing the mouse button.

Finally, you've reached the last stage of creating a button! You must define what is to happen when the button is selected. There are seven general types of buttons. Here you want the "go" type. When one of these buttons is chosen, the current page is moved to another page. There are five types of go buttons, as Figure 3.46

FIGURE 3.46 *The GO TO Button Dialog Box*

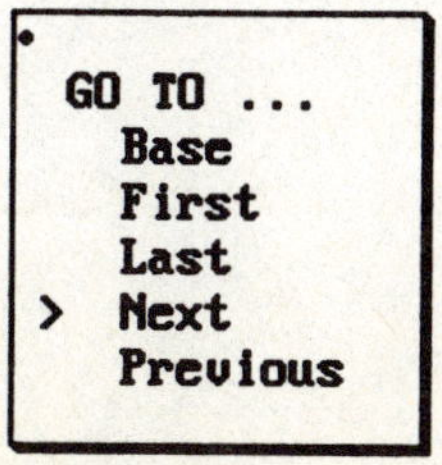

```
GO TO ...
   Base
   First
   Last
 > Next
   Previous
```

shows. Select the fourth one, Next. This button moves to the next page in the folder. If you are at the last page, it moves to the first page, not the base page.

Now it is time to create a new page. As you might suspect, it is as simple as selecting New from the Page pull-down menu. This is the easiest LinkWay object to create, because there are no involved choices.

The new page should look almost the same as the base page, except that the status line on the bottom changes. The word Base has been replaced by the number 1 and the letters Id= followed by a number are to its right. The number in parentheses is the page's sequence number, its location within the current folder. This is the first page, therefore its number is 1. Every page is assigned a unique ID number when it is created. That is, the numbers are unique to the current folder. Pages in other folders can have the same ID number. This number is used to identify a unique page. You can change a page's position within a folder, thus changing its sequence number, but you cannot change its ID number.

Create two more new pages, for a total of three pages in this folder.

If this were a real application, you would add more buttons, fields, and pictures to each of these pages. But the purpose of this lesson was simply to show you how easy it is to create a new LinkWay folder.

LinkWay is fun to use because you, the user, can create your own applications. In many ways these applications will look like programs that a professional has created. The power of LinkWay is equal to the depth of your creativity.

CHAPTER 4

IBM LinkWay's Other Programs

The programs described in this chapter are distributed with IBM LinkWay. You can use some of these programs independently of IBM LinkWay, but most of them are executed directly by IBM LinkWay.

Using the LWEDIT Text Editor

The document button is one of the seven general types of buttons. When you select a document button, the current page disappears and the LWEDIT text editor appears. LWEDIT is a separate program that edits text files stored in the ASCII format. The ASCII standard is the usual means of storing textual data in files and is commonly used when you want to export the file for use by another program.

A *text editor* is a program you use to create, modify, and print text files. A *text file* is one long string of characters broken up into lines and paragraphs. A *character* is any letter, number, or symbol that your keyboard can create. Some characters, such as the space, are invisible. Each line is ended by a carriage return, which is created by pressing the ENTER or RETURN key. The name *carriage return* is a remnant of the lingo of manual typewriters; it means the end of the current line and moving the printhead or "carriage" to the first character on the next line. Paragraphs are separated from one another by blank lines.

The text cursor, a small blinking line underneath a character, determines the current position within the file. Most actions affect the character just above the text cursor.

Unlike most text editors, LWEDIT does not deal with tabs created in other text editors. Most text editors place a special code symbolizing a tab inside the text file. When you press the TAB key in LWEDIT, the program inserts a series of spaces. LWEDIT does not understand the tab symbol and behaves strangely when it finds one. Everything on a line after a tab symbol, including the tab, is invisible until the text cursor moves over the invisible characters. If you are using files created in other text editors, you may have to replace all of the tabs with an equivalent number of spaces.

LWEDIT can hold approximately 25,000 characters. It does not open files that are larger, but the F4 key described later in this chapter enables you to add a portion of a large file to the current file.

You can also start LWEDIT from the DOS prompt by typing **LWEDIT** followed by the text file name.

If you don't specify a file name, LWEDIT asks for one. LWEDIT automatically creates a file if no file by the name you enter exists.

Once you start the program, you may view, edit, and print text files. If the current access level is read, you cannot modify the file. Placing a space followed by a capital **X** after the file name when you start the program from DOS is equivalent to opening it in read only mode.

The top line of the screen contains the file name and a short message, `F1=Help`. If you press the F1 key for help, a list of keys and their actions appears. Press any key to make the list disappear. The second line contains a horizontal line with several small vertical lines attached. Each vertical line represents a tab stop. Pressing the TAB key moves the cursor to the next tab stop. Line 23 of the display is the mirror image of the second line. Line 24 displays messages. If you press the **INSERT** key, the word `Insert` appears on this line, which indicates that you are in insert mode. Otherwise, you always use the default—text replace mode. Line 25 of the screen is used for prompts and errors.

When you first open the file, there will be a blinking line or box at the first character in the file. This is the text cursor, which indicates the current character. If you are in text replace mode a typed character replaces the current character. Typing a character while you are in insert mode places it before the current character.

Some keys have special purposes for cursor movement or editing. These keys are

Arrows Move the cursor one space in the indicated direction.

HOME Moves the cursor to the beginning of the current line.

END Moves the cursor to the end of the current line.

PAGE UP Moves forward 20 lines, one screen.

PAGE DOWN Moves backward 20 lines, one screen.

TAB Moves the cursor to the next tab stop. The first tab stop is at column 5, the second is at column 10, and the rest are at 10-column intervals starting with column 20.

INSERT The LWEDIT program is in either of two modes—insert or text replace mode. When you are using insert mode the word `Insert` appears in the lower right corner of the screen. Press the INSERT key to switch between the two modes.

While you use insert mode, typing a character inserts it before the text cursor. If you fill up the line, all characters after the cursor move to the next line.

While you use text replace mode, typing a character replaces the character beneath the text cursor and moves the cursor ahead one space.

DELETE Removes the current character from the line; remaining characters move left to fill the space. This only affects characters on the current line.

F1 Displays a list of keys and their actions. The list remains until a key is pressed.

F2 Saves a copy of the current file. If this is the first save since LWEDIT was started, a copy of the old file is made with the same name but with the extension .BAK. If you wish to revert to the previous version of a file, exit the program and use the DOS command COPY to copy the file with the .BAK extension to its original extension.

F3 Exits the program. The question `Do you want to quit without saving changes (Y-N) ?` is displayed if you have modified the text but not saved it. To keep your changes press **N**, then use the F2 command above to save the file. If you press **Y**, none of the changes you have made since the last save are kept.

F4 Copies the contents of the file you specify into the current file at the line above the text cursor. If the file is too large, a prompt asks whether you wish to have a partial load. Press + to accept it; press any other key to abort the file load.

F5 Displays a line at the bottom of the screen prompting you to enter a *text string,* a series of characters. If there is a string present already, you may replace it by typing in a new one. Press **ENTER** when the string you wish to search for is displayed. The search starts from the current text cursor position. If the string is found, the cursor moves to the first character in the string. If the string isn't found, the cursor does not move and a message telling you this displays on the bottom line of the screen for several seconds.

F6 Compresses spaces within the current paragraph. A paragraph is composed of lines of words separated by spaces. Paragraphs are separated by blank lines. Pressing F6 compresses the current paragraph, starting at the text cursor, until the end of the paragraph. If there is empty space on a line and a word on the next line can fit in the space, the word fills the space. Extremely long words may cause the compression to behave oddly. The end of a word may not be visible. Using the cursor keys will not expose the hidden characters. To see the end of the line, cut it into two lines by moving the cursor to the point where you want the line cut and press **ENTER**. You must use the insert mode to do this.

SHIFT-F6 This key combination functions similarly to F6, except that the F6 command always tries to fit lines into 80 characters. With this key, however, you choose the width of the line. The width is equal to the position of the text cursor. If the text cursor is before column 20 it is moved to that column.

As an example, if the text cursor is at column 60 and you press SHIFT-F6, LWEDIT tries to compress the current paragraph into an area 60 columns wide.

F7 Copies the current line to a temporary buffer called the *pick stack*. The copy remains there until you push the F7 key again or use the SHIFT-F7 key.

SHIFT-F7 Inserts the line in the temporary buffer before the current line. If the buffer is empty, nothing happens. Once the line has been inserted, the buffer is emptied. To make more than one copy of a line you must use the F7 and SHIFT-F7 keys repeatedly.

F8 Prints the file on the system printer. If you are using a nonstandard printer, such as a printer on a network, specify the /P option when LinkWay is started. Otherwise, if the printer is not ready DOS may display strange characters on your screen.

F9 Deletes the current line. This command is irrevocable.

SHIFT-F9 Adds the next line to the end of the current line. Only as many words as will fit are added. This action is similar to F6, except that it only works on the current and next lines.

F10 Inserts a new line after the current line. The text cursor is automatically placed at the beginning of the new line.

SHIFT-F10 Breaks the current line into two at the text cursor. The text cursor remains where it is. A similar effect may be achieved in insert mode by pressing ENTER.

Printing Files

When you press the F8 key, the current file is printed on the system printer. The file is printed in text mode, not graphics mode.

You may insert formatting commands into a text file that take effect when the file is printed. These commands all start with two periods, so they are called *dot commands.* The first four dot commands require a parameter, which is a number immediately following the command.

- **..F** Defines the form length, the length of a single page. The default is 6 lines per inch, 66 lines on an 11-inch page.
- **..B** Defines the number of blank lines at the bottom of each page. The default is 11 lines. This command determines the amount of blank space separating pages.
- **..L** Defines the left margin, the number of spaces added to the beginning of each line. The default is 0 spaces.
- **..N** Sets the page number of the first page. The default is 0, which turns off page numbering.
- **..P** Starts a new page (that is, it inserts a "forced page break").

Escape Codes

The ASCII standard specifies 96 printable characters, numbered 32 to 127. The characters numbered 0 to 31 are called *control characters.* They are used to control the printer. Each type of printer has a different set of control codes.

Just to confuse things, control codes are stored as escape codes within LWEDIT text files. Some printers also have escape codes. The printer's escape codes usually start with the control character ESCAPE and contain several characters more.

Therefore, a control code is an ASCII character with an index between 0 and 31. A printer escape code is an ESCAPE control code—ASCII character 27—followed by one or more ASCII characters.

To put a control code into your text file, press the **ESC** key and then type the decimal number of the control code. An upside-down triangle represents the ESC character.

If you need to enter the ASCII value of the ESCAPE control code, press the **ESC** key and type **27**.

The LWEDIT program assumes that all of the numbers following an ESC character are part of the escape code. There must be at least a space or letter between an escape code and a number. You cannot have a number immediately following an escape code.

No matter how many characters are in the escape code, it is converted into a single character when printed. Some escape codes don't even print a character; they just affect all further characters printed.

The following chart shows some of the control codes for the IBM Proprinter III:

7 BELL
14 Turns on double-wide printing
15 Turns on condensed printing
18 Sets 10 characters per inch (CPI)
20 Cancels double-wide printing

See your printer manual for a complete list of its control codes.

The following example shows how to turn on double-wide printing and then turn it off:

```
This ▼14 word ▼20 is very big.
```

The following example is specifically for the IBM Proprinter II or IBM Proprinter III. Inside LWEDIT it looks like

```
This is a normal line.
▼14This is a double-wide line.
▼27GThis line is printed in emphasized text.
▼14▼27GThis line is printed in double-wide emphasized text.
▼27I▼0This is printed in standard mode.
▼27I▼1This is fastfont, 12 CPI.
▼27I▼2This is printed in the Near Letter Quality resident font.
▼27I▼3This is printed in the NLQ II resident font.
```

If you enter this example into an LWEDIT file and print it, the escape codes take effect and each line is printed in a different style. Remember that these codes are specific to the IBM Proprinter II and may not work on your printer. You must print this file from within LWEDIT.

Some printer manuals use hexadecimal values for their control codes, so you must convert them to decimal first.

LWEDIT's use of control codes reveals another difference between it and most other text editors. The escape code is quite literally stored in ASCII format as the escape character followed by the decimal number stored. In an LWEDIT file, the control code ESCAPE-14 is stored as the three characters 27, 31, and 34. The ASCII value 27 stands for the ESC key, 31 is the character 1, and 34 is the character 4. Most text editors store escape codes as their decimal equivalent. In this case, that equivalent is the character number 14, an unprintable but shorter character. If you use LWEDIT control codes, most text editors will not understand them.

Using the LWPAINT Program

Picture Pop-Up buttons and picture objects display previously created pictures. LWPAINT is one of the programs that creates these pictures.

Inside LinkWay, a picture is just another object. You may change how a picture is displayed, but you cannot change the contents of a picture.

What you see in LinkWay does not have to be the entire picture. It is as if the object were a window showing some portion of a picture file. Because of this virtual window, you may use the same picture file for different objects, showing a different portion of the picture for each object. As an example, a page with several small picture objects could use the same picture file as a source, the object windows showing a different area of the picture.

The size and shape of a picture depend on the graphics mode you use. You cannot change the mode of a picture as you do a folder. Pictures are only visible within folders of the same graphics mode. Each graphics mode has a different sized picture, and all pictures of the same mode have the same size.

The *pixel* is the basic unit of a picture. The word *pixel,* also known as a *pel,* is a contraction of *picture element.* Each picture is composed of between 64,000 and 307,200 pixels, depending on the graphics mode. Each pixel can display a range of colors, which also depends on the graphics mode. When a new picture is created, all pixels are set to the background color.

Even though the number of pixels may change, the screen of your computer does not change size when you change modes. The size of the pixels changes.

Resolution is the measure of a pixel's size. With the exception of the MCGA Mono mode, which uses square pixels, pixels are oblong—their height and width are different.

CGA pictures contain 320 pixels per screen horizontally and 200 vertically. Each pixel can display one of 3 colors or the current background color.

MCGA 256 color mode pictures also have 320 horizontal and 200 vertical pixels. However, each pixel may hold one of 262,144 colors. Each picture has a maximum of 256 colors. Thus, each MCGA 256 Color picture contains a subset of the available colors. This subset is defined by a palette. If you wish to use a nonstandard palette, it must be stored in a separate palette file. This file has the same file name as the picture and uses the extension .P13. If you try to display a picture without its palette file, the pixels are shown in their default colors. If you change the background color of a LinkWay page the palette is reset to the standard palette and possibly changes the displayed colors of any pictures.

Whenever you load another picture, its palette replaces the current palette. The last palette file to be loaded will be used for all pictures on the current page. Every time you load another picture there is a chance that the colors in previously loaded pictures may change because the palette is changed.

EGA+VGA pictures have 640 columns and 350 rows of pixels. Each pixel is one of 15 colors plus the current background color.

MCGA Mono pictures have 640 columns and 480 rows of pixels. This is the highest resolution mode; thus, it has the smallest pixels. This mode can only display two colors: the background and foreground colors. Using this mode is a trade-off between the visual impact of colors and the sheer number of pixels.

Pictures cannot be converted from one mode to another, because they have different resolutions and color sets. Programs that change a picture's resolution have never worked very well. The process really requires human intervention.

Each graphics mode has a different file extension for its picture file. The extensions are

.PCC CGA 320 by 200, 4-color pictures
.PCE EGA+VGA 640 by 350, 16-color pictures
.PCH VGA/MCGA 640 by 480, monochrome pictures
.PCM VGA/MCGA 320 by 200, 256-color pictures

In addition, the palette files for the MCGA 256 color mode have the extension .P13.

When you draw something on the screen, you set the color of each pixel. You are not drawing objects. You cannot move, change, or delete individual objects, because there are none. You can set pixel colors with the available tools. In LinkWay, overlapping objects are XORed together; their appearance is a combination of the two objects. In LWPAINT, new pixels replace existing pixels; when you draw over something, the new supersedes the old. When you erase a pixel, its color is set to the background color.

Drawing a picture in LWPAINT is not like placing objects in LinkWay. When you draw something in LWPAINT, it remains there until you erase its individual pixels. You cannot move an object once it is drawn, because it ceases to be an object and becomes a collection of pixels with no special relationship between them.

You have more control over what the picture looks like in LWPAINT, but using this program takes a bit more effort. It is difficult to correct mistakes. You can undo everything created with the current tool, but when you select another tool your previous artwork is frozen.

The LWPAINT Menu Bar

As Figure 4.1 shows, the LWPAINT menu bar contains commands for five pull-down menus: Picture, Draw, Tools, Options, and Color. The Picture options control the broad, general features of the program, such as opening pictures, saving pictures, and exiting the program. The Draw and Tool menus have overlapping purposes. Their options deal with setting the pixels on the picture. The Options pull-down menu controls the behavior of the program. When you choose the Color pull-down menu, a box shows all of the available colors, and the number of the colors varies, depending on your display adapter.

The Picture Pull-Down Menu

The options in this menu, shown in Figure 4.2, affect the program or the whole picture. If you wish to create a new picture, open an

FIGURE 4.1 *The LWPAINT Menu Bar*

```
Picture Draw    Tools   Options   Color
```

FIGURE 4.2 *The Picture Pull-Down Menu*

```
Picture Draw    Tools   Options   Color
Open
New
Print
Quit
Save
Exit Paint
```

old picture, print a picture, save a picture, or exit the program this is the menu to use.

Open

When you use the Open option and a picture is already open, first a small dialog box displays, asking `Save Picture As...`. The bottom line of the box contains the word `Cancel`. If you move the mouse cursor over this word and press the mouse button, you are returned to the current picture without changing anything. It is a safety feature to give you a way out if you select this option by mistake.

After you have saved the current picture, a file dialog box with the title `Open Picture` displays. Figure 4.3 shows the box. You are given a list of pictures created in the current graphics mode. Use the triangular arrows to scroll the list up and down. Select the name of the file you wish to load by clicking the mouse or enter a file name by selecting the line containing two parentheses and typing the name. If you do not wish to load a picture, select Cancel. Close

FIGURE 4.3 *Open Picture Dialog Box*

the dialog box by selecting the close circle or pressing the mouse button while the mouse cursor is outside of the box.

If you do not have an open picture, the options under Draw or Tool will not work.

New

Use this option to create a new picture. Enter the name of the new picture. A message box warns you if you try to create a new picture with the same name as an existing picture, and you have to select New to try again.

Print

This option calls the LWPRINT program, described later in the chapter, to print the current picture on the system printer.

Quit

Choose this option to quit the program without saving changes you have made to the current picture since the last save. A dialog box opens that displays `Quit without saving picture` and your choices are YES and NO. If you select YES, any changes you have made to the file since it was last saved are irrevocably lost. If you select NO, you are returned to the program. Select Save or Exit Paint to save the current picture.

Save

The Save option stores the current picture in a disk file. You are prompted for a file name; a default name is displayed. To change the default, select the name with the mouse and type in the new name. Save the file and close the dialog box by selecting the close circle in the top left corner or pressing the mouse button while the mouse cursor is outside of the box. You may select Cancel to return to the program without saving the file.

Exit Paint

Select this option to exit LWPAINT. If there is a picture open, you are prompted to save it first. The prompt is the same as for the Save option.

When you exit, the screen returns to the display just before LWPAINT was called. If you started LWPAINT from DOS, you are returned to the DOS prompt.

The Draw Pull-Down Menu

All of the options shown in Figure 4.4 for the Draw menu change pixels on the picture in the current color. Each option creates a different effect, ranging from the Pencil, which sets individual pixels, to the Cube, which draws a two-dimensional representation of a cube.

The Draw menu options all use the current color set in the Color pull-down menu. You may change the color at any time.

Different LWPAINT options have different cursors, represented in Figure 4.5. If you choose the Pencil option, the cursor changes from the familiar arrow to *cross hairs,* two perpendicular lines crossing at their centers rather like a plus sign. Every cursor has a *hot-*

FIGURE 4.4 *The Draw Pull-Down Menu*

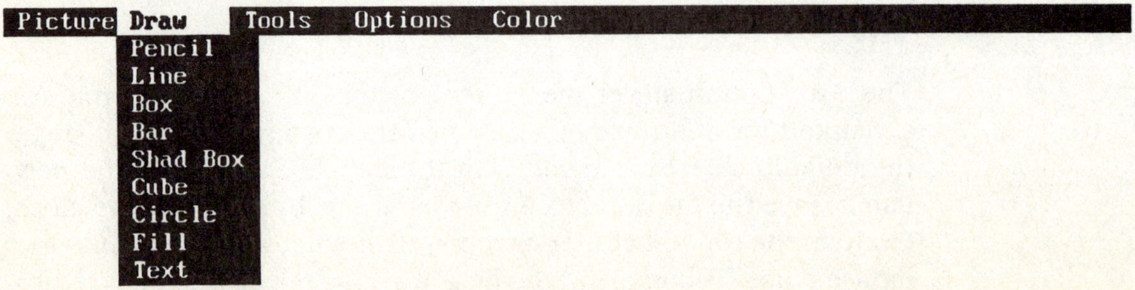

```
Picture Draw     Tools   Options   Color
        Pencil
        Line
        Box
        Bar
        Shad Box
        Cube
        Circle
        Fill
        Text
```

spot, which represents the physical location of the cursor. The icon, or picture representing the cursor, follows the hot-spot. The hot-spot of the arrow cursor is the tip of the arrow, and the hot-spot of a cross hairs cursor is the intersection of the two lines. When you are using the Pencil and press the mouse button, the pixel under the hot-spot, the intersection of the two lines, changes color.

Pencil

The Pencil option sets the color of individual pixels. When you press the mouse button, the pixel under the hot-spot changes to the current color. If you hold the mouse button down as you move the mouse, you create a line following the mouse's movements.

Line

When you select the Line option, a cross hairs cursor appears. The first time you press the mouse button, you define the start point of the line. Now, when you move the mouse a ***rubber band line*** is drawn from the current mouse position to the start point. The line stretches, like a rubber band, to follow the mouse movements. When you press the mouse button a second time, a line is drawn in the current color from the start position to the current position of the mouse, and the cursor changes to a cross hairs one again. To set the width of the line, use the Set Width choice in the Options pull-down menu.

FIGURE 4.5 *The LWPAINT Cursors*

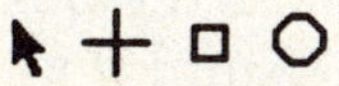

Box

The Box option is similar to the Line command, except that it draws a box from the start point to the mouse position. When you select this option, the cursor becomes a small box. The hot-spot is the top left corner of this box. When you press the mouse button, the start point is defined as the pixel underneath the top left box corner.

As you move the mouse, a rubber band box is drawn following the movements of the mouse. When you press the mouse button a second time, the box is frozen in place and drawn in the current color. Unlike the Box/Line option in the LinkWay Page pull-down menu, the second corner of the box may be placed in any direction relative to the start point.

The width of the sides is also set by the Set Width choice in the Options pull-down menu.

Bar

The Bar option works just like the Box command, except that the interior of the box is filled with the current color.

Shadow Box

The Shadow Box option works just like the Box option, except that the right and lower edges are three pixels thick and the other two edges are one pixel thick. The Set Width option does not affect this command.

Cube

The first face of the cube is defined in the same manner as the Box option. But when you press the mouse the second time the cursor becomes a box the same size and shape as the box you just created. When you press the mouse button the third time the four corners of the original box and the cursor are connected.

Circle

The cursor for the Circle option is a small circle (refer again to Figure 4.5 to see how it looks); the hot-spot is the center of the circle. When you press the mouse button the first time, a circle appears centered around the original circular cursor. Move the mouse to change the size and shape of the circle. Press the mouse button to leave the circle in place. Despite the name, you can also make ellipses.

Fill

The Fill operation is known as a *flood fill,* because it "floods" an area of pixels of one color with a new color. Pressing the mouse button selects the pixel under the center of the cross hairs cursor. The color of the pixel becomes the interior color. All adjacent pixels that are the interior color will be changed to the current color. Diagonal pixels are not considered adjacent. Only the pixels above, to the right of, below, and to the left of the current pixel are changed.

Think of the interior color pixels as the lowlands in the middle of a flood. All of the other pixels are the high land and therefore saved the ravages of the flood. If an area of interior colored pixels is separated from the main flood waters by a group of other pixels, it will not be touched. Pixels of other colors serve as the banks of the river that prevent the flood from spreading.

Colors can get a bit confusing with MCGA 256 Color pictures. Each pixel is assigned a number that is not related to its actual appearance. The number is an index into a list of colors in a palette. The same color may be listed more than once in a palette. Even though two pixels may look alike, their index numbers may be different. The flood fill operation looks at the pixel index, not its color. Therefore, some areas may not be filled when it looks like they should be.

This operation is very memory hungry. It is a recursive function, which means that it calls itself repeatedly, using more memory each time. For every pixel it checks, the flood fill must check its four neighbors. If you try to fill a large, complex area, the function stops when it runs out of memory, not completing the fill operation.

Text

The Text option draws text. The text is not stored in a field, so you cannot edit the text once it is created. The current font, which is set in the Options menu, and the current color are used.

The arrow cursor is used for this option. Press the mouse button once to enter text. The position of the cursor does not have to be the final position of the text. The right edge of the screen limits the length of the text. If you want a lot of text on one line, start it at the left edge of the screen.

Press **ENTER** when you are finished. The cursor becomes the block of text. Move the mouse to place the text and press the mouse button a second time when it is in the correct position.

The Tools Pull-Down Menu

The Tools menu options, shown in Figure 4.6, are similar to those in the Draw pull-down menu.

FIGURE 4.6 *The Tools Pull-Down Menu*

```
Picture Draw   Tools   Options   Color
               Undo Last
               Eraser
               Clear All
               Fan
               Ribbon
               Airbrush
               Copy
```

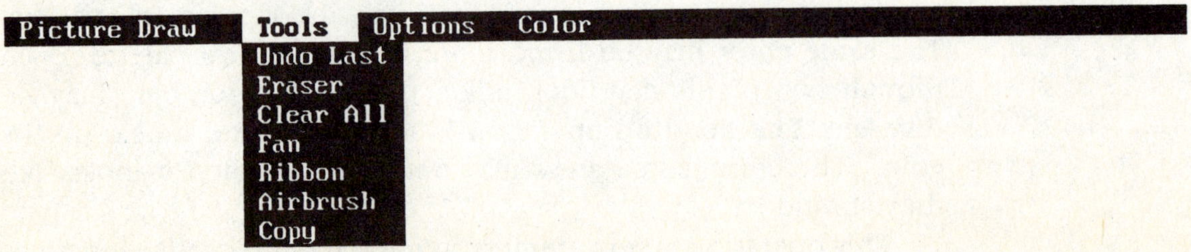

Undo Last

Whenever you choose a new tool or option in the Draw pull-down menu, a copy of the screen is made. If you select Undo Last, the copy replaces the current screen. Any changes since you selected the current tool will be canceled. The moment you select a new tool, you surrender the chance to undo your mistakes.

This option works only once per tool selection, because only one copy of the screen is saved. Selecting this option will have no effect until you draw something new.

Eraser

When you select the Erase option, the cursor becomes a small square. The size of the square depends on the Set Width choice on the Options pull-down menu. When you press the mouse button, the pixels under the cursor are set to the current background color.

Clear All

The Clear All command displays a menu that prompts you to select YES or NO to the question, `Clear Picture?`. If you select YES, the entire picture will be erased, and all of the pixels will be set to the current background color. If you select NO, nothing happens.

Fan

When you press the mouse button down, the center of the cross hairs cursor becomes the start point. As you hold the mouse button down and drag the mouse, lines are drawn from the start point to the current mouse position. An example of the pattern, which resembles a three-dimensional graphic, appears in Figure 4.7. Lines are continuously drawn until you release the mouse button.

Ribbon

The Ribbon option also displays a cross hairs cursor. While you press the mouse button, a series of vertical lines are drawn, all the same length. The lines follow the mouse movement. The top and bottom of each line are connected to their predecessors, giving the appearance of a ribbon. You can also close the pattern to form a loop, as shown in Figure 4.8.

FIGURE 4.7 *Sample Graphic Drawn with the Fan Command*

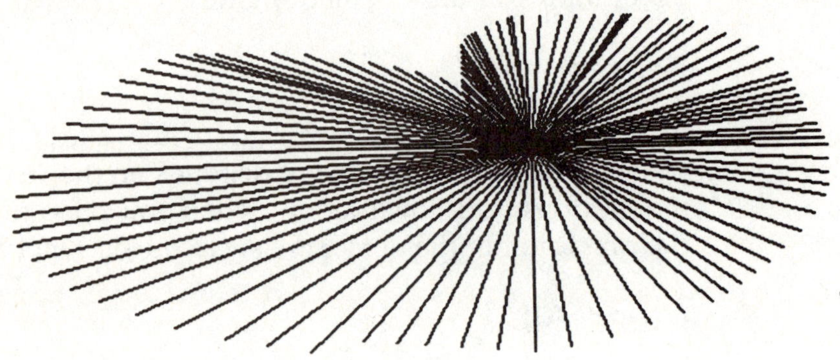

FIGURE 4.8 *Sample Graphic Drawn with the Ribbon Command*

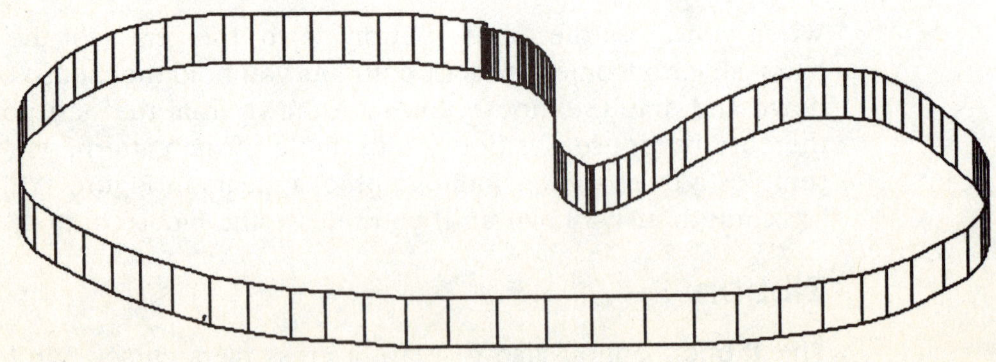

Airbrush

After you select the Airbrush option, you can press the mouse button so that random pixels in an area around the arrow cursor become the current color. This option gives the impression of spray-painted color, as Figure 4.9 shows. If you hold the button down and keep the mouse stationary, a filled-in area gradually appears. If you move the mouse, pixels appear in a circle following the mouse movement.

The Set Width choice in the Options pull-down menu affects the size of the circle of pixels.

Copy

The Copy option of the Tools menu displays the same as the Box command described earlier. The cursor becomes a small box. When you press the mouse button for the first time, the top left corner of a box is locked into place. Moving the mouse displays a box that follows the cursor. Pressing the mouse button a second time defines a box. Now, when you move the mouse, the box follows its movement. If you press the mouse button, a copy of the original rectangle will be drawn at the mouse's location, as Figure 4.10 shows. This duplication continues until you select another tool.

FIGURE 4.9 *Sample Use of the Airbrush Command*

The Options Pull-Down Menu

The choices in the Options menu control general, picture-wide attributes. Figure 4.11 shows the full menu.

Bg Color

When you select Bg Color, a dialog box with two choices opens; select YES or NO for the prompt `New Background`. LWPAINT provides eight background colors. When you select YES, the next background

FIGURE 4.10 *Characters Duplicated with the Copy Command*

Hello World!
World!
World!
World!

FIGURE 4.11 *The Options Pull-Down Menu*

Picture Draw Tools Options Color
Bg Color
Set Width
Font
Show Grid
Set Mode

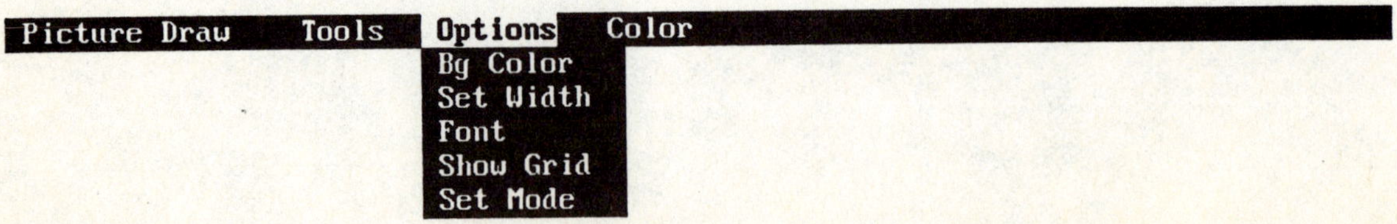

color is shown. Select NO when the background color you wish is visible.

The background colors may visually match some of the foreground colors, but they are different internally. If the foreground color of an area of the screen matches the background color, you cannot see the boundaries between the two. But, if you try to fill the background area, the foreground area is not affected, and vice versa.

Set Width

The Set Width option sets the thickness of lines, the width of box borders, and the size of the Eraser and Airbrush for all future operations. It does not affect anything previously drawn. If you look at the dialog box in Figure 4.12, note the three rectangles. The topmost rectangle has the thinnest sides. If you select it, all of the subsequent operations are small; lines are thin, the Eraser is small, and the Airbrush also is small. Conversely, if you select the bottom, thickest rectangle, everything is drawn in its large format.

Font

When you choose the Font option, a dialog box with the title Select Font, shown in Figure 4.13, is opened. Select a font name with the

FIGURE 4.12 *The Set Width Dialog Box*

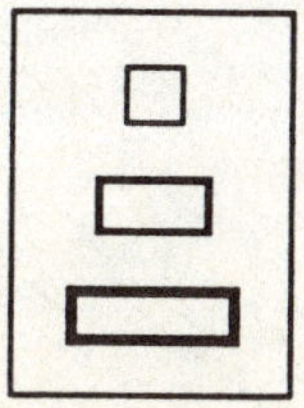

mouse or type the name using your keyboard. Press the **ENTER** key or the mouse button outside the box to choose the font. Select Cancel to continue using the current font.

Only the fonts in the \LINKWAY directory are shown, not those in the current directory. You can, however, type in the name of a font that is not listed but is in the current directory.

The extension .FMF is automatically added to the name you type in.

Show Grid

When you choose the Show Grid option, the screen is covered with a grid so it resembles Figure 4.14. The grid remains displayed until you press the mouse button.

Each square of the grid is approximately the size of a character in the system font—the font used to draw the menu bar.

Unlike most graphics programs, in LWPAINT you cannot choose the spacing of the grid; the size of the rectangles is fixed.

FIGURE 4.13 *The Select Font Dialog Box*

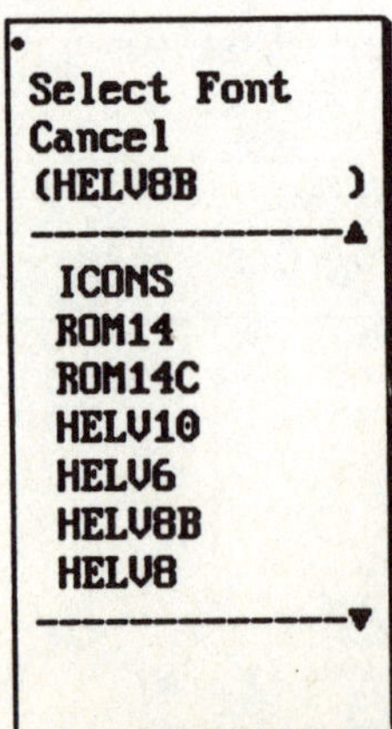

You can use the grid to align objects on the screen. Unfortunately, the grid does not stay on the screen, so you must repeatedly turn it on and off.

Set Mode

If you wish to create another picture in a different graphics mode, choose the Set Mode option. If a file is open, you are prompted to

FIGURE 4.14 *The Grid Display*

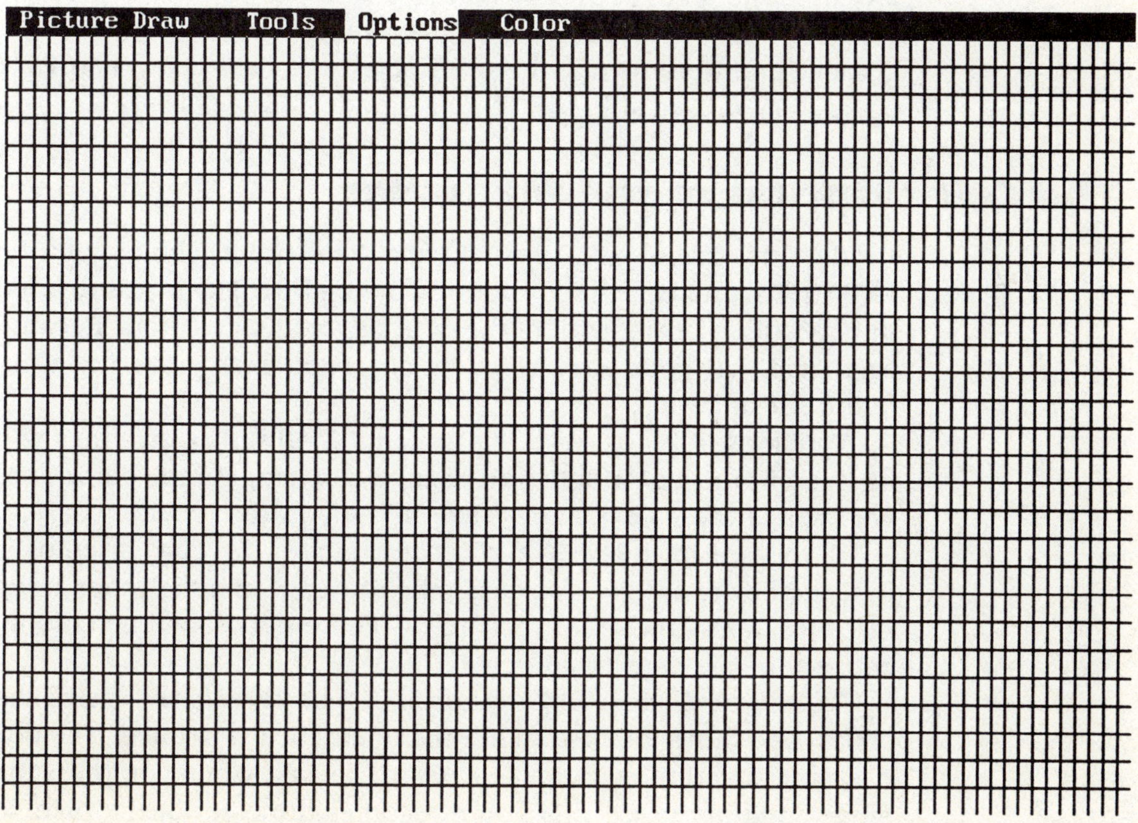

save it first. The current file is closed, and you are prompted to choose the new graphics mode. You must then select Open or New from the Picture pull-down menu when you want to start a new picture.

You cannot change the graphics mode of pictures once they have been created. Thus, it is worth the effort to plan ahead when you choose a graphics mode.

Remember that the CGA mode is the oldest and therefore the most common graphics adapter mode. But it also provides the lowest resolution. The EGA+VGA mode is a good compromise. The EGA standard predates the IBM PS/2 model line. It should be usable on a large number of computers. The two MCGA/VGA standards, MCGA Mono and MCGA 256 color, were introduced with the IBM PS/2 systems. Because AT and XT users must buy new display adapters and monitors to use the VGA standards, not many non-PS/2 computers will be able to use these modes.

The Color Option of the Menu Bar

Unlike the other pull-down menus, the Color choice on the LWPAINT menu bar directly opens a dialog box. The box is divided into rectangles to show all of the currently available colors. Because each graphics mode has a different color set, each mode has a different list of colors.

To choose a color, select its rectangle. All future drawings will be done in this color until you change it. Changing the color does not change the color of any pixels already in the picture.

If you are in the MCGA 256 color mode, the current color is indicated by two dots—one along the top edge and the other along the left edge of the color rectangles. These dots show the column and row of the current color.

To choose a color already displayed on the screen, press the **SHIFT** key, either before or after the dialog box is opened. The box disappears, and the cross hairs cursor appears. When you press the mouse button, the current color becomes the color of the pixel at the center of the cursor.

For the really brave (hackers), a feature enables you to create your own palettes. See Appendix D, "File Formats," for more information about the file format.

Using the LWCAPTUR Program

You are not restricted to creating pictures in the LWPAINT program; you may also use other programs to manipulate LinkWay graphics. Before you start the other program, you must load the LWCAPTUR program into memory. This is as simple as typing **LWCAPTUR** at the DOS prompt. If the program loads correctly, you see the message `LWCAPTUR installed`. From then until you turn off your computer or use the LWREMOVE program, whenever you press the PRINT SCREEN key a copy of the current screen is placed in a picture file. A prompt appears at the top left corner of the screen with a suggested file name. The first time LWCAPTUR is used, the name will be PIC000, the second time, PIC001, and so on. You may change the name if you wish. Press **ENTER** when the prompt displays the file name you wish to use.

The graphics mode is automatically determined and the file extension added to the file name. See the earlier discussion about the LWPAINT program for more information about the formats and the file extensions that identify the files. If the current graphics mode is one that LinkWay does not understand, LWPAINT creates a file but LinkWay won't be able to use it. If you are using MCGA 256 color mode, a second file is created for the palette with the extension .P13. If you do not keep the palette file with the picture file, the colors change when you display the picture.

To remove the LWCAPTUR program from memory to free memory space, reboot your machine or type **LWREMOVE** at the DOS prompt.

The LWPALETT Program

If you capture an MCGA 256 Color picture with the LWCAPTUR program just described, use the LWPALETT program to adjust the palette file before it is used in LinkWay.

LinkWay uses the first 18 colors in the palette for special purposes such as drawing text on the menu bar. Therefore, LinkWay must ensure that these colors will work well together. Having white characters on a white menu bar doesn't help their legibility at all!

To use LWPALETT, just type **LWPALETT** at the DOS prompt. The program asks you for the name of a palette file to check. The processing is automatic once you have typed in the file name and pressed the **ENTER** key.

LWPALETT works only on computers that can display MCGA 256 color images.

Graphics Printing with the LWPRINT Program

The LWPRINT program prints the current contents of the screen on the system printer. You may execute the program directly from DOS by typing **LWPRINT**; you can select Print from the LinkWay Page pull-down menu or the LWPAINT Picture pull-down menu; or you can run it by including the CPRINT command in a script.

The menu bar is not printed; it is hidden first.

The output is determined by the current graphics mode. In all four modes, the background color is printed as white. In CGA mode the three foreground colors are printed as shades of gray. In the other modes, the foreground colors are printed as black.

If you try to print a page that is completely filled with graphics, the hard copy is all black. The printer can only produce two colors: black and white. Thus, background color pixels are white, whereas everything else is black.

The LWPRINT program works with IBM Proprinter and Epson-compatible printers. If you buy the LinkWay Toolkit, you get a program compatible with Hewlett-Packard LaserJet® printers.

CHAPTER 5

General Programming with LinkWay

LinkWay exists in a DOS environment and is subject to the limitations of the operator. This chapter provides a brief summary of the DOS environment as it impacts your programming.

Directory and File System

The DOS file system is composed of *directories* that group and store files. Any directory can have *subdirectories,* which are lower-level directories.

The structure of a file system is similar to an upside-down tree. The topmost directory is called the *root.* Directories are the branches and files the leaves.

The full name of a DOS file is composed of a drive name, a path, the file name, and the extension.

The drive name is a single letter followed by a colon. The first floppy disk drive is called A: and the second, B:. The first fixed or hard disk is called C:, and each successive drive is given the next available letter. Whenever you use DOS or run a program under DOS, there is always a current drive. If you do not specify another drive name, the current drive (the one where LinkWay is stored) is assumed.

The path is a series of directory names, each preceded by a backslash, \. A single backslash represents the root directory. Thus

**** The root directory on the current drive
C: The root directory on the drive C

Likewise, each subdirectory name is preceded by a backslash.

\LINKWAY\WORK\PROJECT1 PROJECT1 is a subdirectory of WORK, and WORK is a subdirectory of LINKWAY, and LINKWAY is a subdirectory of the root.

Absolute paths start with a backslash. The first directory name in an absolute path must be a subdirectory of the root.

\DOS C:\LINKWAY Each of these two entries is an absolute path, because each starts with a backslash.

A path name that does not begin with a backslash is relative to the current directory. Thus, on this command line the full path name is used to show a file being copied from one subdirectory in the current directory to another subdirectory in the current directory:

```
COPY \LINKWAY\WORK\PROJECT1\TEST.LWM \LINKWAY\WORK\PROJECT2
```

However, this shortened version performs the same copy:

```
COPY PROJECT1\TEST.LWM PROJECT2
```

The directories PROJECT1 and PROJECT2 are subdirectories of the current directory, \LINKWAY\WORK.

The second command line is an example of relative paths. Both directories are found relative to the current directory \LINKWAY\WORK.

The file name is a series of one to eight characters. It cannot contain the characters ^ \ [ ] : | < > + = ;* ?, the comma, the double quote ("), the single quote ('), or the space character.

A file name may have an optional extension of one to three characters following the file name. A period separates the file name and the extension. LinkWay uses the file extension to determine the file type. Following are samples of the conventional file extensions for different types of files:

README A filename without an extension

SOUND.ASM An assembly language source file

SPEECH.BIN A binary program

GO.BAT A batch file

PIC000.PCM An MCGA 256 color picture file

LWREMOVE.COM A file related to the .BIN file. .COM files are executable files you can run by typing their name at the DOS prompt

LINKWAY.EXE A compiled executable file

Files and directories are always assumed to be on the current drive. You do not have to specify the drive letter unless the file or directory is on another drive.

If you do not specify a path, the file is assumed to be in the current directory. The current directory is set by the CD (change directory) DOS command. Type the directory path after the CD command. You cannot change directories to a file, only to another directory. Study the following command line examples and their descriptions.

`CD \LINKWAY` \LINKWAY becomes the current directory.

`CD \LINKWAY\WORK` \LINKWAY\WORK becomes the current directory.

`CD PROJECT1` \LINKWAY\WORK\PROJECT1 becomes the current directory. The path is relative to the current directory, because it does not begin with a backslash.

LinkWay does not store file paths but just the file name. If a file is not in the current directory, the proper environment variable or command line argument must contain its path.

The contents of the proper environment variable are automatically added to the file name. For example, if LinkWay is looking for a file that isn't in the current directory, it looks in the directory stored in the LWPATH environment variable. Environment variables are DOS objects that have a name and value. DOS assigns memory space to these variables independently of any program so the variables can be available to all programs.

LinkWay's Environment Variables

The DOS command SET creates environment variables and assigns values to them. To generate environment variables, type the command **SET** followed by the variable name, an equal sign, and the value. The name is composed of alphanumeric characters, starting with the first nonspace character following the SET command and extends to the equal sign. There may be spaces after the first character and before the equal sign, but two names are equivalent if and only if the number of spaces between the characters and the equal sign are equal. For example, the command

```
SET LWDOC=C:\DOCS
```

sets the value of the environment variable LWDOC to C:\DOCS.

The LWPATH environment variable contains the path of the directory holding the LinkWay system files. When a font or icon file cannot be found in the current directory, the directory stored in this variable is searched also. When a system file or home folder is loaded, this directory is searched for the file. As an example, type **SET LWPATH=C:\BIN** before LinkWay is started or type **LINKWAY /LWPATH=C:\BIN** to start the program.

The directory C:\BIN is searched for all system files if they cannot be found in the current directory. This directory also is searched for folders that cannot be found in the current directory. The default value for this variable is \LINKWAY. If you do explicitly set or change the variable, the LinkWay program searches the directory \LINKWAY on the current disk for the files it needs.

The value of the LWDOC environment variable is added to the name of all documents within LinkWay. As you've seen in Chapter 3, the Document button is one of the seven button types. The Document button puts the LinkWay program on hold, switches to a text editor, and enables you to edit a text file. The file name used by the text editor LWEDIT is the variable and file name concatenated together. The combination of the two must be a valid file name.

When LinkWay looks for a picture file, it checks the current directory first, and then the directory specified by the LWPIC environment variable.

As a programmer, you may need several different environments for different projects. Use batch files and different directories to isolate your projects from one another.

Command Line Arguments

When you start LinkWay you may specify command line arguments that control LinkWay's operations. *Command line arguments,* also called *parameters,* are values placed in the DOS command line after the command name. If the parameter begins with a forward slash it is a flag or signal to the program. Flags have names consisting of one or more characters immediately following the backslash. There are two types of flags: those with values and those without. In the LinkWay program, the flags /LWPATH, /LWPIC, and /LWDOC have precedence over the environment variables of the same name.

Flags with values are set by typing a forward slash, followed by the flag name, an equal sign, and the value. No spaces are allowed in a flag; the flag name must follow the forward slash immediately, the equal sign must follow the name, and so on.

Following are all of the flags that the LinkWay program understands:

/C Forces the screen into 4 color CGA mode when LinkWay is started. You may change the mode once the program has started.

/Z Permits only the CGA adapter mode to be chosen. The higher resolution modes use more memory. This option prevents these higher modes from being used, freeing up memory.

/X Prevents the EGA+VGA 16 color mode from being used, saving 50K of memory.

/E Forces the screen into EGA 16 color mode. This assumes that your display and adapter can display the EGA mode.

/V Indicates that a VGA graphics adapter is installed in a computer that does not normally have such a card. If you are using LinkWay on an IBM PC or XT that has a VGA display adapter, use this option.

/M Forces the screen to use MCGA 256 color mode, if it is available. If it isn't, the highest usable resolution is used.

/P Specifies that your printer is not attached to the default printer port. If printing is redirected to another port, a network printer, or a file, LinkWay may crash when trying to print. If this option is set, it is your responsibility to ensure that the printer is ready.

/Snnn Places a new buffer size in 1K units immediately after the /S option; no spaces are allowed. Normally at startup a 50K buffer is the maximum folder size. The minimum size is 4K, the maximum 250K. A smaller buffer allocates more memory for DOS functions called from within the program. This argument must be used if you use folders larger than 50K.

/N Enable National Language Support (NLS). Allows double-capacity fonts using characters numbers 32 to 323. Normal LinkWay fonts contain 95 characters, numbered from 32 to 127. These additional characters may be used for non-English languages. This feature uses approximately 36K.

Consider the following sample command line, which uses the `/Snnn` and `/X` arguments:

```
LINKWAY /S110 /X /LWDOC=\DOCS test
```

Here, `/S110` is a flag with the value 110 and `/X` is a flag without a value. `/LWDOC=\DOCS` is the command line equivalent to an environment variable of the same name. Therefore, the value, `\DOCS`, is used instead of the value of the environment variable. The `test` is a normal parameter. When the LinkWay program starts the folder, `test` is opened rather than the MAIN folder.

How Pages Are Drawn

The objects on a page are drawn in the following order:

1. A copy of the base page is made.
2. Box/line drawings are made on the current page.
3. Pictures are inserted in order of creation.
4. Fields and buttons are inserted in order of creation.

Pictures are displayed in order of creation. The oldest picture objects are displayed first. Newer pictures are drawn over older pictures.

Fields and buttons are drawn in exclusive-or (XOR) mode. Exclusive-or is a logical or boolean mathematical operation. Logical operators work with true/false values. The XOR operation takes two true/false parameters and returns a single true/false value according to a simple formula: If both parameters are the same, return a false; otherwise, return true.

In terms of monochrome/black-and-white graphics, black pixels represent false values and white represent true. If you draw a white pixel over a white pixel, the result is a black, false pixel. If you draw a black pixel over a black pixel, the result is also a black pixel. The XOR operation only returns true when the pixels are different colors. So, if you draw a white object over a black background, the object is shown in white. If you draw a black object over a white background, it is also shown in white.

So what is the significance of this operation? Just this. When you place a picture object on a page you know that the picture window completely replaces anything behind it. When you put a button or field object on a page, its appearance depends on the pixels already drawn. What you see is a combination of the new and the old, as Figure 5.1 shows. If you put a field over a busy picture, chances are you won't be able to see what the field says. Placing fields and buttons can be a trial-and-error procedure. You may have to move them to a place where they are visible.

When you switch from black-and-white pictures to color pictures, the impact of the XOR function gets much more complicated. This discussion is for programmers who have some knowledge of binary arithmetic. The color of a pixel is stored as a binary number. Table 5.1 shows the values of colors for decimal, hexadecimal, and binary numeric systems. When two color pixels are XORed together, their color values are XORed as well, creating a third color value. Unless you know the binary value of each color, it is difficult to predict what two colors will become when they interact, with two exceptions. Black is usually represented by the value zero. A number XORed with zero is unchanged. White is usually represented by the binary value −1, which means that all of the bits are set to 1. A color value XORed with white becomes inverted; all of the 1s are changed to 0s, and all of the 0s are changed to 1s.

The following are examples of EGA colors being XORed together:

Brown	XOR	Light Gray	=	Blue
(0110)		(0111)	=	(0001)
Light Yellow	XOR	Red	=	Light Green
(1110)		(0100)	=	(1010)
Bright White	XOR	Magenta	=	Light Green
(1111)		(0101)	=	(1010)

Experiment a bit: Place a couple of fields, buttons, and pictures over

FIGURE 5.1 *Overlapping Buttons and Fields*

TABLE 5.1 *EGA Color Values*

Color	Decimal Value	Hexadecimal Value	Binary Value
Black	0	00h	0000
Blue	1	01h	0001
Green	2	02h	0010
Cyan	3	03h	0011
Red	4	04h	0100
Magenta	5	05h	0101
Brown	6	06h	0110
Light Gray	7	07h	0111
Dark Gray	8	08h	1000
Light Blue	9	09h	1001
Light Green	10	0Ah	1010
Light Cyan	11	0Bh	1011
Light Red	12	0Ch	1100
Light Magenta	13	0Dh	1101
Light Yellow	14	0Eh	1110
Bright White	15	0Fh	1111

each other. See how two fields of different colors create patterns in a third color. Notice that parts of buttons look normal, but other parts look like the background.

CHAPTER 6

Object-Oriented Programming with LinkWay

Programs in conventional programming languages consist of linear sequences of commands that are executed in a specific order. They are lists of actions. Commands either perform an action on data or control the command sequence.

Overview of Objects

The basis of object-oriented programming is, obviously, the object. An *object* is a unique part of a program, a combination of data and control elements. Objects that have similar behaviors are grouped in classes. Objects inherit properties from their class, such as appearance, placement, extent, operators, and actions. Objects may also inherit properties from other classes of objects. The properties of an object define its behavior. Objects are independent of each other. Independence creates modularity, the ability to copy and reuse objects in other applications.

There are five major classes of objects in LinkWay: folders, pages, buttons, pictures, and fields.

When you set the background color of a folder, all of the pages in the folder inherit that color.

Pages inherit a list of the current fonts from the folder. If you change the available fonts, all of the pages in the folder are affected.

The *extent* of an object is the number of areas in which it is visible. Objects on the base page of a folder are visible on every page of the folder. Their extent is the whole folder. Objects on pages are seen only on that page. Their extent is a single page.

An *instance* of an object is one specific object. When you refer to an instance you do not mean a class of objects but a specific, individual object.

An operator performs an action on an object. For example, in arithmetic the basic operations are addition, subtraction, multiplication, and division. These operations take two operands and return a value. Operations that affect objects may change the object or return a value.

LinkWay programs are known as *applications.* An application is an act of putting to use. When you run a LinkWay application you are putting objects to use. You are using the objects to get things done. The different classes of objects have different uses, and their properties are based on their use.

Pages are components of folders. A page can only exist within a folder. Pages inherit properties such as graphics mode, background color, and access level from their folder. The pages have three properties: sequence number, ID number, and box/line drawings on the page. The *sequence number* is the page's relative position within the folder. The base page has sequence number 0, the first page is 1, and so on. A unique *ID number* is assigned to every page when it is created. The ID number for a page never changes. To see the ID number of the current page, select the Status option from the Option pull-down menu.

Figure 6.1 shows the three types of objects—buttons, pictures, and fields—that are a subclass of pages; each page is a collection of these objects. Objects on the base page are shown on every page in the folder. When you create a new object, it is added to the list of the objects on the current page.

To work with button, field, and picture objects you must set your access level to Format.

In the Format access level whenever you try to select an object a dotted rectangle is displayed around the object instead of an action. You have selected the object itself rather than the object's action. This is shown in Figure 6.2. It is like picking up a hammer and looking at it rather than using it to pound in a nail. You are working with the object's image instead of using it.

While you use the Format mode you must press the mouse button twice in quick succession (double-click the button) to select an object's action.

When an object is selected, as shown in Figure 6.2, you may perform operations on it. These operations are listed in the Object pull-down menu. You may change or delete any objects on the

FIGURE 6.1 *The Object Type Dialog Box*

```
OBJECT TYPE
> Button
  Picture
  Field
```

FIGURE 6.2 *Selecting an Object*

current page. Objects on the base page are selectable, but not changeable. If you are not on the base page you may still select base page objects but you may not change them.

There are three classes of objects on a page: buttons, fields, and pictures. When you create an object, you must specify its class. You cannot change an object's class once it has been created.

To create an object, select New from the Object pull-down menu. You must choose the object class from the Object Type dialog box.

Buttons

The names of the seven button types are Go, Link, Find, Text Pop-Up, Picture Pop-Up, Script, and Document. The types share four properties: name, position, size, appearance, and area. These properties are independent of the button type.

The button type name describes a class of buttons. A button instance may have a specific name that is completely unrelated to the button type or the button type name.

Buttons have one of three appearances: an icon, a sign, or none at all. Signs are the button name surrounded by a shadowed box, as shown in Figure 6.3. An icon is a small picture that represents the button's action. Icons are numbered from 1 to 96. Icon 95 is invisible but functions nevertheless as an icon.

Buttons with no visual appearance can be placed over other objects to make them behave like buttons. If you have a picture of a map you can insert a group of invisible buttons. When the buttons are selected, they can show information about the area of the map they cover. Invisible buttons with empty scripts can be used to cover buttons that the user should not select. When the user tries to select the forbidden button, the invisible button is selected instead.

After you determine the button type, you must select the button area. At this point the mouse cursor changes into a small rectangle the size and shape of a character cell. Position the cursor and press the mouse button to select the first corner of a rectangle. Now you use the mouse cursor to specify the diagonally opposite corner of the rectangle. Move the mouse to specify the button area and press the mouse button when you are satisfied. The button sign or icon is displayed in the first corner you specified.

To select a button, the mouse cursor must be inside the *selection area.* The selection area of an invisible button is the entire button area. The selection area for an icon button is the smallest rectangle surrounding the icon. The selection area for a sign button is the rectangle surrounding the name. The button area has no relationship to the selection areas of sign and icon buttons.

When you select a Text Pop-Up button, a rectangle the size of the button area is displayed over the current page.

When you select a Picture Pop-Up button, the button area defines a window into the picture file. The size and shape of the window determine how much of the picture is shown. The picture can be shifted so that any portion of it is seen through the window. The location of the window is unrelated to the contents of the picture.

If you create an invisible Picture Pop-Up button, the button area defines both the button selection area and the window where the picture is shown.

FIGURE 6.3 *Selecting a Button's Appearance*

Button Types

The Go, Link, and Find button types shown in Figure 6.4 perform familiar actions. These button types work in the same manner as their counterparts in the Go to pull-down menu. When one of these buttons is selected, control is transferred to a new page.

Text Pop-Up buttons display a rectangle the same size as the target area. The target area may be any combination of rows and columns, up to a total of 400 characters. The Text Pop-Up may hold up to 3000 characters. Arrows at the top right and bottom right of the rectangle enable the user to scroll through the text. Pressing ESC, F2, the close circle in the upper left corner, or the mouse button while the mouse cursor is outside of the box closes the Text Pop-Up. If the current access level is above Read, you can edit the text.

When you select a Picture Pop-Up button, a window the size and position of the button area is opened and a portion of a picture file is shown. The window is a maximum of 400 character cells in size in any combination of rows and columns. It is automatically reduced to 400 characters when the button is created if the original window is too large. The name of the picture file is chosen at creation from a file dialog box. If the file cannot be found when the

FIGURE 6.4 *Choosing the Button Type*

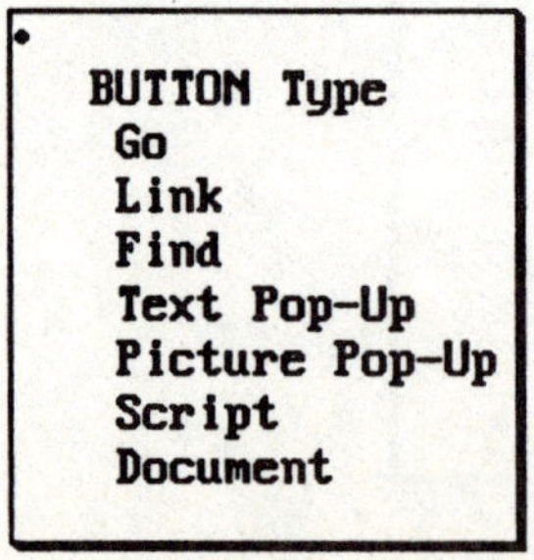

```
BUTTON Type
 Go
 Link
 Find
 Text Pop-Up
 Picture Pop-Up
 Script
 Document
```

button is selected, a shadowed box is displayed, the same size and position as the target area, and the file name is printed in the upper left corner. If the option Blank is chosen in the File dialog box, LinkWay displays a rectangle the size and shape of the target area using the current background color when you select the button. This is a way you can hide part of a page, especially the base page. Press a keyboard key or mouse button to close the Picture Pop-Up.

Selecting a Document button type puts the LinkWay program on hold and invokes the text editor LWEDIT. The document is an ASCII text file; its file name is specified when the button is created. If you do not specify a file name, LWEDIT asks you for one. If the access level is above Read, changes may be made to the file. The LWEDIT program needs 80K for itself. If there isn't enough memory to load LWEDIT, the program will not run. It can edit files up to 25K of characters. Use the arrow keys to move the cursor. Press **F1** for help, **F2** to save the current file, and **F3** to exit. See Chapter 4 for more information about LWEDIT.

The last button type is the entry into another level of LinkWay programming, the Script. A *script* is a textual list of actions and commands in the LinkWay Script Language. Selecting a Script button executes the series of commands. Scripts are stored in predefined Text Pop-Ups or in text files. If you are using Format mode and you select a Script button, a 30-character-wide Text Pop-Up appears in the center of the screen. Each script may be up to 3000 characters. See Chapters 7 and 8 for more detailed information about scripts.

A Button Creation Summary

The following shows the steps you follow to create a button.

Type	**Steps**
Go	1. Select New from the Object pull-down menu.
	2. Select Button from the Object Type dialog box.

3. Define the button area.
4. Select Go from the Button Type dialog box.
5. Enter the button name by selecting a space between the two parentheses, typing in the name, pressing the **ENTER** key, and pressing the mouse button while the mouse cursor is outside of the dialog box. This step is optional.
6. Select either the sign, an icon, or None for the button appearance.
7. Select the page the button will transfer control to, as shown in Figure 6.5.

Link

1. Select New from the Object pull-down menu.
2. Select Button from the Object Type dialog box.
3. Define the button area.
4. Select Link from the Button Type dialog box.

FIGURE 6.5 *The Go To Button Dialog Box*

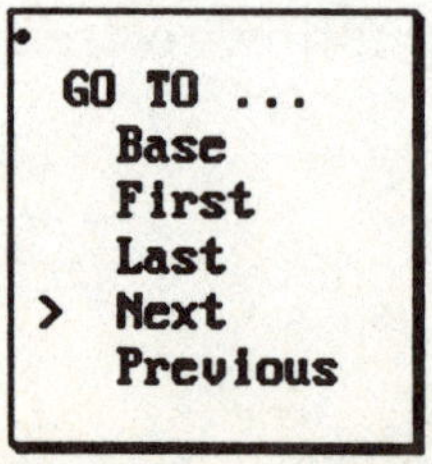

```
GO TO ...
  Base
  First
  Last
> Next
  Previous
```

5. Enter the button name by selecting a space between the two parentheses, typing in the name, pressing the **ENTER** key, and pressing the mouse button while the mouse cursor is outside of the dialog box. This step is optional.

6. Select either the sign, an icon, or None for the button appearance.

7. Enter the page ID and the optional folder name into the Link Information dialog box shown in Figure 6.6. Press the mouse button while the mouse cursor is outside of the box to finish defining the button.

Find

1. Select New from the Object pull-down menu.

2. Select Button from the Object Type dialog box.

3. Define the button area.

4. Select Find from the Button Type dialog box. You see the Find Button dialog box shown in Figure 6.7.

FIGURE 6.6 *The Link Information Button Dialog Box*

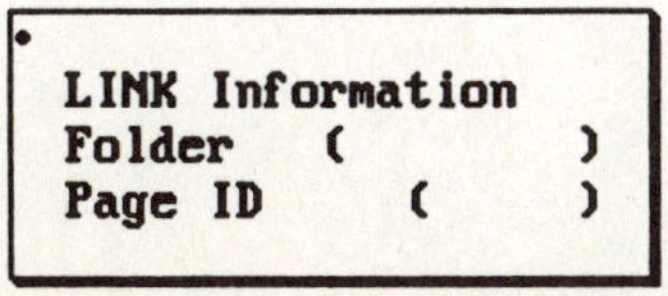

```
LINK Information
Folder   (        )
Page ID     (     )
```

5. Enter the button name by selecting a space between the two parentheses, typing in the name, pressing the **ENTER** key, and pressing the mouse button while the mouse cursor is outside of the dialog box. This step is optional.

6. Select either the sign, an icon, or None for the button appearance.

7. Enter the search string, the optional field name, and the optional folder name into the Find Information dialog box. Press the mouse button while the mouse cursor is outside of the box to finish defining the button.

Text Pop-Up

1. Select New from the Object pull-down menu.

2. Select Button from the Object Type dialog box.

3. Define the button area. Remember that the size of the Text Pop-Up is defined by its button area.

FIGURE 6.7 *The Find Button Dialog Box*

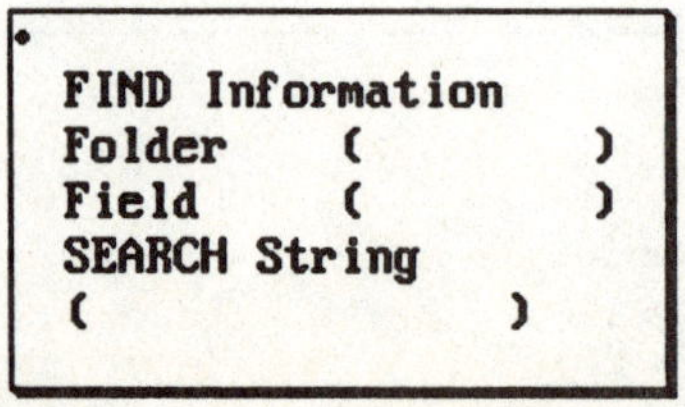

```
FIND Information
Folder    (          )
Field     (          )
SEARCH String
(                )
```

4. Select Text Pop-Up from the Button Type dialog box.

5. Enter the button name by selecting a space between the two parentheses, typing in the name, pressing the **ENTER** key, and pressing the mouse button while the mouse cursor is outside of the dialog box. This step is optional.

6. Select either the sign, an icon, or None for the button appearance.

7. Immediately after you select the button appearance, the Text Pop-Up opens. Continue as if you had just selected a Text Pop-Up button. Add or edit text. When you are finished, press the mouse button while the mouse cursor is outside the pop-up.

Picture Pop-Up

1. Select New from the Object pull-down menu.

2. Select Button from the Object Type dialog box.

3. Define the button area. Remember that the button area determines the picture window.

4. Select Picture Pop-Up from the Button Type dialog box.

5. Enter the button name by selecting a space between the two parentheses, typing in the name, pressing the **ENTER** key, and pressing the mouse button while the mouse cursor is outside of the dialog box. This step is optional.

6. Select either the sign, an icon, or None for the button appearance.

7. After you select the button's appearance, a File dialog box with the title Picture File opens. You can select a picture file from the list, type in a file name, or select Blank. If you select Blank, a rectangular area the size of the button area and the current background color is drawn on the current page. This is a way of covering the background drawn on the base page. If every page in a folder except one has the same background, it is easier to put the background on the base page. Then you can use a blank picture on the page whose format is the exception in order to cover the background.

8. After you select the picture file you are asked to adjust the picture, the portion of the file that is visible in the window. A portion of the picture is shown in the window and a dialog box with the title Adjust appears on the screen. There are eight choices in this dialog box; each moves the picture relative to the window. The window does not move, just the visible portion of the picture is adjusted.

Script

1. Select New from the Object pull-down menu.

2. Select Button from the Object Type dialog box.

3. Define the button area. Script buttons are defined in the same way as Text Pop-Up buttons, except that Script buttons are always in the center of the screen and are always 30 characters wide.

4. Select Text Pop-Up from the Button Type dialog box.
5. Enter the button name by selecting a space between the two parentheses, typing in the name, pressing the **ENTER** key, and pressing the mouse button while the mouse cursor is outside of the dialog box. This step is optional.
6. Select either the sign, an icon, or None for the button appearance.
7. Immediately after you select the button appearance, the script opens. Continue as if you had just selected a Text Pop-Up button. Add or edit text. When you are finished, press the mouse button while the mouse cursor is outside the script area.

Document

1. Select New from the Object pull-down menu.
2. Select Button from the Object Type dialog box.
3. Define the button area.
4. Select Document from the Button Type dialog box.
5. Enter the button name by selecting a space between the two parentheses, typing in the name, pressing the **ENTER** key, and pressing the mouse button while the mouse cursor is outside of the dialog box. This step is optional.
6. Select either the sign, an icon, or None for the button appearance.

7. Immediately after you select the button appearance, the Document File Name dialog box shown in Figure 6.8 opens. Enter the name of the document file here. If you don't enter a name here, the LWEDIT program prompts you for a file name.

Fields

Field objects are used to display and store textual information. Unlike a Text Pop-Up button, a field is always visible. Fields have eight properties: size, position, font, name, characters per line, number of lines, locked/unlocked, and color.

The size and position are set the same way as you set a button target area. The cursor becomes a small dotted rectangle the size of a character cell, and you press the mouse button to select the current location as the first corner. Now the mouse defines the diagonally opposite corner of the rectangle as you press the mouse button when the rectangle is the proper size and shape. All text in the field is constrained to this rectangle.

Now you must choose one of the four current fonts displayed in the Field Font dialog box in Figure 6.9. Four lines of text, each line starting with the letters *ABC,* are displayed in four sizes on the screen. Select the line that contains the font you wish to use. You may change this list of fonts by choosing Fonts from the Option pull-down menu. Note that all of the fields in the current folder

FIGURE 6.8 *The Document Button Dialog Box*

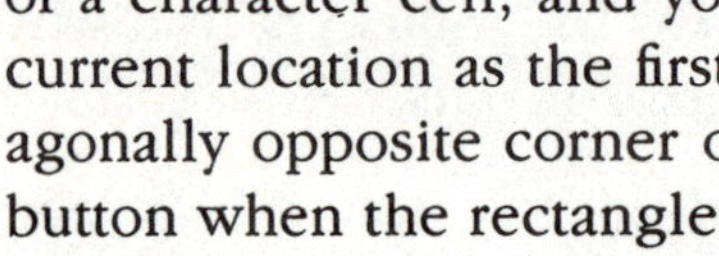

```
Document File Name
(                )
```

use these same four fonts, so if you do change the current fonts all fields in the folder change fonts.

Next you see the dialog box in Figure 6.10, which opens with fields for the name, number of characters per line, number of lines, and a choice of Unlocked or Locked. The field name is optional and is used by the Find command and scripts. The dialog box displays suggested values for the number of characters per line and the number of lines. These values are based on the size of the field and the size of the font. You may change these values using the mouse button to select the field, then typing in the new number.

FIGURE 6.9 *The Field Font Dialog Box*

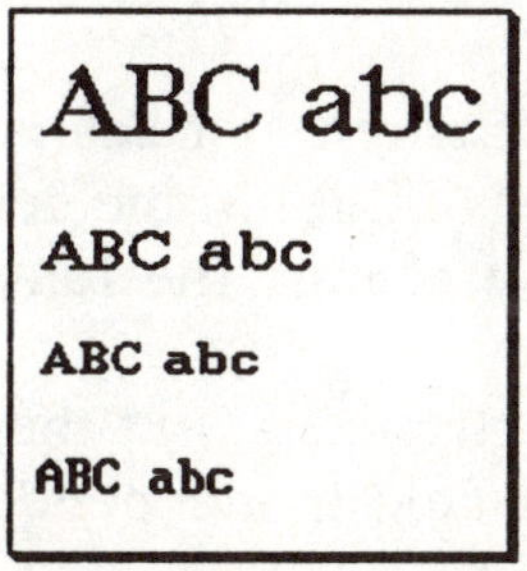

ABC abc
ABC abc
ABC abc
ABC abc

FIGURE 6.10 *The Field Information Dialog Box*

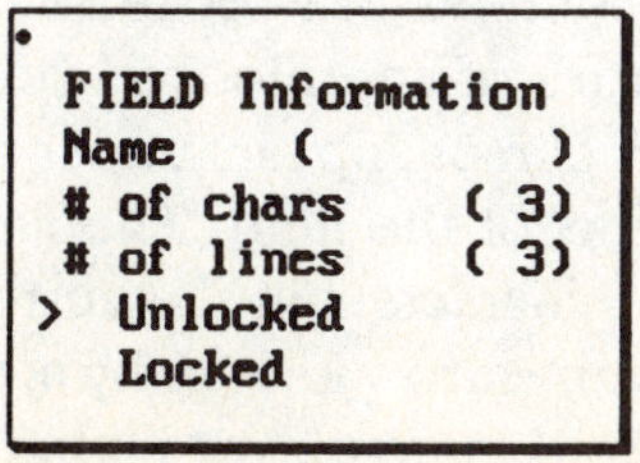

```
FIELD Information
Name      (          )
# of chars      ( 3)
# of lines      ( 3)
> Unlocked
  Locked
```

There is a maximum of 99 characters per line and 20 lines per field. Characters that do not fit into the field are not displayed, but they are not discarded; changing the field size may bring them into view.

The relationship between the number of characters per line, the number of lines, the size of the field, and the size of the font is complex. Because the LinkWay fonts are proportional, each character can be a different width.

Remember two rules as you determine how many characters will fit onto one line. The characters must fit into the field boundaries. The period character is narrow. More periods can fit onto one line than can a series of wide characters like the capital *M*. If the field is 100 pixels wide and a period character is 3 pixels wide, then 33 periods can fit onto one line. If the capital *M* is 14 pixels wide, only 7 of them fit on one line. The second rule limits the number of characters permitted on one line. This value is independent of the field width.

The character height of the current font defines the number of visible lines. The actual number of lines in the field may be larger than the number visible. If you change the fonts in a field, the number of visible lines changes.

Shrinking a field may hide characters, but they are not erased or lost. The visible portion of a field is independent of the actual number of characters in the field.

Unlike changing the size and position of the field, reducing the number of characters in the field *does* erase extra characters. If the field has 20 characters per line and 5 lines, there is space for 100 characters. Reducing the characters per line to 10 cuts the total characters to 50; all subsequent characters are lost.

You cannot change the contents of a locked field. If the mouse cursor is inside the boundaries of an unlocked field and you press the mouse button, a field text cursor appears under the mouse cursor and you can edit the contents of the field. The field text cursor is a vertical line taller than the characters in the current font. You can move this cursor by pressing the arrow keys or by moving the mouse. If the mouse is inside the field and you press the button, the field text cursor moves to the character nearest the mouse cursor. Pressing the INSERT key repeatedly inserts spaces before the text cursor, until the maximum number of characters per line is reached. Typed characters replace the character immediately to the right of the text cursor.

Next you select the color of the text. A rectangle appears with all of the available colors displayed. Choose a color by moving the mouse over a cursor and pressing the mouse button. The apparent color is a combination of an internal color value and the current background color. When the field is created, the internal color value is assigned in such a way that the text color appears to be the color you chose. If you change the background color or place a field over a picture, the color of the text may change and this may make the text illegible.

When a field is drawn, it does not replace the graphics behind it. The pixels you see are a combination of the previous pixel color and the field text color. The intersection of two fields of different text colors can result in displaying pixels of a third color. If you are not careful as you place fields, you may put them in a place where their contents are totally disrupted by the background picture. It is best to place fields over areas of a single solid color.

A Field Creation Summary

1. Select New from the Object pull-down menu.
2. Select Field from the Object Type dialog box.
3. Define the field boundaries.
4. Select a font from the dialog box.
5. Enter the field name, number of characters, number of lines, and unlocked/locked state. Entering a name is optional. You do not have to change the default values for the number of characters and lines. These values are calculated when LinkWay looks at the font you chose and the size of the field boundaries. The unlocked/locked state is a toggle; if you choose one the other is automatically turned off. To continue, select the circle in the top left corner or press the mouse button while the mouse cursor is outside of the box.

6. Select a text color. Remember that the color you see is a combination of an internal text color and the current background color. If you change background colors, your text color may change.

Pictures

Pictures are stored in files and displayed when a page is displayed. Pictures can be made in the LWPAINT program. You can start LWPAINT outside of LinkWay by typing **LWPAINT** or inside LinkWay by selecting Paint from the LinkWay Option pull-down menu. If you run LWPAINT inside LinkWay, the program may run out of memory. See Chapter 4 for more information about LWPAINT.

Pictures have three properties: the size and position of the window, the name of the picture file, and the portion of the picture visible through the window.

The window is defined by selecting the two corners of a rectangle. The cursor becomes a small box the size of a character cell. When you press the mouse button, you define the first corner of the window. A rubber band box is drawn that stretches to follow the movements of the mouse. Press the mouse button a second time to freeze the window in place.

Once you have specified the window you must specify the picture file. When the Picture File dialog box shown in Figure 6.11 appears, you can choose a picture file from the list or type in another name. Only pictures created in the current graphics mode are shown.

Instead of choosing a picture file you may choose the word Blank on the second line or type the character # as a file name. This creates a blank area on the screen that is the same color as the background. Use this option to cover an area of the base page that you do not want to be visible on the current page.

And, last, you must specify the portion of the picture to be visible through the window. After you choose the picture file, the image appears in the window. Use the Adjust dialog box shown in Figure 6.12 to adjust the visible portion of the window. The box has eight choices that move the picture up, down, left, and right either one unit or eight units. The units are the size of a system font character cell. The characters in the menu bar are drawn in the system font. If you select Down 1, the picture moves down the height of the

FIGURE 6.11 *The Picture File Dialog Box*

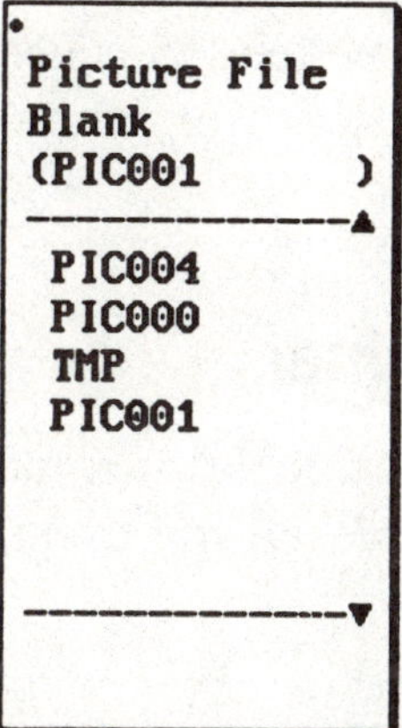

FIGURE 6.12 *The Adjust Dialog Box*

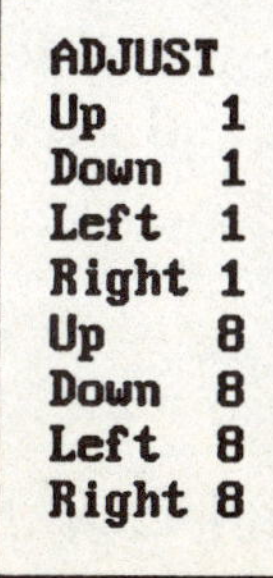

menu bar. If you select Right 8, the picture moves eight character spaces to the right.

Remember that the whole picture remains there, and you are just looking at a portion of it. The position of the window is independent of the area of the picture that is visible.

MCGA 256 color pictures may have palettes. If a picture has a palette, it replaces the current palette whenever you load the file. In other words, when a palette is loaded, it takes precedence over previous palettes. If there are several pictures displayed on one page, the palette of the last file to be loaded is used. Whenever you change palettes, there is a chance that the colors in the previously displayed pictures will change.

A Picture Creation Summary

1. Select New from the Object pull-down menu.
2. Select Picture from the Object Type dialog box.
3. Define the picture window.
4. Select the file name with the Picture File dialog box.
5. Adjust the portion of the picture that is visible in the window.

The Remaining Options of the Object Pull-Down Menu

The options below New on the Object pull-down menu (see Figure 6.13 for these options) are all operations on previously created objects. You must select an object before you select these options, because they are operations on objects and they need something to work with.

Move

The Move option moves the selected object without changing its size. The object's outline follows the movement of the mouse. Press the mouse button when the object is in the proper place.

Move+Size

The Move+Size option both moves and resizes the currently selected object. This is the same mechanism used to define button areas, picture windows, and field boundaries. The cursor becomes a small box. Pressing the mouse button defines the first corner. Move the mouse to set the size of the rectangle. Press the mouse button a second time to freeze the rectangle.

Edit

Choosing Edit enables you to change the properties you set when the selected object was created. The same dialog boxes are used. If you do not wish to change a value, press the mouse button outside of the dialog box.

About the only property you cannot change with this option is the class of an object. You cannot convert a Link button to a Text Pop-Up button, a field to a picture, and so on.

Cut

The Cut option of the Object menu is similar to the Cut option in the Page pull-down menu. Instead of placing a copy of the current page in file, however, it places a copy of the currently selected object

FIGURE 6.13 *The Object Pull-Down Menu*

```
Folder     Page       Object     Go to      Option
                      New
                      Move
                      Move+Size
                      Edit
                      Cut
                      Paste
                      Delete
```

in a file. The default object file name, which you can change, is SCRAP. Press the mouse button while the mouse cursor is outside of the box to choose the name displayed between the parentheses in the Cut Object dialog box shown in Figure 6.14. Object files and page files have different file extensions and formats. The two cannot be interchanged.

This command is used to copy objects between folders and pages. Once an object has been placed in an object file, the Object menu's Paste option can be used to insert it in the new location.

Paste

The Paste option places a copy of the object stored in the specified file onto the current page. Paste performs the opposite action to the Cut option just described. Figure 6.15 shows the dialog box you use for this operation. The object is returned to the same position as before.

FIGURE 6.14 *The Cut Object Dialog Box*

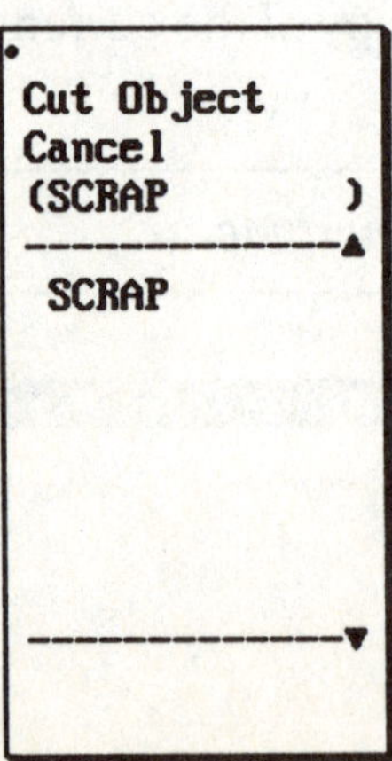

Delete

The Delete option irrevocably deletes the currently selected object from the page. You must confirm that you want the object deleted by selecting YES from the confirmation dialog box shown in Figure 6.16. If you select NO, nothing will happen.

How Objects Are Selected

When you press the mouse button, LinkWay checks the list of objects on the page to see whether the mouse cursor is over one. Buttons

FIGURE 6.15 *The Paste Object Dialog Box*

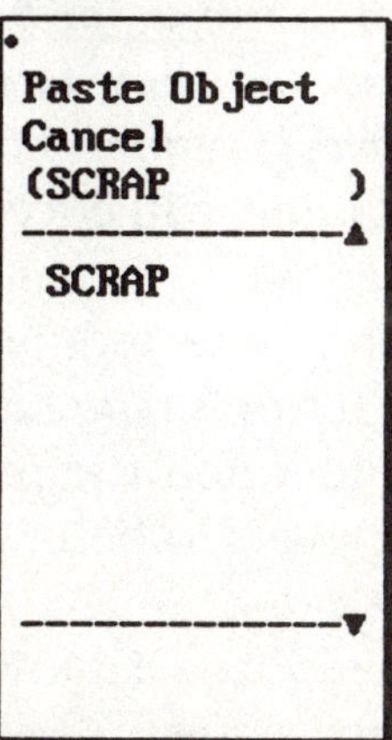

FIGURE 6.16 *The Delete Object Dialog Box*

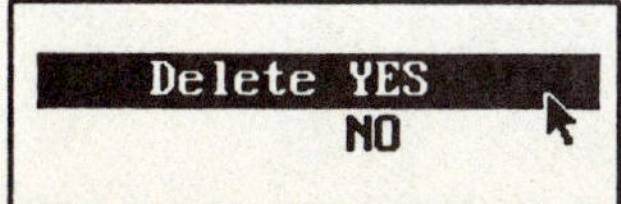

have the highest priority and are checked first, then fields, and finally pictures (only applicable in Format access level).

If the mouse cursor is inside the target area of two objects of the same type, the object created first is selected. If a button, field, and picture overlap, pressing the mouse button selects the button. If two or more buttons overlap, the first button created is selected. The objects in a page are stored in a list, and new objects are added to the end of the list.

To make an object "younger," that is, appear later in the list of objects, cut the object, delete it, and paste it back in. This takes the object out of the list, and puts it back at the end of the list. The oldest object is the first object in the list. To make an object older you must make all of the objects created before it younger. To see the order of creation, press the **TAB** key; each object in turn is outlined. The oldest object will be outlined first.

If two buttons are close together or their target areas overlap, selection is more intuitive if the lower button is older than the upper button. The overlapping area most likely will cover part of the lower button. If the upper button is older and the mouse cursor is in the overlapping area, the upper button is selected. Because the mouse cursor appears to be in the lower button's target area, this confuses the user. If the lower button is older and the mouse cursor is in the overlapping area, the cursor appears to be in the lower object's target area, and the correct object can be selected.

Now what does this mean? Simply, if LinkWay has to choose between two buttons, it chooses the oldest. The two button target areas intersect over the lower button. If the mouse cursor is in this intersection area, you want the lower button to be selected. To ensure that it is selected, it must be older.

CHAPTER 7

Variables, Constants, and Expressions

Scripts are a series of commands written in the script language. Scripts are usually associated with buttons: Selecting the proper button executes the script. Scripts are composed of up to 100 lines of 30 characters each. You may place more than one command on a line, but usually this causes your script to become less readable. Script editing is done within a text pop-up window, 9 lines high and 30 characters wide.

Upper- and lowercase letters are considered equivalent in script commands. All commands are terminated with semicolons (;). Some commands have *parameters,* which are values that define or affect the operation of the command. The values may be numbers, object names, or strings of characters beginning and ending with double quotes (''). Parameters are separated from each other by commas (,).

`mbar;`
`Mbar;`
`MBAR;`
	Display the menu bar, equivalent to selecting Menu Bar from the Option pull-down menu.

`PROMPT "Hello!";`	Display the string `Hello!` on the bottom line of the screen.

Commands can be divided into six general types: control, user interface, page manipulation, object manipulation, miscellaneous, and variable handling.

A program is a sequence of commands. The next command to be executed is usually the next command in the sequence. Flow of control (or control, for short) commands alter the order of execution.

LinkWay application programs are user oriented; the user interface commands provide communication between the user and the scripts.

As you saw in earlier chapters, the page is the basic unit of every application. Users see a collection of pages and do not need to know that pages are stored in a particular folder, or even that the next page may be in the next folder. Page manipulation commands enable you to create, delete, and change pages.

Every page is created to store objects. Object manipulation commands provide a way for scripts to deal with objects.

Variables

Variables are one type of LinkWay object. Their purpose is to hold information. However, unlike fields they are not visible to the user and are changeable only within scripts.

Variables have three properties: a name, size, and value. The name and size are defined when the variable is created. They can only be created inside of scripts. See the VAR command for more information about creating variables.

Subscripts may be used with variables. If you place the number n in parentheses directly after the variable name, the value of the variable is the nth character in the variable. If two numbers, n and l, separated by a comma are placed in parentheses, the value of the expression is a string starting with character n and ending with character $n + l$. The value l represents the length of the subscript.

You may assign values to variables using subscripts. The first value in the subscript represents the first character to be replaced. The second value, *l,* represents the number of characters to replace.

Constants

There are two types of constants: numeric and string.

Numeric constants represent decimal numbers in the approximate range of −10,000,000 to +10,000,000, with up to 2 decimal places. Examples of numeric constants are

```
10000000
-10000000
1234
+1234
-1234
3.14
-31.45
```

String constants are a series of characters delimited or bounded by double quotes (''). The string constant begins with the character after the first double quote and does not end until the second double quote. A string constant beginning on one line of a script may end on another line. A *character* is any letter, number, or symbol that you can type on your keyboard. All characters between the quotes are part of the string constant—especially spaces. You cannot place a literal double quote directly into a string. You can, however, use the CHR() function and the string concatenation operator (both described later in the chapter) to put any character in a string.

```
"This is a string constant"
"Notice that the spaces will be included
in the string constant, and the constant
ends when at the second double quote, not
the end of the line."
```

Expressions

An *expression* is a combination of operands and operators.

Operands are numeric constants, string constants, variables, system variables, and functions.

Operators

There are two types of operators: ***binary operators,*** which require two operands, and ***unary operators,*** which require one operand.

The value of an expression is the result of the action of the operators on the operands.

Expression	Value
2 + 2	4
2 * 3	6
12 / 4	3

Arithmetic Operators: + (Addition), − (Subtraction), * (Multiplication), and / (Division)

Arithmetic operators are binary operators; they require two operands. The value of an expression is the mathematical result of the action of the operator on the operands. Division is an integer operation; the remainder is not kept. Table 7.1 shows the results of a common operation using arithmetic operators.

The Unary Negative Operator: −

The unary negative operator is the same symbol as for subtraction, and it performs a similar action. It reverses the sign of the expression it precedes. Only one operand is affected.

```
VAR N(15);
SET N = 123;
PROMPT -N;              The number −123 is displayed.
PROMPT 200 - -N;        The number 323 is displayed.
```

`PROMPT 200 + -N;`	The number 77 is displayed.
`PROMPT -(200 + N);`	The number −323 is displayed.
`PROMPT -(N - 200);`	The number 77 is displayed.

String Concatenation Operator: :

The string concatenation operator, the colon, is used to append one string to another. It takes two string operands and returns a single string composed of the first string immediately followed by the second string.

```
VAR S(64);
SET S = "The bear went over the mountain " :
   "to see what he could see."
```

The variable S is set to the value

```
"The bear went over the mountain to see what he could see."
```

When you use variables as operands, you must remember that the entire variable is used. In the preceding example the variable S would be padded with spaces up to its length of 64 characters.

```
VAR S(8), R(8), T(16);
SET S="SHORT";
```

TABLE 7.1 *Examples of Arithmetic Operators and Their Operations*

Operand	Operator	Operand	Result
2	+	2	4
5	−	7	−2
100.5	*	3	301.5
423	/	8	52

```
SET R="PHRASE";
SET T= S : R;
```

The variable T will be set to the value

```
"SHORT   PHRASE  ".
```

Here the value is the combination of two 8-character variables, a total of 16 characters. There are three spaces added to the word SHORT to fill variable S, and two to variable R.

See the function TRUNC() later in this chapter for information about avoiding those extra spaces.

Relational Operators: <, <=, >, >=, =, and !=

Relational operators perform comparisons between two operands. The comparisons are made in either of two ways: If one or more of the operands is a number, the two are compared as if they were all numbers; otherwise, they are compared as strings.

An operand is considered to be a number if the first character is a number, plus sign (+), or negative sign (−).

If one operand is considered a string and the other is a number, the value of the string is 0.

If a comparison is true, the result is 1; otherwise, it is 0.

Numeric comparisons are the familiar mathematical operations. The symbol != represents not equal and is the opposite of the equals operation. Following are some examples of numeric comparisons:

X < Y	Return true if X is less than Y.
X <= Y	Return true if X is less than or equal to Y.
X > Y	Return true if X is greater than Y.
X >= Y	Return true if X is greater than or equal to Y.
X = Y	Return true if X is equal to Y.
X != Y	Return true if X is not equal to Y.

In LinkWay the difference between numbers and strings is very hazy. Numbers are stored as strings. Therefore, in some situations a number behaves like a string and in other situations like a number. If you treat a number like a number, that is, if you use a mathematical operator on it, the number behaves like a number.

String Relational Operators: $<, $<=, $>, $>=, $=, and $!=

The string relational operators force a string comparison, whereas the relational operators just described are numeric if either operand is a number.

String comparisons are based on the ASCII system, which assigns a number, called the *index,* to every character. The index of the space character is 32, the letter *A* is 65.

Each character in both operands is compared in turn. If every character is equal, the strings are equal. If any character is not equal, the indexes of the first characters that differ are used for the comparison. Here are some examples.

`"abcde123*" = "abcde123*"`	The result is true, because all of the characters are equal.
`" abcde123*" = "abcde123*"`	The result is false, because the first string begins with a space.
`" abcde123*" < "abcde123*"`	The result is true, because the first character that differs, the space, has a lower value than the lowercase letter *a* in the ASCII system.

Logical Operators: & (Logical AND) and | (Logical OR)

Logical operators are binary operators that use numbers as operands.

Logical operators work with true or false values. If an operand is 0, it is considered false. Otherwise, the operand is true, that is, all nonzero numbers are considered true.

Logical operators return one of two possible values: 0 for false, and 1 for true. The & (and) operator returns true (1) if both of its operands are true (nonzero). Otherwise, & returns false (0). Table

7.2 shows typical logical operations between two operands, along with their results.

The | (OR) operator returns false (0) if both of its operands are false (0). Otherwise, | returns true (1). Table 7.3 shows results of common operations with OR.

These operators extend the power of the IF command (described later) by allowing complex logical operations.

```
IF A >= 0 & A < 10
        PROMPT "The variable A contains a single digit";
ELSE
        PROMPT "This is not a single digit.";
```

TABLE 7.2 *Common Operations with the & Logical Operator*

Operand1		Operand2	Result
0	&	0	0
0	&	3	0
24	&	0	0
12	&	397	1

TABLE 7.3 *Common Operations with the | Logical Operator*

<table>
<tr><th>Operand1</th><th></th><th>Operand2</th><th>Result</th></tr>
<tr><td>0</td><td>|</td><td>0</td><td>0</td></tr>
<tr><td>0</td><td>|</td><td>3</td><td>1</td></tr>
<tr><td>24</td><td>|</td><td>0</td><td>1</td></tr>
<tr><td>12</td><td>|</td><td>397</td><td>1</td></tr>
</table>

```
IF A < 0 | B < 0
        PROMPT "One of these variables is less than zero"
```

Operator Precedence Rules

Expressions may be concatenated together to form new expressions. The precedence of the operators determines which expressions are executed first. For example, the multiplication operator has a higher precedence than the addition operator, so it is executed first, as the following sample operation shows:

2 * 3 + 7	The result is 13, because the multiplication operator is executed first.

Parentheses may be used to change the order of execution, as the following operation shows:

2 * (3 + 7)	The result is 20.

Table 7.4 shows the operators in their order of precedence. Operators with the highest precedence are executed first. If a choice must be made between two operators of equal precedence, the leftmost operator is executed first.

7 − 2 + 11	The number 2 is subtracted from 7 first. Then 11 is added to the result.

TABLE 7.4 *Operator Precedence Chart*

Precedence	Operator
5	− (unary minus)
4	*, /
3	+, −, : (string concatenation)
2	<, <=, >, >=, all relational operators
1	&, |

Expression	Description
(7 − 2) + 11	These two expressions are equivalent. The parentheses just emphasize the order of execution.
7 − (2 + 11)	If you wanted this equation you must use parentheses. The result of this expression is −6.

All mathematical operators have higher precedence than relational and logical operators, so they are executed first.

Expression	Description
7 * A < 10	The result is true if the expression 7 * A is less than 10.
(7 * A) < 10	This expression is equivalent to the previous expression; the parentheses do not change the order of execution, because the mathematical operation multiplication has a higher precedence than the comparison.
7 * (A < 10)	The relational operator < returns a value of 1 if A is less than 10; otherwise, it will return 0. This expression returns 7 if A is less than 10; otherwise, it returns 0.
7 * A < 10 & B > 100	The result is true if the expression 7 * A is less than 10 and B is greater than 100. The multiplication operator has the highest precedence, so it is executed first. Then the two relational operators are executed. And, finally, the logical operation containing & is executed.
SET N = 5;	Assign the value 5 to the variable N.
3 * −N − 12 / 4	The operations are performed in the following order: First, 3 * −(5) − 12 / 4 is computed. N is replaced by its value. Second, 3 * (−5) − 12 / 4 is computed. The unary minus takes effect.

Third, (−15) − (3) is performed. The multiplication and division operators are executed.

Fourth, −18 is performed. The subtraction operator is executed for final result of −18.

More About Operands

Fields may be used as operands if they have names. The name cannot contain spaces. Remember that a field is an object and that its name is one of its attributes. The value of a field is another attribute that consists of every character in the field, including the spaces used to fill it up. If a field definition has 3 lines of 40 characters each, there are 120 characters in the field, no matter how many are actually visible.

Three types of buttons may be used as operands also: Text Pop-Ups, Scripts, and Links. These buttons must have names that contain no spaces.

Unlike fields, Text Pop-Ups and Scripts do not have a specific number of characters. The string of characters in a Text Pop-Up or Script button ends at the last nonspace character. This does not mean that spaces between words are dropped. Every nonspace character in the Text Pop-Up will be included, as well as every space character between them. Space characters that do not have other characters following them, such as the spaces at the end of the Text Pop-Up or Script button, are not included.

Link buttons return a string of 13 characters. The first 8 are the name of the folder the link is pointing to. If the folder name consists of fewer than 8 characters, the remainder is filled with spaces. The last 5 characters contain the page ID of the link, and again, spaces are added to make at least 5 characters.

Functions

A *function* is a one-word operand that contains a parameter. The parameter is an expression that evaluates to a number, string, character, or variable name. Optionally, you may place the parameter between parentheses. The parentheses make a script more readable. Functions may not be used as commands, but only as operands, that is, as part of an expression.

ASC() Function

The syntax for the ASC() function is

```
ASC(expression);
```

Every character is assigned a number; this is its ASCII index. The ASC() function returns the ASCII index of the first character in the expression. Numbers are converted to strings.

Following are examples of the ASC() function:

`ASC("Abcdef");`	The value 65, the letter *A* is returned.
`ASC("A");`	The value 65 is returned.
`ASC("a");`	The value 97, the letter *a* is returned.
`ASC("0123");`	The value 48, the character 0 is returned.
`ASC(789);`	The value 55, the character 7 is returned.

See Appendix H, "The ASCII Character Set," for the complete list of ASCII codes.

CHR() Function

The syntax for the CHR() function is

```
CHR(expression)
```

The CHR() function is the inverse of the ASC() function. Given an ASCII index value, CHR() returns the appropriate character. This function is very valuable when you are working with characters that serve special purposes, such as the double quote (").

Following are examples of the CHR() function:

```
PROMPT "He said, " : CHR(34) : "How are you today?" : CHR(34);
```

Because the double quote is used to delimit strings, it cannot be used inside of a string. Instead, the CHR() function may be used. The double quote has the ASCII value 34. The result of this expression is the string (quotes included)

```
He said, "How are you today?"
```

FSIZE() Function

The syntax for the FSIZE() function is

```
FSIZE(expression)
```

If the expression evaluates to the DOS name of a file, the result of the function is the size of the file in bytes (one byte equals one character). The file name may include a path. If the file does not exist, the result is 0.

Following are examples of the FSIZE() function:

```
PROMPT FSIZE("\autoexec.bat");
                                        The result on my computer is 730.
PROMPT FSIZE("\LinkWay\LinkWay.exe");
                                        The result on my computer is 79557.
IF FSIZE("\autoexec.bat") > 0
   LOAD buffer,"\autoexec.bat";
```

LEN() Function

The syntax for the LEN() function is

```
LEN(expression)
```

This function returns the length, in characters, of the expression, not counting trailing spaces. The expression may be a string, a variable, a Link button, a Text Pop-Up button, a Script button, or a field. To calculate the length of an object, it must have a name. The name cannot contain space characters.

Following are examples of the LEN() function:

`LEN("abcdef")`	The result is 6.
`VAR buf(12);`	
`SET buf =`	
`"abcdefghi";`	
`PROMPT LEN(buf);`	The result is 9.
`PROMPT LEN(select);`	The length of the contents of the button, field, or variable named "select".

TRUNC() Function

The syntax for the TRUNC() function is

```
TRUNC(expression)
```

This function truncates the expression by removing any trailing spaces.

Following are examples of the TRUNC() function:

`TRUNC("Hello?    ")`	The result is `Hello?`
`TRUNC("123456    ")`	The result is `123456`.
`TRUNC(7890)`	The result is `7890`.

When you concatenate the contents of a field, the TRUNC() function can be used to strip off the extra spaces used as padding.

CHAPTER 8

Script Commands

The LinkWay command descriptions in this chapter are composed of four parts, the last of which is optional. The first line is the title of the command. The second part, composed of one or more lines, shows the syntax for how to enter the command. The third part is a description of the command's actions, with examples of its use. Finally, some commands have a list of related topics.

Conventions for Command Lines

For brevity and conciseness, the following words are used as variables for important concepts in the *syntax lines* (diagrams of proper command formats) in this chapter:

button The name of a button on the current page
command A reference to another script command
expression The string value of an expression

field The name of a field on the current page
folder The name of a folder
object The name of an object
value The numerical value of a expression
variable The name of a variable

You should replace these words with the appropriate names or commands. Variables appear in lowercase in all the syntax lines in this book.

Most script command lines contain *parameters,* which are values or expressions following the command name. These parameters affect the operation of the command by specifying the details on how the command should work. An expression can be a value, a literal string, a number, or a combination of all three.

Square brackets, [], enclose *optional* parameters—those items not required in every instance of the command. Do not type the brackets. If you use the optional parameters, you must use all the characters enclosed in the brackets.

For example, the CUT command has a single optional parameter:

```
CUT [expression];
```

There are two ways of using this command:

```
CUT;
CUT "OLDPAGE";
```

Again, if you do use an optional parameter you must type all the characters in the square brackets, especially commas. Notice that you replace the word *expression* from the syntax line with the command's actual parameter.

As another example, the LinkWay DOS command has two optional parameters:

```
DOS [#] expression [#];
```

There are four ways of entering this command:

```
DOS expression;
DOS # expression;
```

```
DOS expression #;
DOS # expression #;
```

The two optional parameters—the first and second #s—are independent of each other. You may have any combination of the two.

The FIND command also has two optional parameters:

```
FIND expression[,field[,folder]];
```

There are three ways of using this command:

```
FIND expression;
FIND expression,field;
FIND expression,field,folder;
```

Notice that the FIND syntax line contains *two* sets of square brackets, one inside the other. These are called ***nested brackets.*** Each set of nested brackets is called a *level.* The first level in the FIND command example is

```
,field[,folder]
```

and the second level is

```
,folder
```

If you specify the second level of brackets, you must specify the first level. Levels are dependent on each other. If you specify a level, you must specify its predecessor.

If you specify the parameter `field`, then `folder` is optional. If you specify the parameter `folder`, then `field` is required.

The following command is illegal and won't execute:

```
FIND expression,folder;
```

Here, LinkWay assumes that the parameter folder is the name of a field, not a folder.

BCALL Command

Syntax

```
BCALL variable;
```

Purpose and Examples

This command executes a precompiled, specialized assembly language program stored in the parameter *variable*. LinkWay's operation is interrupted only long enough for the program to run.

Preparing a program for use with the BCALL command is a three-step process:

1. Create and compile the program into a .COM or .BIN file.
2. Load it into memory with the LOAD command.
3. Execute it with the BCALL command.

The assembly language program must comply with several rules:

- Its origin must be 0, use the "ORG 0" command
- It is called with a FAR CALL, and must return with a FAR RETURN.
- The segment and stack registers must return with their start values.
- Approximately 1K of stack space is available to the program.

If the first command is a short JMP to a location further into the program, the area immediately after the JMP may be used to pass information between the program and your LinkWay application.

The program is stored in a LinkWay variable. Subscripts may be used to access individual bytes of the program before and after it is executed. The first byte in the routine is byte 0, but it is character subscript 1 in the variable.

Creating the assembly language program consists of four steps:

1. Entering the code
2. Compiling the code into an object file
3. Linking the object file
4. Converting the executable file into a binary file

The code should start with the following statements. Remember to replace the word `name` with the name of your routine.

```
PROG SEGMENT BYTE PUBLIC PROG
name PROC FAR
```

```
ASSUME CS:PROG,DS:PROG
ORG 0
```

The code should end with the following statements. Again, replace `name` with the name of your routine.

```
        RET
name    ENDP
PROG    ENDS
END
```

After the text file with the code is created, you must create an object file. This example uses the Microsoft® Macro Assembler (MASM) v5.00.

```
MASM name;
```

Once the object file has been created, you link it to create the executable file. Most versions of DOS are shipped with the LINK program. Always make sure that you are using the most recent version of LINK possible. See your documentation for more information about linking and libraries.

```
LINK name;
```

The LINK program should print out a warning stating `no stack segment`. Ignore this message, because you are creating a .COM or .BIN file that cannot have a stack segment. In fact, in a .COM file everything—including the code, program data, uninitialized memory, stack, and program segment prefix—is in one segment. The compiled and linked file must be smaller than 64K.

After you have created the object file, it must be converted to a binary file with the EXE2BIN program, which is also shipped with DOS. To run this program, enter

```
EXE2BIN name
```

If this program cannot convert your code, it prints out an error message to that effect, and your file cannot be used within LinkWay. The file must conform to the limitation of the .COM format: one segment for each element. High-level language compilers generally cannot conform to this standard.

To summarize, your text editor created an .ASM file, MASM created an .OBJ file, LINK created an .EXE file, and EXE2BIN created the .BIN file that will be used in your LinkWay application.

Now, to use the program in LinkWay you must create a script button. Inside the script you need a minimum of two commands:

```
LOAD ROUTINE,"name.BIN";
BCALL ROUTINE;
```

where `name` is replaced with the name of your file.

The LOAD command creates a copy of the file in memory and the BCALL command executes a FAR CALL to the address of the first byte of the variable.

This example is for those who have some knowledge of assembly language programming. It does not attempt to be a full tutorial.

```
PROG SEGMENT BYTE PUBLIC 'PROG'
SOUND PROC FAR
ASSUME CS:PROG,DS:PROG                          ; CREATE ONE SEGMENT
ORG 0                                           ; SET ORIGIN TO 0
JMP         short GO                            ; JUMP PAST DATA

ALREG       db          0
AHREG       db          0
BLREG       db          0
BHREG       db          0
CLREG       db          0
CHREG       db          0
DLREG       db          0
DHREG       db          0
GO          label       near
            mov         al,byte ptr ALREG
            mov         ah,byte ptr AHREG
            mov         cl,byte ptr CLREG
            mov         ch,byte ptr CHREG
```

```
            mov         dl,byte ptr DLREG
            mov         dh,byte ptr DHREG

START:
            mov         bl,byte ptr BLREG
            mov         bh,byte ptr BHREG
STSOUND:
            mov         al,10110110b        ; Put the magic number into
            out         43h,al              ; the speaker port.
TONE:
            mov         ax,bx               ; 1/tone is stored in
BX
            out         42h,al              ; put low-byte in tone port
            mov         al,ah               ; put high-byte into AL
            out         42h,al              ; and put it into tone port
            in          al,61h              ; Port 61 turns the speaker
            or          al,3                ; on and off, other services
            out         61h,al              ; use it so only bits 0 and
                                            ; 1 may be changed safely.
            mov         cl,byte ptr CLREG
            mov         ch,byte ptr CHREG
                                            ; Set the delay between
                                            ; changing the tone value.
WAITING:
            loop        waiting;
            mov         ah,0bh              ; get keyboard status with
            int         21h                 ; the BIOS keyboard routine
            inc         al                  ; which returns FF if a key
            jz          CLEANUP             ; has been pressed.
            dec         bx                  ; decrease the 1/tone value
            jnz         STSOUND             ; start over
            dec         dx                  ; decrease iteration value
            jnz         START               ; and reset tone value
CLEANUP:
            in          al,61h              ; turn off speaker
```

```
            and         al,11111100b
            out         61h,al
            mov         byte ptr DLREG,dl
            mov    .    byte ptr DHREG,dh
                                              ; Put the remaining
                                              ; iteration value back
            RET
SOUND       ENDP
PROG        ENDS
END
```

Eight bytes are reserved at the beginning of the routine, after the JMP, for communication between the routine and your LinkWay application.

In the following example the program is stored in a variable called ROUTINE. Use subscripts with that variable to set the values for the program's use.

```
LOAD ROUTINE, "SOUND.BIN";
SET ROUTINE(3)  = CHR(0);      /* ALREG, not used */
SET ROUTINE(4)  = CHR(0);      /* AHREG, not used */
SET ROUTINE(5)  = CHR(0);      /* BLREG, low byte of pitch */
SET ROUTINE(6)  = CHR(3);      /* BHREG, high byte of pitch */
SET ROUTINE(7)  = CHR(0);      /* CLREG, low byte of delay */
SET ROUTINE(8)  = CHR(3);      /* CHREG, high byte of delay */
SET ROUTINE(9)  = CHR(16);     /* DLREG, low byte of repeats */
SET ROUTINE(10) = CHR(0);      /* DHREG, high byte of repeats */
BCALL ROUTINE;
VAR remain(11);
SET remain = asc(routine(10)) * 256 + asc(routine(9));
IF remain > 0
   MSG "A key was pressed."
```

The preceding assembly language routine plays a siren-like, warbling sound on your computer's speaker. The pitch and delay values determine the sound. High-pitch values are low-pitched sounds. The delay value determines how long each pitch is played; the result is hard to characterize, other than to say it takes longer to finish each note.

Because all LinkWay variables are string variables, numbers are represented as ASCII strings. The number 500 is represented by the characters 5, 0, and 0 (ASCII values 53, 48, and 48). The statement

```
SET ROUTINE(3) = 0
```

places the value 48, the ASCII index of the character 0, in that location of the variable.

To place a numerical value in a location you must use the CHR() function:

```
SET ROUTINE(3) = CHR(0);
```

This statement would place the value 0 in the location of that variable.

Related Topics

See also: DOS command and EXTERN command.

BEEP Command

Syntax

```
BEEP;
```

Purpose

This command causes the computer to make an audible tone. Use it to get the user's attention, but don't use it too often or the user will tire of it.

CLONE Command

Syntax

```
CLONE;
```

Purpose and Examples

This command creates a new page that is an exact copy of the current page. The new page is inserted directly after the current page. After the CLONE command is executed, the cursor is moved to the new page.

Note: The base page may not be cloned.

If the folder has run out of space, LinkWay does not create a new page; the current page is not changed; and you won't see an error message. The only way a script can detect this situation is by saving the ID number of the current page before cloning and comparing it to the ID number after copying. If the two IDs are the same, a new page has not been created. See Chapter 9 for a discussion about the ID variable. The system variable ID is automatically changed if a new page is created, as the following code shows.

```
VAR ID(5);
SET X = ID
CLONE;
IF X = ID
   MSG "The Cloning failed!";
ELSE
   MSG "A clone has been created!";
```

Related Topics

See also: CUT command, DELETE command, PASTE command, and ID system variable.

CPRINT Command

Syntax

```
CPRINT;
```

Purpose

This command prints a picture of the current page on the system printer. The printer must support an IBM-compatible graphics print mode.

In CGA mode, the background color is white, and the three foreground colors are printed as shades of gray. In the other graphics modes, the background is white and all other colors are printed as black. If a page contains a lot of graphics, the CPRINT command will not be of much use, because all of the foreground colors are printed as black. For graphics pages, then, the majority of the printed pages would be printed as black with CPRINT.

To print the file, LinkWay automatically loads the LWPRINT program.

Related Topics

See also: PRINT command.

CSAVE Command

Syntax

```
CSAVE;
```

Purpose and Examples

This command forces LinkWay to update the current folder's file.

When it opens a folder, LinkWay places a copy of the folder in the computer's memory. Any changes you make to the folder are made to the copy; the original stored in the file is not changed. When you close a folder or exit LinkWay, the copy in memory replaces the original in the file.

The CSAVE command tells LinkWay to save any changes made to the folder.

For example, a button that moves to the next page could have the following script:

```
CSAVE;
GO SEQ+1;
```

so that any changes made to the current page are immediately saved.

CUT Command

Syntax

```
CUT [expression];
```

Purpose and Examples

This command is the opposite of the PASTE command. CUT places a copy of the current page in a file. If the parameter `expression` is empty, the file is called SCRAP.PG. If not, the extension .PG is added to the parameter `expression` and the page stored in that file. The value of `expression` must be a valid DOS file name.

The first example that follows places a copy of the current page in the SCRAP.PG file; the second example places a copy of the current page in the file TEMP.PG.

```
CUT;
CUT "temp";
```

Related Topics

See also: CLONE command, DELETE command, and PASTE command.

DELETE Command

Syntax

```
DELETE;
```

Purpose and Examples

This command irrevocably deletes the current page from the current folder. If you delete the last page, the second to the last page becomes the current (and last) page. If you delete any page other than the last, the current page becomes the page after the deleted page.

In the following example, the system variable COUNT contains the current number of pages in the folder. The value of COUNT is also the sequence number of the last page in the folder, so this command will take us to the last page.

```
PROMPT "There are " :
   COUNT : " pages";
GO COUNT;
DELETE;
PROMPT "There are now " :
   COUNT : " pages";
```

Related Topics

See also: CLONE command, CUT command, PASTE command, and COUNT system variable.

DO Command

Syntax

```
DO field;
DO button;
```

Purpose and Examples

The DO command simulates the result of a user selecting a button or field object with the mouse. The parameter for this command, `field` or `button`, is the name of the object. The object must have a name to be selected.

The parameters `field` and `button` are the names of their respective objects. They are *not* strings, so don't use double quotes around the name. You cannot concatenate two strings together to create an object name. If you need to select an object with a string containing the object's name, use the OBJECT command.

When a script button is selected, the flow of control transfers to the script and does not return to the script that called it. All other buttons continue with the current script when the selected script is finished.

```
DO NEXTPAGE;
```

In this example, the button NEXTPAGE is a LINK button. The new page is displayed and control is returned to the script.

```
DO DIAL;
```

In this second example, the button DIAL is a script button. Control does not return to this script.

When a field is activated, it is as if the user selects the first character of the field. All field keyboard commands operate for the activated field.

```
DO PHONE;
```

If PHONE is the name of a field, the text cursor will appear at the beginning of the field. If PHONE is the name of a button, its script is executed.

Related Topics

See also: SCRIPT command, MOUSE command, OBJECT command, and OBJECT system variable.

DOS Command

Syntax

```
DOS [#] expression [#];
```

Purpose and Examples

This command executes the DOS command you specify in the parameter expression as if you had typed it at the DOS prompt. You can use any command that fits into the memory available.

Your `expression` can be a string enclosed in quotes, the name of a variable, or a combination of both using string concatenation. Variables are replaced by their contents.

If your command has textual output, insert a number sign, # (also called a pound sign or crosshatch), before the expression. Your display then appears in 80-column text mode before the command and returns to graphics mode when the command is completed.

If your command changes the display in any way, use a second number sign after the expression but before the semicolon. This tells LinkWay to redraw the current screen after the DOS command is finished.

LinkWay resumes immediately after the DOS command is finished. If the command does not pause, you probably will not be able to see its effect before the screen is redrawn.

To execute a command, LinkWay must load the transient part of the COMMAND.COM command processor as well as the program you want to run. If there isn't enough memory left, the program is aborted. Your screen will appear as if nothing happened.

Remember that LinkWay assumes that files are in the current directory or in a directory specified by an environment variable. If you change directories and your files are not in a directory specified by an environment variable, LinkWay may not be able to find them.

```
DOS "dir";
```

This example displays a listing of the current directory on the screen. Some types of adapters will display the text directly over the current page. LinkWay is asking the DOS portion of your system to display a list of files. The characters in the quotes are sent to DOS. If the quotes weren't there, LinkWay would look for a variable named dir.

```
DOS #"dir";
```

In the second example, the user wants the directory listing shown in 80-column text mode.

```
DOS #"dir"#;
```

Here, when the listing is complete, the current page will be completely redrawn.

```
DOS "copy \config.sys \config.bak";#
```

The next example shows how a DOS command may copy a file from within LinkWay, then print out the message `1 File(s) copied` on the screen.

```
DOS "copy \config.sys \config.bak > nul";
```

This final sample command prevents the DOS-generated copy message from being displayed.

To redirect the output, the phrase `> nul` is added to the command and prevents most messages from being displayed. When in doubt, use the number signs to make sure that the screen is redrawn when the DOS command is finished.

Related Topics

See also: BCALL command and EXTERN command.

EXTERN Command

Syntax

```
EXTERN expression,variable;
```

Purpose and Examples

This command executes the DOS program specified by the parameter `expression`. The program is given four command line arguments:

1. The segment address of the first page in the folder
2. The number of pages in the folder
3. The segment address of the parameter `variable`
4. The size of the parameter `variable`

The parameter `expression` must be the name of a program either in the current directory or in a directory specified by the PATH environment variable.

The parameter `variable` must be the name of a variable. It is not a string. You cannot place quotation marks around the name. You cannot make the name by concatenating two strings together. The variable must be created before you call this command.

The address of a memory location is composed of two parts: the segment address and the offset address. The absolute address is calculated by multiplying the segment address by 16 and adding it to the offset address.

Because variables and pages all start on paragraph boundaries, their offsets are always 0 and there is no need to communicate with them.

Here is a sample program written in Microsoft C v5.1 for use as an external command. You must use the large memory model to compile the program.

```
#include <dos.h>
#include <memory.h>
#include <stdio.h>
#include <stdlib.h>
#include <string.h>

void main(int argc, char **argv)
{
   unsigned   varseg, varlen;
   char       *var = NULL;
   if(argc >= 5) {
   /* There must be 4 arguments plus one for the program name */
      varseg = (unsigned)atoi(argv[3]);
      /* variable segment address */
```

```
        varlen = (unsigned)atoi(argv[4]);
        /* variable length in bytes/characters */
        var = calloc(1, varlen + 2);
        /* temporary data buffer */
        if(var == NULL) {
        /* A very real possibility that there is no memory */
           goto end;
        }

        movedata(varseg, 0, FP_SEG(var), FP_OFF(var), varlen);
        /* move contents of variable to buffer */
        strrev(var);
        /* reverse buffer */
        movedata(FP_SEG(var), FP_OFF(var), varseg, 0, varlen);
        /* move buffer to variable */
    }

end:
    if(var != NULL)
        /* If buffer was allocated free it */
       free(var);
}
```

Here is an example of the compiled program's use inside LinkWay:

```
VAR s(8);
SET s = "abcdef";
EXTERN "reverse",s;
```

The variable s now contains the string " fedcba". Notice that the number passed to the EXTERN is the size of the variable, not the size of its contents.

This program reverses the contents of the variable s. It creates a temporary buffer for the variable, reverses the buffer, and copies the data back into the variable.

Unlike in multiuser systems, the memory of your computer is not protected from unauthorized changes. A program may change anything in memory, including the current page or folder. It might also crash the computer. Be very careful when you change data in memory.

Unlike the LinkWay DOS command described earlier, the EXTERN command does not put the display in text mode or redraw the screen when it is finished executing. Any output from the called program is likely to obscure or alter the current page in a random manner. If the current page needs to be redrawn, use the following command after the program is executed:

```
GO SEQ;
```

LinkWay probably consumes most of your computer's memory. Called programs must run in what memory is left. If there isn't enough memory for the program, LinkWay will probably resume execution as if you hadn't called an external program.

Related Topics

See also: BCALL command, DOS command, SET command, and VAR command.

FIND Command

Syntax

```
FIND expression[,field[,folder]];
```

Purpose and Examples

This command searches the remaining pages of the folder for the string specified by the parameter `expression`. The search starts with the first page, not the current page. The page on which the string is found becomes the current page. If the string is not found, the current page is not changed.

If the optional parameter `field` is defined, only fields with that name are checked. If the parameter `field` is blank, all fields, text pop-ups, and scripts are searched. Upper- and lowercase letters are equivalent.

If the optional parameter `folder` is defined, the specified folder is opened and then searched. The parameter `field` must be defined or blank to use the `folder` parameter.

If the parameter `expression` is blank, the previous search is repeated starting at the next page. Otherwise, all searches start at the first page in the folder.

All three parameters are strings. To specify a blank parameter, use two double quotes with nothing between them. You must place commas between parameters, even if they are blank.

The following examples illustrate various formats of the FIND command line.

```
FIND "Mr. Goodbar"
```

This command searches all fields in the current folder for the string `Mr. Goodbar`.

```
FIND "Mr. Goodbar","LName";
```

This command searches all fields named `LName` for the string `Mr. Goodbar`.

```
FIND "Mr. Goodbar","LName","Address";
```

This command searches all fields named `LName` in the folder Address for the string `Mr. Goodbar`.

```
FIND "Mr. Goodbar","","Address";
```

This command searches all fields in the folder Address.

```
FIND "Mr. Goodbar";
FIND "mr. goodbar";
FIND "MR. GOODBAR";
```

Case is ignored by the FIND command, so these three searches are equivalent.

```
VAR s(8),flds(8),fldr(8);
```

```
SET s="Mr. Goodbar";
SET flds="LName";
SET fldr="Address";
FIND s,flds,fldr;
```

In this last example, variables are shown being used instead of strings.

Related Topics

See also: ID system variable, GO command, LINK command, and RETRACE command.

GO Command

Syntax

```
GO value;
```

Purpose and Examples

Use the GO command to move to a page number value. This command differs from its menu bar equivalent. It expects a page sequence number, not a word such as first or last. The base page is 0, the first page is 1, and so forth. If the parameter value is greater than the number of pages, no change is made.

These examples show variations of formats for the GO command:

```
GO 0;
```

This command goes to the base page.

```
GO 1;
```

This command goes to the first page.

```
GO SEQ;
```

Use this command to go to the current page. This command redraws the current page.

```
GO SEQ+1;
```

The system variable SEQ contains the sequence number of the current page, so this command transfers the cursor to the next page.

```
GO COUNT;
```

The system variable COUNT contains the number of pages in the folder. This is also the sequence number of the last page in the folder. This command transfers to the last page.

Related Topics

See also: SEQ system variable, COUNT system variable, LINK command, FIND command, and RETRACE command.

IF/ELSE Commands

Syntax

```
IF expression command1;
[ELSE command2;]
```

Purpose and Examples

The IF/ELSE commands are known as conditionals. If the value of the parameter expression is true (nonzero), command1 is executed. If the expression is false (0) and the optional ELSE statement exists, command2 is executed. Instead of a single command, multiple commands may be executed by surrounding them with curly braces, { and }.

The IF command is similar to the common English phrasing, "If this is true, then do that." Adding the ELSE command changes the phrase to, "If this is true, then do this; otherwise, do that."

If you are not using the braces, you must include a semicolon at the end of the IF command and before the ELSE command. If you are using braces, there must *not* be a semicolon between the brace and the ELSE command.

The value of the parameter expression is usually set by a relational operator—an operator that compares two values. Relational operators return either of two values: 0 for false and 1 for true.

```
VAR A(5),B(5);
SET A="FORMULA";
SET B="MOTOR";
IF A $= B
   MSG "string A is equal to B";
ELSE
   MSG "A is not equal to B.";
IF A $!= B {
   MSG "variable A is not equal to variable B";
   SET A = B;
   MSG "Now it is!";
} ELSE {
   MSG "variable A is equal to variable B";
}
```

In scripts, the text formatting does not matter. As far as LinkWay is concerned, a script is one long stream of characters. The formatting for IF/ELSE commands (indenting lines between IF and ELSE statements) is popular because it makes the commands easier to read. There is a drawback, however. Scripts have a maximum of 3000 characters. If you want to use the space efficiently, you must group as many commands as possible on every line.

Related Topics

See also: JUMP command and Relational Operators.

INPUT Command

Syntax

```
INPUT expression,variable;
```

Purpose and Examples

This command accepts user data typed at the keyboard and stores the data in a variable.

This command displays a dialog box that contains three lines. The first line contains a close circle. Selecting this circle has the same action as pressing the ENTER key, described later. The second line displays the parameter expression. Usually this is a question. The third line is a field of spaces bounded by parentheses. When the dialog box first opens, there is a text cursor over the first space of the field.

To enter your answer, just start typing. You can insert up to 32 characters in the field.

The following keys have special actions for the INPUT command:

ENTER,↑,↓	Close the dialog box and put whatever is in the field into the variable.
ESCAPE	Close the dialog box without changing the contents of the variable.
Arrow keys	Move the cursor in the appropriate direction.
INSERT	Insert a space before the text cursor.
DELETE	Delete the current character.

You can always type in 32 characters. If the variable is larger than 32 characters, only as many characters as will fit are placed in the variable.

JUMP/LABEL Commands

Syntax

```
JUMP label;
@label
```

Purpose and Examples

These two commands are used as a pair. A *label* is a marker placed inside of a script. The JUMP command transfers execution to a specified marker/label. Each label must have a name, a string of characters following an @ symbol. Label names may not have spaces in them and they are not followed by semicolons. If names are repeated, only the first label in the script will be recognized.

The JUMP command transfers the flow of control to the first label it finds with the specified name. There is no limit to the number of JUMP commands for each label.

If a script gets caught in an infinite loop, there is no way of breaking out of a JUMP/LABEL combination. You can press the ESCAPE key to cancel the script to halt execution of the script immediately. The remainder of the script is not executed.

```
VAR x(5);
SET x = "1000";
@LOOP
  PRINT x;
  SET x = x + 1;
  IF x < 10
    JUMP LOOP;
```

Related Topics

See also: IF/ELSE Commands.

LINK Command

Syntax

```
LINK expression[,folder];
```

Purpose and Examples

When you create a new page, it is assigned a unique ID number. The LINK command moves to a new page, the page whose ID number is the value of the parameter expression. If you specify the parameter folder, the folder is opened first. If it isn't specified, the page within the current folder is selected. If there is an error, for example, either the page or the folder doesn't exist, nothing happens. You do not even see an error message.

Folders have a maximum size. The LINK command provides a way for the programmer to overcome that limit by putting segments of applications in different folders.

Using LINK is not the same as opening a folder. When a folder is opened, the base page is checked for a button with the name AUTOEXEC, which is then executed. The LINK command moves directly to the specified page without going through the base page.

The following examples show variations of the LINK command format.

```
LINK 1;
```

This command transfers control to the page whose ID number is 1.

```
LINK 3,"main";
```

This command transfers control to the page whose ID number is 3 in the specified folder.

The ID and FOLDER system variables can be used to confirm that a LINK command is executed properly, as in the following:

```
VAR newID(5),newFOLD(8);
set newID = 3;
set newFOLD = "main";
LINK newID, newFOLD;
IF ID = newID & FOLDER $= newFOLD
   PROMPT "FOUND IT!";
ELSE
   PROMPT "You are lost!";
```

Related Topics

See also: GO command, FIND command, RETRACE command, FOLDER system variable, and ID system variable.

LOAD Command

Syntax

```
LOAD variable,expression;
```

Purpose and Examples

This command creates or replaces a variable and assigns to it the contents of the file whose name is the parameter expression. The parameter variable follows the same rules specified for the VAR command, for the name of a variable. The parameter expression must be the name of a DOS file.

This command assigns space to the variable, so you do not have to enter the VAR command. The length of the variable is determined by the length of the file, up to a maximum of 32,000 characters.

The variable may be used as a script with the SCRIPT command or as an assembly language routine with the BCALL statement.

```
LOAD s,"script.txt";
SCRIPT s;
```

This example loads a text file into memory and executes it like a script.

```
LOAD a,"sound.bin";
BCALL a;
```

This command loads a binary file into memory and executes the file with the BCALL command.

The following example shows a way of letting your scripts create scripts of their own. This is an artificial intelligence technique.

```
VAR s(512),total(5);
SET total = 10;
SET s = "VAR n(5); " :
        "SET n = 0; " :
        "@L1 " :
```

```
        "PROMPT n; " :
        "SET n = n + 1; " :
        "IF n < " : total : " JUMP L1;";
WRITE "script.txt",0,LEN(s),s;
LOAD sc,"script.txt";
SCRIPT sc;
```

Related Topics

See also: BCALL command, DOS command, SCRIPT command, EXTERN command, VAR command, and WRITE command.

MBAR and NOMBAR Commands

Syntax

```
MBAR;
NOMBAR;
```

Purpose

These commands control the display of the menu bar.

The MBAR command displays the menu bar. If the menu bar is already visible nothing happens.

The NOMBAR command turns off the display of the menu bar. If it is invisible already, nothing happens.

Related Topics

See also: SHOW/NOSHOW commands.

MENU Command

Syntax

```
MENU variable,value,expression;
```

Purpose and Examples

This command displays the menu shown in Figure 8.1, which is similar to the pull-down menus on the menu bar. As the mouse cursor passes over each line of the menu, the line is highlighted. Pressing the mouse button selects that line, and its number is returned in the variable specified by the parameter. The first line returns 1, the second 2, and so on. Pressing the ENTER key or pressing the mouse button while the mouse cursor is outside of the menu closes the menu and returns 0. There is a maximum of 16 lines, and the parameter expression must be less than or equal to 240 characters.

The width of each line is equal to the parameter value. The number of lines is equal to the number of characters in the parameter expression divided by the width. The first line begins with the first character, the second line with character width + 1, the third with 2 * width + 1.

If the width is six characters, the first six characters will be displayed on the first line, the second six on the second line, and so on. If the length of expression is not a multiple of the width, the last line is not displayed; each line of the menu must have width characters.

FIGURE 8.1 *The MENU Command*

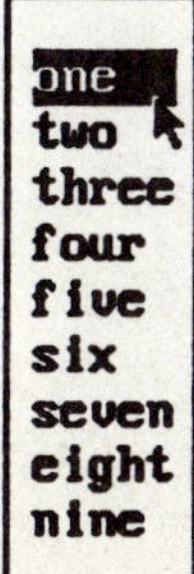

```
var a(2);
menu a,5,"one  two  threefour five six  seveneightnine "
```

The menu displays nine lines, each five characters wide. Line 1 starts with character 1. Line 2 starts with character 6, width of 5 + 1. The words *one, two, four, five,* and so on, are less than five characters each, so spaces are added after them to ensure proper spacing. The words *three, seven,* and *eight* are five characters each, so there are no spaces after them.

The following example shows an easier way to create a menu. It uses the string concatenation operator to concatenate six strings of equal length. Each line in the script becomes a line in the menu. You can see immediately if all of the lines are the same length. You can also center the contents of each line.

```
var a(2);
menu a,7,
  "  one  " :
  "  two  " :
  " three " :
  "  four " :
  "  five " :
  "  six  ";
```

Related Topics

See also: OBJECT command, OBJECT system variable, and VAR command.

MODE Command

Syntax

```
MODE [value][,expression];
```

Purpose and Examples

This command changes the display mode and default folder. The `value`, if present, specifies a graphics mode from one of the following choices:

4	CGA mode
16	EGA+VGA mode
17	MCGA Mono mode
19	MCGA 256 color mode

The `expression`, if present, must evaluate to the name of a folder.

When LinkWay is started, the first folder shown becomes the default folder, and its graphic mode becomes the default graphics mode.

There is always a default folder name and default graphics mode. There may not be an actual folder in the default graphics mode.

If a graphics mode is specified in this command, it becomes the new default graphics mode. If this new mode cannot be supported by your graphics display, the highest resolution mode available is used instead.

If a folder name is specified, it becomes the new default folder.

If neither parameter is specified, the default folder is opened in the default mode.

When the command is executed, the current script is halted, the current folder is closed, the mode is changed to the new default mode, and an attempt is made to open the default folder. When the default folder cannot be opened, a message box announces this; no folder is opened; and the default folder name does not change.

The following examples give an idea of the variety of MODE command formats.

```
MODE;
```

This simple command switches to the default folder in the default graphics mode.

```
MODE 4,"MAIN";
```

This command makes the MAIN folder the current and default folder in the CGA mode.

```
MODE 17;
```

This command switches to the default folder in MCGA Mono mode.

```
MODE ,"CALENDAR";
```

With this command you make the CALENDAR folder the default and open it.

MOUSE Command

Syntax

```
MOUSE;
```

Purpose and Examples

This command displays the mouse cursor and pauses execution until you select an object by pressing a mouse button or keyboard key. If the mouse cursor is over an object on the current page, four system variables contain properties of the object. The variables are OBJECT, ONAME, OTYPE, and OWID.

See the discussion in Chapter 9 about the system variables for more information.

This command can also pause execution of a script until a mouse button or keyboard key is pressed.

Related Topics

See also: OBJECT command, WAIT command, OBJECT system variable, ONAME system variable, OTYPE system variable, and OWID system variable.

MSG Command

Syntax

```
MSG expression1[,expression2];
```

Purpose and Examples

The MSG command displays a message, which is stored in the command's parameters in a dialog box (see Figure 8.2). The dialog box remains until the user presses a keyboard key, selects the close circle, or presses the mouse button while the mouse cursor is outside of the box.

The second parameter, `expression2`, is optional.

The MSG command is a simple means of confirming that the user is aware of a message. He or she must perform an action before the program can continue.

```
MSG "Hello","How are you?";
```

This command displays the message shown in the figure.

Related Topics

See also: PROMPT command.

FIGURE 8.2 *The MSG Command*

```
Hello
How are you?
```

OBJECT Command

Syntax

```
OBJECT expression;
```

Purpose and Examples

This command performs a task similar to that of the MOUSE command: It selects an object. Instead of asking the user to choose an object with the mouse, however, this command selects an object by name. If the expression evaluates to the name of an object on the current page, four system variables—OBJECT, ONAME, OTYPE, and OWID—contain properties of the object.

See the discussion of the system variables in Chapter 9 for more information.

Related Topics

See also: MENU command, MOUSE command, OBJECT system variable, ONAME system variable, OTYPE system variable, and OWID system variable.

PASTE Command

Syntax

```
PASTE [expression];
```

Purpose and Examples

This command performs the opposite action of the CUT command. The command takes a page out of a file and inserts it after the current page. The inserted page becomes the current page. If the parameter expression is omitted, the page comes from the file SCRAP.PG;

otherwise, it comes from the file specified by the parameter `expression` plus the extension .PG. You do not have to specify the file extension; it is automatically added.

If the folder is full, no page is inserted. See the discussion of the CLONE command for information about detecting this state.

```
PASTE;
```

The page stored in the file SCRAP.PG is inserted after the current page; then it becomes the current page.

```
PASTE "temp";
```

This example shows how a page stored in the file TEMP.PG is used instead of the page in SCRAP.PG.

Related Topics

See also: CLONE command, CUT command, and DELETE command.

PRINT Command

Syntax

```
PRINT expression;
```

Purpose and Examples

The PRINT command prints the value of the expression on the system printer. A carriage return/line feed combination is printed after the expression every time. If you want to use control codes in the expression, use the function CHR();

```
PRINT "Hello, How are you?";
PRINT "Line 1" : CHR(10) : "Line 2";
PRINT "This is underlined" : CHR(13) :
     "__________________";
```

The ASCII character number 10 is the value for a line feed. It moves the paper in the printer ahead one line without moving the carriage left or right.

The ASCII character number 13 is the value for a carriage return. It moves the carriage to the beginning of the current line. The carriage return character can be used to underline text. After the text is printed, print the carriage return character and a series of underline characters. The carriage returns to the beginning of the line without advancing the paper, and the underline characters are printed under the text. The PRINT command always advances the paper; therefore, your entire underline must occur in one PRINT command.

If the printer is not ready or not turned on, the program may halt. If this happens, either turn the printer or check to make sure that it is online.

Related Topics

See also: CPRINT command.

PROMPT Command

Syntax

```
PROMPT expression;
```

Purpose and Examples

The value of the expression is displayed on the bottom line of the display. If the expression is the empty string—two double quotes with nothing between them—the prompt area is erased. The text in the prompt area remains displayed until another prompt command or another page is displayed. The user does not have to acknowledge this message in any way.

```
PROMPT "Please select an object";
```

```
PROMPT "";                              Clear the prompt area.
```

Related Topics

See also: MSG command.

QUIT Command

Syntax

```
QUIT;
```

Purpose

This command exits the current script, saves any changes made to the current folder, and exits LinkWay. Once the QUIT command is executed, there is no turning back; LinkWay will be exited. Fortunately, the current folder is automatically saved.

Related Topics

See also: CSAVE command and STOP command.

READ Command

Syntax

```
READ expression,offset,length,variable;
```

Purpose and Examples

This command reads a specified number of characters/bytes from a file and places them in a variable.

The parameter `expression` must be a DOS file name; path names may be used. The parameter `offset` is the index of the first byte or character to read; byte 0 is the first in the file. The parameter `length` determines the number of bytes to read. The data is placed in the specified variable.

If the file does not exist, a warning message is displayed and script execution stops. If the size of the variable is greater than the length, the remainder of the variable is filled with spaces. If the length is greater than the size of the variable, only as many bytes as will fit into the variable are read.

```
VAR buffer(2048);
READ "\LINKWAY\READ.ME",0,2048,buffer;
```

The FSIZE() function may be used to calculate the length of a file before it is read.

```
READ "\LINKWAY\READ.ME",0,FSIZE("\LINKWAY\READ.ME"),buffer;
```

Related Topics

See also: LOAD command, WRITE command, and FSIZE() function.

/* and */ (Remarks)

Syntax

```
/* This is a remark */
```

Purpose and Examples

Remarks, or comments, are strings of text explaining concepts within a script. They aren't really commands. They perform no action. They are instructions to the LinkWay program to ignore everything in the remark.

The beginning of the remark must begin with the two symbols: / (the slash) followed by * (the asterisk). The two symbols */, an asterisk followed by a slash, signal the end of the remark. Everything between the two markers will be ignored by LinkWay.

Here is a sample comment.

```
/* Real programmers don't use comments */
```

You cannot use nested remarks—remarks inside of other remarks. The following example will not work.

```
/* Outer remark.
    /* This line will be ignored.
        Inner remark is ignored, too.
    */
*/
```

The last line causes an error, because LinkWay does not recognize the beginning of the remark. The previous line's nested comment ending in */ is mistaken for the end of the whole remark.

No matter what your emotional involvement is with the application you are writing, chances are that after a month or two you may forget just why you did what you did. Insert remarks to explain for posterity what your scripts do, how they do it, and why. If you had to experiment to get a script to work correctly, use a remark explaining what works, and what doesn't. If you have to change anything later, you will be grateful for those reminders.

RETRACE Command

Syntax

```
RETRACE;
```

Purpose

LinkWay keeps track of the last 10 pages that you have visited. The list is kept in reverse order; the most recent page is on the top of the list. The list is circular; every time a new page is added, the oldest page is dropped from the list.

The RETRACE command takes you to the most recent page in the list. Every time you call the RETRACE command, you move back one page in the list. You cannot go forward through the list, toward the more recent pages. You can only go backward, toward the oldest pages. When you reach the end of the list, the RETRACE command has no effect.

If a page is in a different folder, RETRACE saves any changes made to the current folder and opens the previous folder.

If the previous page or folder has been deleted or its display mode has been changed, RETRACE cannot get past this page and remains at the current page. The list of pages essentially ends at deleted folders or pages.

Related Topics

See also: FIND command, GO command, and LINK command.

SCRIPT Command

Syntax

```
SCRIPT variable;
```

Purpose and Examples

This command treats a variable as if its contents were a script. The contents of the variable may be created through any normal means, such as the SET command or LOAD command. The maximum size of a script is 3000 characters.

```
VAR S(200);
SET S = "beep;"
SCRIPT S;
```

Control does not necessarily return to the current script, depending on the contents of the script.

Related Topics

See also: DO command and LOAD command.

SERIAL Command

Syntax

```
SERIAL value,expression;
```

Purpose and Examples

There are two common types of communications ports: serial and parallel. Printers are generally connected to parallel ports. Laser disk players, modems, and some types of mice are connected to serial ports.

The SERIAL command transmits a series of characters through the specified serial communications port. The port is specified by the value parameter. The IBM BIOS (Basic Input/Output Services) supports two ports named COM1 and COM2.[1] A value of 1 specifies COM1 and 2 specifies COM2.

Each character of the parameter expression is sent sequentially. Control codes may be added with the string concatenation operator and the CHR() function.

The serial parameters—baud rate, parity, stop bits, and data bits—should be set with the DOS MODE command before you enter LinkWay.

Video disc players, modems, and other serial communications devices are controlled with this command.

```
SERIAL 1,"1000SE" : CHR(13);
```

This command searches to frame 1000 on a Pioneer LV-4200 Laser Disc Player.

```
SERIAL 1,"2000PL" : CHR(13);
```

This command plays from current frame to frame 2000.

[1]There are many add-on cards that support more than two ports. But the IBM BIOS only supports the first two ports. Also, there is no standard for supporting these additional ports.

Related Topics

See also: CHR() function.

SET Command

Syntax

```
SET variable = expression;
```

Purpose and Examples

This command assigns the value of an expression to a variable. The variable must exist before a value is assigned to it. Use the VAR command to create variables.

A *simple expression,* also known as an *operand,* is just a string of characters inside double quotes or a number.

```
SET s = "a simple expression";
SET s = "123";
SET s = 123;
```

A *complex expression* is the combination of simple expressions and operators. See Chapter 7 for a discussion of expressions.

```
SET s = "one simple" : " plus another simple";
SET s = "314" + 54;
SET s = (((A $= "ANSWER") * 7) + n) / 2;
```

Variable values are always stored as strings of characters. However, if a variable or expression is used like a number, its value is treated like a number.

```
VAR test(100);
                                        contents of TEST
1. SET TEST = 11 + 8;                      "19"
2. SET TEST = "11" + 8;                    "19"
3. SET TEST = "11" + "8bbbb";              "19"
```

```
4. SET TEST = "11" : "8bbbb";                    "118bbbb"
5. SET TEST = "11" + "8";                        "19"
6. SET TEST = "this is a string"         "this is a string"
7. SET TEST = "this" : " is" : " another" "this is another"
```

The addition operator (+) works with numbers, so the operands are treated as numbers and the result is a number. In the third example, the second operand has some letters following the number. These letters are ignored when the addition is performed.

The concatenation operator (:) chains two strings of characters together to form one string. The first string is followed immediately by the second. In the fourth example, the concatenation operator is used, so the operands are treated as strings. The result of the operation is a string.

Related Topics

See also: VAR command and string concatenation operator.

SHOW/NOSHOW Command

Syntax

```
SHOW;
NOSHOW;
```

Purpose and Examples

These commands tell LinkWay to start or stop updating the screen.

When you move to a new page, the page is displayed automatically. The NOSHOW command temporarily prevents LinkWay from redrawing pages. The SHOW command resumes page redrawing. In any event, page redrawing will return when the script ends.

If you open a new folder, use the commands SHOW; GO 0; at the end of your script to ensure that the new folder is started properly.

If your script is visiting a series of pages collecting information, you may not want the user to see all of the page changes. Not only is such a display messy, but it also consumes time to draw a page.

The only commands that are displayed when NOSHOW is in effect are MSG, INPUT, and PROMPT. These commands are shown over the frozen page, not the current page.

Do not use the DO command with fields while the display is frozen; the user will not be able to see any changes made to the field.

Related Topics

See also: FIND command, GO command, LINK command, and RETRACE command.

STOP Command

Syntax

```
STOP;
```

Purpose and Examples

This command halts execution of the current script immediately. If the current script was called from another script, both are stopped.

```
VAR X(5);
SET X=1;
@START
   /* YOUR COMMANDS HERE */
   SET X=X+1;
   IF X<=10 JUMP START;
```

Related Topics

See also: QUIT command.

VAR Command

Syntax

```
VAR name1(length1)[,name2(length2),...];
```

Purpose and Examples

This command defines one or more variables. Variables have three properties: their names, lengths, and contents. The name and size of a variable are determined with this command. A variable's contents are also known as its *value*. The SET and LOAD commands assign values to variables. The variable's value is global, accessible to all scripts in the folder.

Each variable must have a name composed of a string of up to eight characters beginning with a letter. Upper- and lowercase letters are equivalent in the name.

The number of characters a variable can hold is specified by the length value, which must range from 1 to 32,000. You may have a maximum of 60 variables at one time. When a variable is created it is filled with spaces.

DOS provides the memory for variables from its pool of memory, so if DOS runs out of memory you will not be able to create variables until you clear out some memory. The VCLEAR command is used to erase a variable from memory.

The program, the graphics display driver, the fonts, and folders all compete for DOS' memory, so don't be surprised if you do run out of memory.

Reusing a variable name replaces the previous variable size with the new. The value of the variable after resizing is unpredictable.

Selecting Open from the Folder pull-down menu erases all variables from memory. Using the Link or Find command does not affect variables.

The following sample program shows how variable v is created with space for 12 characters, is filled with the string between the quotation marks, displays C on the bottom line of the screen, and displays the string EFGHI on the prompt line.

```
VAR v(12);
SET v="ABCDEFGHIJKL";
PROMPT v(3);
PROMPT v(5,5);
```

Related Topics

See also: LOAD command, SET command, and VCLEAR command.

VCLEAR Command

Syntax

```
VCLEAR;
```

Purpose and Examples

This command erases all variables and frees the memory they consumed for use by DOS. This command is irrevocable—all variables and their values are lost. Choosing Open from the Folder pull-down menu also erases all variables.

```
VCLEAR;
```

Use this command to ensure that your application has all of the memory possible and that no variables will accidentally retain values from the previous application.

Related Topics

See also: SET command and VAR command.

WAIT Command

Syntax

```
WAIT expression;
```

Purpose and Examples

This command pauses your script until the specified amount of time has passed or the user presses a keyboard key.

The value of the `expression` is the number of seconds to pause script execution. The time may be expressed in hundredths of a second.

```
WAIT 15;   Wait 15 seconds
WAIT 11.5; Wait 11.5 seconds
```

Related Topics

See also: MOUSE command.

WRITE Command

Syntax

```
WRITE expression,offset,length,variable;
```

Purpose and Examples

This command performs the opposite action of the READ command: instead of transferring data from a file to memory, this command transfers the contents of a variable in memory to a file.

The `expression` must be a DOS file name; paths are permitted.

The data is written in `offset` bytes from the beginning of the file. If the offset is 0, the data is written at the beginning of the file.

The parameter `length` determines how many bytes are written. If the value length is greater than the size of the variable the extra characters are filled with spaces.

This command may be used to write to other DOS devices, such as LPT, PRN, and COM. Just use the device name without the colon instead of the file name. When writing to a special device the offset value is meaningless.

In the following example, the WRITE command writes the string contained in the variable buffer into a file called TEMP.TXT starting at byte 0 of the file. The LEN() function returns the size of the variable.

```
VAR buffer(100);
SET buffer = "When in doubt, punt!";
WRITE "temp.txt",0,LEN(buffer),buffer;
WRITE "LPT1",0,LEN(buffer)-15,buffer(15,5);
```

The second WRITE command writes the string `punt!` to parallel port 1.

Related Topics

See also: READ command.

CHAPTER 9

System Variables

System variables are similar to normal variables except that the system, LinkWay, is responsible for their creation and contents. Unlike functions, values may be assigned to some system variables. They may not have subscripts.

This chapter describes each system variable in alphabetical order, giving its purpose, examples of its use, and related topics, if any.

COUNT System Variable

Purpose and Examples

This variable always contains the number of pages in the current folder, not including the base page. You may not assign a value to this variable.

```
PROMPT "There are " : COUNT : " pages in this folder";
GO COUNT;                      The current page becomes the last page.
```

Related Topics

See also: GO command.

FOLDER System Variable

Purpose and Examples

This variable contains the name of the current folder without its extension. Folder names have a maximum of eight characters.

```
MSG "The name of this folder is ",FOLDER;
```

ID System Variable

Purpose and Examples

Contains the current page ID number. When you create a page, it is assigned a unique ID number in the range of 1 to 65535. A page's sequence number may change, but its ID number never changes. Once an ID number has been used it is retired, never used for another page. If you do manage to create 65,535 pages, you have to start over with another folder.

```
VAR currID(5);
SET currID = ID;
FIND "this string";
IF currID = ID
   MSG "Cannot find the string";
```

The FIND command moves to the next page with a field or button that contains the search string. If the search string is not found, the current page remains active. The script fragment in the example shows a method of confirming the FIND command that found what it is looking for.

Related Topics

See also: FIND command and CLONE command.

LWPATH System Variable

Purpose and Examples

Contains the value of the LWPATH environment variable. Environment variables are created at the DOS prompt outside of LinkWay. If a folder, font file, or icon file cannot be found in the current directory, the directory specified by the LWPATH variable is checked also.

This value may be used to determine whether a folder exists.

```
IF FSIZE("folder")
  LINK 0,"folder";
IF FSIZE(LWPATH:"folder")
  LINK 0,"folder";
MSG "Cannot find","folder";
```

Related Topics

See also: LWPATH environment variable.

OBJECT, ONAME, OTYPE, and OWID System Variables

These variables are used in conjunction with the MOUSE and OBJECT commands described briefly in Chapter 8 for the script commands.

The MOUSE command enables the user to select an object with the mouse by pressing the mouse button while the mouse cursor is over an object. The OBJECT command selects an object on the current page by name. The object must have a name to be selected. When an object is selected, these variables contain information about it.

The variables ONAME, OTYPE, and OWID remain empty if there is no object currently selected.

The ONAME system variable contains the first word of the name of the selected object. Words are separated by spaces. Two buttons with the names CHOICE 1 and CHOICE 2 both return CHOICE as their name.

The OTYPE variable contains a one- or two-letter code representing the object's type. The codes are

F	Field
P	Picture
BT	Text Pop-Up Button
BS	Script Button
BL	Link Button
BG	Go Button
BP	Picture Pop-Up Button
BF	Find Button

The OWID system variable contains the width of field and text pop-up objects. If the object is a field, the value is the maximum number of characters per line. If the object is a text pop-up, the value is the width, in characters, of one line.

The following example asks the user to select an object with the mouse, then it displays information about the object.

```
PROMPT "Select an object";
MOUSE;
IF OTYPE = ""
   MSG "Invalid Object";
ELSE
```

```
MSG "OBJECT NAME: " : ONAME,
"OBJECT TYPE: " : OTYPE;
```

The OBJECT system variable (not the command) represents the object itself. The contents of fields, text pop-up buttons, script buttons, and link buttons may be changed by means of this variable. The variable may also be used in expressions.

In the following example, variable I is defined and assigned the value 1. The `@LOOP` statement defines the label LOOP. The object whose name is `CHOICE` is selected, followed by the number in `I`. The value in `OBJECT` is multiplied by the value in `I`, then 1 is added to `I`. The final `IF` statement repeats the processes while `I` is less than or equal to 3.

```
VAR I(5);
SET I = 1;
@LOOP
   OBJECT "CHOICE" : I;
   SET OBJECT = OBJECT * I;
   SET I = I + 1;
   IF I <= 3
      JUMP LOOP;
```

The following statements perform the same actions as the example just given.

```
SET CHOICE1 = CHOICE1 * 1;
SET CHOICE2 = CHOICE2 * 2;
SET CHOICE3 = CHOICE3 * 3;
```

This may seem like a lot of work to multiply 3 numbers, but this will work for any number of objects, not just 3. If you had 31 fields, 1 for each day of the month, it would take 31 SET commands to assign values to each field.

A common programming structure is a menu of choices, each choice representing an action. The MENU and OBJECT commands can be used together to create this structure.

All of the strings under `MENU` in the following are exactly 12 characters wide. Spaces are added to both sides to center the text.

The second-to-last line of the code shows the OBJECT command, and the last line uses the OBJECT variable.

```
VAR r(2);
MENU r,12,
         "  New File  " :
         "  Open File " :
         " Close File " :
         "  Save File " :
         "   Save As  " :
         "   Delete   ";
OBJECT "CHOICE" : r;
DO OBJECT;
```

Here again, the next-to-last code line uses the OBJECT command, whereas the last line uses the OBJECT variable. Six objects, called CHOICE1, CHOICE2, and so on, must exist. They may be buttons or fields.

Note that an object called CHOICE0 may exist, and if nothing is selected from the menu, you can program this choice to provide a help facility.

Related Topics

See also: DO command, OBJECT command, MENU command, and MOUSE command.

OFF X and SEG X System Variables

These variables delve deeply into the depths of IBM PC/AT/XT computers.

The memory of a computer is composed of many locations that may hold data, one byte or character in each location. Each location is numbered sequentially; this is its *address.* Absolute addresses in the IBM PC range from 0h to FFFFFh[1] (1024K). But a five-digit

[1]The lowercase *h* signifies a hexadecimal number, a base 16 number rather than a decimal or base 10 number.

hexadecimal digit would not fit in the registers of early PCs, so the address was divided into two parts, the segment and the offset. The absolute address is calculated by multiplying the segment by 16 (Fh) and adding the offset. The segment address always points to a memory page, a block of 16 bytes. The offset address is relative to the segment address.

The OFF system variable contains the offset of the variable X. The SEG system variable contains the segment of the variable X.

What does this have to do with you, the LinkWay programmer? The BCALL and EXTERN commands execute external programs. These programs can use and modify the variables in your application if they know the variable's address. Information is passed to the external program when it is loaded into memory. Part of that information probably is the location of your variables.

Variables are always created on page boundaries, so the OFF variable always contains 0. This may change in the future, so you should probably continue to use the OFF variable in addition to the SEG variable.

Related Topics

See also: BCALL command and EXTERN command.

SEQ System Variable

Purpose and Examples

Each page has a sequence number, which is essentially its position within a folder. The base page is number 0, the first page is number 1, and so on. The SEQ variable always contains the sequence number of the current page.

The command

```
GO SEQ;
```

may be used to redraw the current page.

Related Topics

See also: GO command.

TIME System Variable

Purpose and Examples

This variable always contains the current time and date in the following format:

```
Mon Mar 20 08:31:46 1989
```

You can use the following examples to display the time or date.

```
VAR T(24);
SET T = TIME;
PROMPT "The time is " : T(12,8);
PROMPT "The date is ":T(5,3):". ":T(9,2):", ":T(21,4);
```

You must use the variable `T` because you cannot use subscripts with system variables.

CHAPTER 10

LinkWay Programming Tips

This chapter presents a variety of hints for better or faster programming with LinkWay. The tips are arranged in alphabetical order by topic.

BCALL and EXTERN: These two commands enable you to execute specialized programs from inside LinkWay. Unfortunately, there is nothing to prevent such application programs from crashing the computer. The computer may crash immediately, soon after the return to LinkWay, or when you exit LinkWay. There are a lot of areas that can cause execution problems. Crashes are often caused by changing an area of memory that shouldn't be altered. Do not change memory allocations unless you know what you are doing.

The Black Hole: Occasionally scripts seem to go into a black hole. The script just stops for no apparent reason. This usually happens when the programmer forgets that the SCRIPT and DO commands can execute other scripts. When they do execute additional scripts, the end of the current script is ignored. Pay attention to any

commands that cause branching that may not return in all conditions. The following annotated code example is taken from the definition for the OBJECT system variable.

`VAR I(5);`	Define variable I.
`SET I = 1;`	Assign the value 1 to variable I.
`@LOOP`	Define the label LOOP (see the JUMP/LABEL command for more information).
`OBJECT "CHOICE" : I;`	Select the object whose name is the word *CHOICE* followed by the number in the variable I.
`SET OBJECT = OBJECT * I;`	Multiply the value in OBJECT by the value in I.
`SET I = I + 1;`	Add 1 to I.
`IF I >= 3 JUMP LOOP;`	Repeat while I is less than or equal to 3.

During the writing of this code fragment, a script button was named CHOICE2. Each time the fragment was executed, it would stop after two tries instead of three. Every time the CHOICE2 button was executed, the script would stop.

Formatting: You can pack commands into a script in many ways. You can use one long, complicated string of characters or a series of neat, elegant lines of code. Whereas neatness won't automatically make your code work better, it is easier to find problems in code that is easy to read. Choose any method of formatting that you like. A commonly used format is similar to that used by some people for programs written in the C language: one command per line, indents for the commands associated with IF/ELSE commands, and indents for the commands between the label and JUMP commands.

Hardware: LinkWay can be used with many optional hardware devices. The LinkWay Toolkit and LinkWay Demonstration folders have examples of folders and buttons for use with these devices. If one of these devices does not work with your computer, keep in mind that newer models are much faster than older models. Some cards and peripherals do not work properly or at all in fast-clock-speed computers. If possible, reset your machine to run at a slower speed to use these devices. If you cannot change your computer's speed, you may be out of luck.

Names: Buttons, fields, variables, system variables, functions, and commands all have names. If you give an object the same name as another object, your code may yield unexpected results. Usually LinkWay tells you that you have an error in your script. The script line won't look like it contains an error, but try a simple solution when you get an error. Give your button/script/field/variable a new name—one that isn't used somewhere else.

CHAPTER 11

Using the LWFONTED Font Editing Program

A *font* is a collection of characters of a similar style and size. The LWFONTED program enables you to change existing font files.

Caution: Change font files at your own risk. If you make a font illegible, you also make your LinkWay applications illegible. Always make copies of fonts before you alter them.

In every LinkWay folder there are four possible fonts. The Fonts choice in the Options pull-down menu prompts you for two of the four fonts: the small and large sizes. You may enter the name of any font file for both choices. The medium-sized font is used to display signs for button names. Be especially careful if you decide to change this font, because the change affects a major portion of your application. The fourth font, the system font, is actually stored in the read-only memory (ROM) of your computer; it cannot be changed.

Fonts are stored in special files. Icons are another form of fonts, and icons are stored in the same type of file. A normal font file contains 96 characters. The characters in a font file are numbered from 32 to 127. Icons are numbered from 1 to 96.

Font files may be stored in the current directory or the directory specified by the LWPATH environment variable or command line argument. The current directory is checked first. If two files have the same name, the file in the current directory is used. You may substitute special-purpose font files for the standard files by putting them in the current directory instead of the LWPATH directory.

A font displays differently in each graphics mode. Each graphics mode has a different resolution and aspect ratio. *Resolution* measures the size of individual pixels. The size of the screen does not change when you change graphics modes, but the size of the pixels does. Most pixels are oblong, either ovals or rectangles. The *aspect ratio* is the ratio between the horizontal and vertical dimensions of a pixel. In the MCGA Mono mode the horizontal and vertical resolutions are the same, which means that the aspect ratio is 1. In the other three modes, the pixels are oblong—wider horizontally than vertically.

A font does not change size when it is moved from one display mode to another. The width and height of a character in pixels does not change. However, because the size and aspect ratio of the pixels change, the appearance of the font also changes. A font looks smaller on a higher-resolution display because the individual pixels are smaller.

The apparent width of the characters changes because of the change in aspect ratio. A character that is square on the MCGA Mono display appears rectangular on other displays. The character itself has not changed; only its appearance is altered.

The default fonts are chosen so that their apparent size and shape are equivalent in each graphics mode. Each character takes approximately the same amount of screen space no matter which mode you use. If you convert a folder from one mode to another, the fonts are converted to the default fonts of the new mode. If the fonts are equivalent, the pages will appear the same. If not, the text will be different.

If you decide to change the fonts in a folder, remember that only four fonts are allowed per folder. The text in every field has to use one of these fonts.

Table 11.1 describes the default fonts for each graphics mode:

The system font, which is used for the menu bar and dialog boxes, depends on your graphic display. You cannot change it, so the table doesn't list it.

The file names follow a simple pattern: an abbreviated name followed by a number.

Each font style has a name. The name is independent of the font's size. The Roman or Times Roman® (ROM) font is more ornate than the Helvetica® (HELV) font.

ROM

HELVETICA

The number following the name is usually the height of the font in pixels. The larger the number, the larger the height of the font.

Some fonts have the letter *C* after the font size. This stands for condensed, and it means that the characters are closer together and sometimes taller and thinner.

TABLE 11.1 *The Default Fonts*

MODE	SMALL	MEDIUM	LARGE
CGA	HELV6	HELV8	ROM14C
MCGA 256	HELV6	HELV8	ROM14C
MCGA Mono	ROM10	ROM14	ROM24
EGA+VGA	HELV10	ROM14	ROM24

Editing Fonts

First, before you start to change a font make a copy of the file. Enter

COPY ROM14.FMF ROM14OLD.FMF

If you make a mistake while you are changing the file, you can always use the copy you just made.

Now, start the program by typing

LWFONTED name

where `name` is the file name of a font. The extension .FMF is automatically added to the name.

Once you have started the program, the LWFONTED Main menu, which resembles the chart of the characters with a dialog box superimposed over them, is displayed. Figure 11.1 illustrates this menu. Follow these steps to edit characters:

1. Press **F1** to edit characters.
2. Use the arrow keys to select a character. When you press an arrow key, a white cursorlike box moves across the chart. On the lower left of the screen, a box displays the current character.
3. When you have reached the character you wish to edit, press the **F3** key to pick up the character and put it into the edit buffer. The top box on the left edge of the screen shows the contents of the edit buffer. You cannot directly change a character; it must be in the edit buffer. This provides simple insurance against accidentally damaging a character format.
4. Press the **F9** key to edit the character in the edit buffer. A new screen is displayed with the character in a large box in the top left corner. Follow the instructions listed to the right of the screen to change the character.
5. Press the **F10** key to return to the character selection menu.
6. The changes you have made are not stored in the font file until you use the **F4** key to put the character back in the file from the edit buffer.
7. When you are finished editing this font, press the **F10** key

to return to the Main menu and press **F10** again to return to MS-DOS.

Always remember to put characters back in the file with F4 after you have changed them. If you do not, your changes will not be saved.

Here is a more detailed list of the options in the LWFONTED program. The caret symbol (^) before a key means you must press the **SHIFT** key while the other key is being pressed.

Key on Main Menu	**Name and Action**
F1	Edit Characters: Press this key to edit the current font file.

FIGURE 11.1 *The LWFONTED Main Menu*

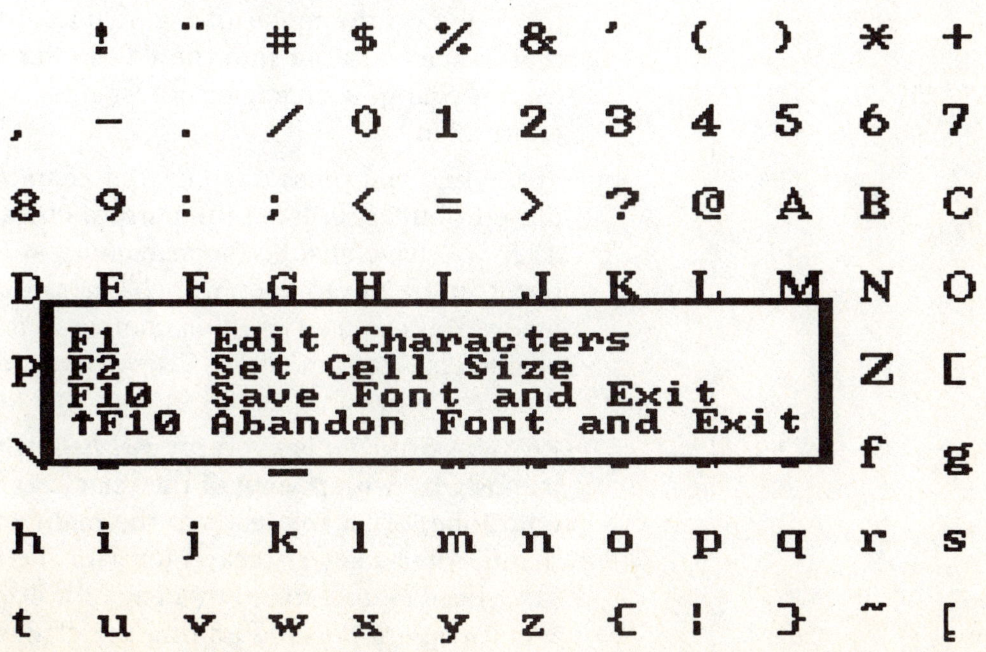

F1 Edit Characters
F2 Set Cell Size
F10 Save Font and Exit
↑F10 Abandon Font and Exit

F2	Set Cell Size: The cell width is not currently used. The cell height determines the line spacing, or the number of pixels between lines of text. Do not change the cell size of icon files.
F10	Save Font and Exit: Press this to save your changes to the current font file.
^F10	Abandon Font and Exit: Press this if you have made a mistake or do not wish to save the current font file.

Key on Edit Characters Menu	**Name and Action**
Arrow keys	Use the arrow keys to select the current character.
F3	Pick: When you press this key, shown on the lower left on the menu in Figure 11.2, the current character is put into the edit buffer. You cannot change a character unless it is in the edit buffer.
F4	Put: When you press this key, the character in the edit buffer replaces the current character. After you have changed a character you must put it in the file to keep the changes you have made. You can also use this command to copy characters. You can select a new character with the arrow keys and replace it with this key.
F9	Fat: The word *fat* is short for *Fat Bits,* which means a blown-up view of the character in the edit buffer. This key leads to the main editing menu. After a key is picked up with the F3 key, press F9 to expand its image for editing. When you are finished editing the character, press the F4 key to put it back into the file.

F10	Main Menu: Press this key to return to the Main menu.

Key on Fat Bits Menu	**Name and Action**
Arrow keys	A small rectangular cursor defines the location of the current pixel. Use the arrow keys as shown in Figure 11.3 to move the cursor.
F1	Dot Set: If you press F1, the current pixel is set to the current color.

FIGURE 11.2 *The Edit Characters Menu*

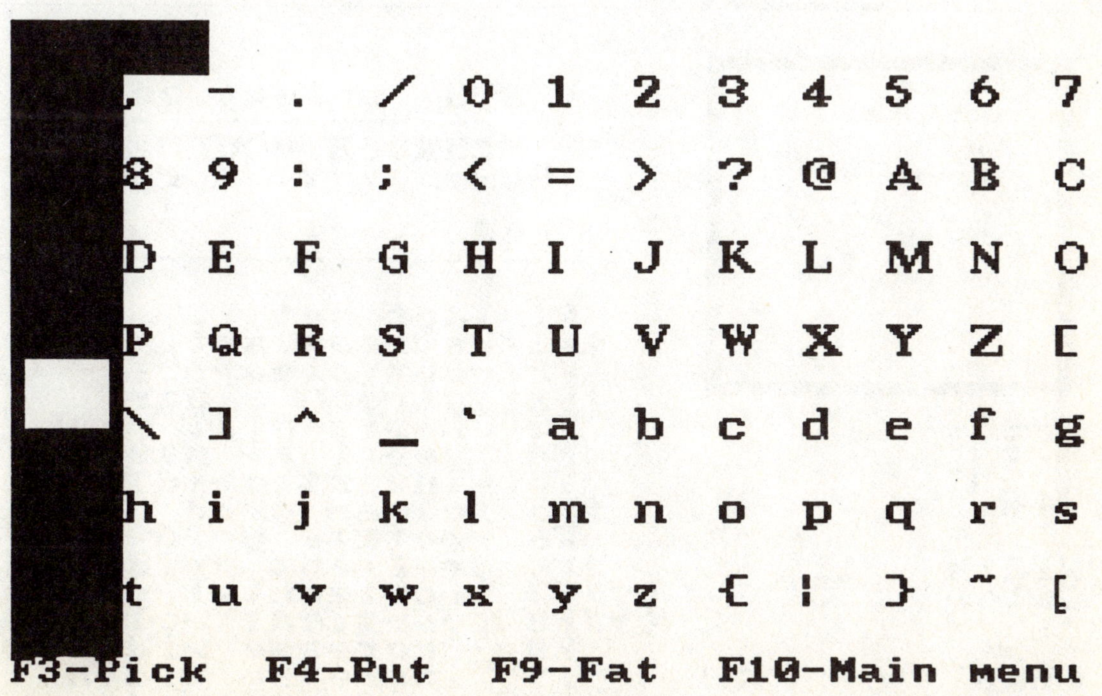

^F1	Stream Set: This is similar to the Dot Set command, except that when you move the cursor it continues to set pixels until you press another key.
F2	Dot Clear: There are three foreground colors and a background color. This key sets the color of the current pixel to the background color.
^F2	Stream Clear: This is a combination of the Stream Set and Dot Clear commands; it sets the pixels under the cursor to the background color until another key is pressed.

FIGURE 11.3 *The Fat Bits Menu*

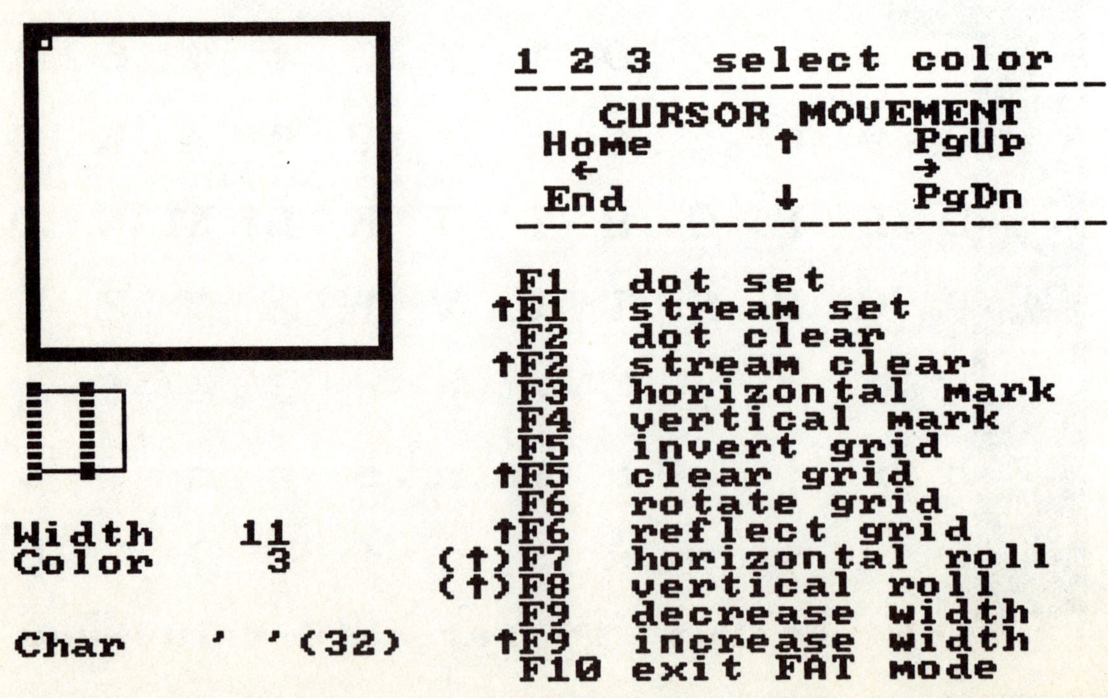

F3	Horizontal Mark: Press this key to leave a mark in the border of the character to the left and right of the cursor.
F4	Vertical Mark: Press this key to leave a mark in the border of the character cell to the top and bottom of the cursor. The mark does not change the character's appearance. It is used to line pixels up.
F5	Invert Grid: There are two pairs of colors, black/white and cyan/magenta. Each color in the pair is the inverse of the other color. This command converts each pixel to its inverse. All of the pixels in the character cell are affected. Black pixels are converted to white and vice versa. Likewise, cyan becomes magenta.
^F5	Clear Grid: This key sets every pixel in the character cell to the background color.
F6	Rotate Grid: This key rotates every pixel in the character cell clockwise around the center of the cell. If the character extends past its current width, it should be changed.
^F6	Reflect Grid: Every pixel on the left is swapped with its opposite on the right. A mirror image of the character is created.
F7 and ^F7	Horizontal Roll: If you press just F7, the pixels are moved to the left. Pixels that run off of the left edge of the screen reappear on the right edge. If you press the SHIFT and F7 keys simultaneously, the pixels move to the right.
F8 and ^F	Vertical Roll: If you press just F8, the pixels are moved up. Pixels that run off of the top edge of the screen reappear on the bottom edge. If you press the SHIFT and F8 keys simultaneously, the pixels move down.

F9 and ^F9	Decrease/Increase Width: The width is shown as two vertical bars on either side of the miniature picture of the character. Its numerical value is also shown below this picture. This value is the number of pixels to move ahead before the next character is drawn. Press the F9 key to decrease the width. Press the SHIFT and F9 keys simultaneously to increase the width. If the character extends past these bars, you should change the width to include the pixels. If the width is too large, there will be a large blank space to the right of the character when it is drawn.
F10	Exit FAT Mode: Press F10 to return to the previous menu.

The right side of the screen in the Fat Bits menu is a list of your choices. In the lower left corner of the screen are several important features. First, there is the miniature view of the character. To its left and right are vertical bars, which represent the character width. All of the characters should fall between these two bars. None of the character's pixels should extend past the bars. The width value and current color number are displayed below this. At the bottom, the standard character symbol and the ASCII index are displayed.

Double-Length Font Files

Normal font files contain 96 characters. Double-length font files contain 192. The ASCII indexes for a normal file range from 32 (the space character) to 127. Double-length files range from 32 to 223. The additional characters may be used for any purpose, including foreign languages.

To create a double-length font file, first create two normal font files. The specifications of the two fonts must be the same. The largest character in both fonts must be the same height and width. Type the following command at the DOS prompt—replacing the words `font1`, `font2`, and `total` with the names of your files—to join the two files together:

```
LWFONTJ font1 font2 total
```

The file font2 will be added to the end of the file font1 and stored in the file total. Do not add the extension .FMF to the file names font1, font2, and total. The extension is added automatically.

To use double-length font files in a LinkWay application, you must specify the \N, National Language Support, command line argument. LinkWay uses an extra 36K of memory when this option is specified because the font files are larger than regular text files.

CHAPTER 12

Using Palettes

Most people have an image of a palette as that strangely shaped piece of wood that an artist uses to hold and mix paints. That is close to what a palette is in the world of computerdom. A palette is a list of colors currently being used. A display may be able to show an enormous number of colors, but only a few at a time. The palette determines which of the many colors are available.

Before you learn about palettes, there are a few concepts you should understand about physics. Yes, physics! This chapter tries to keep these scary concepts nice and simple.

About Color on Computers

Passing quickly over quantum mechanics, suffice it to say that light is composed of different frequencies, just like radio waves. Each frequency is a different color. When you combine lights of several frequencies, you create other colors. White light is really a combination of frequencies; there is no such thing as pure white light.

One theory about vision says that the human eye has three types of *cones,* which are color receptors. Each is sensitive to a different color. They are red, green, and blue (RGB). Color televisions create pictures by displaying combinations of these colors. If you look really closely at a television screen, you will see very tiny red, green, and blue dots.

Computer monitors work similarly to the way that televisions work, except that the picture originates from a computer rather than a camera. Each little dot on the computer display is stored internally as a number that specifies a combination of red, green, and blue light.

The color white is created by having equal amounts of red, green, and blue. You can create most other colors by combining different levels of the three primary colors. The secondary colors cyan, yellow, and magenta are created by combining only two of the primary colors. Cyan is created by equal parts green and blue, yellow is made from red and green, and magenta from red and blue.

The number of visible colors is infinite. However, computers cannot deal with infinity, so computers can only display a portion of the visible spectrum.

The MCGA 256 color mode can display 256 shades of color out of 262,144 shades possible by keeping a table that maps a number between 0 and 255 to a set of RGB values. This table is sometimes called a color look-up table (CLUT) or a palette.

By choosing the colors in a palette carefully, you can display some really amazing pictures. For example, a picture of a forest contains lots of green and very little yellow and red. Therefore, the color palette consists of mostly shades of green.

MCGA 256 pictures can optionally have palette files associated with them. These files are very simple; they list 256 RGB values. Whenever a picture is loaded, LinkWay looks for another file with the same name as the picture file but with the extension P13. This second file contains the palette information. Every time a new palette file is loaded, its values replace those stored in the computer's memory. So, if you have more than one picture on a page, the palette of the last picture to be loaded is used for every picture.

Creating Palette Files

There are three ways to create your own palette files. You can use the LWCAPTUR program to capture pictures created by other paint programs, edit the contents of a palette file, or change the palette from within LinkWay.

If a paint program accepts changes to the palette, you can create a picture with that program and then use the LWCAPTUR program to create the files that LinkWay needs to show the picture.

If you feel extremely brave, you can edit the contents of the palette file. This method isn't recommended, because it requires some knowledge of DOS internals, and there is a small chance that you could corrupt files. The files are exactly 768 bytes long, and the 6-bit RGB values are stored in groups of 3 bytes (3 bytes * 256 colors = 768 bytes). Each color value is stored in a single byte; therefore, there are 2 unused bits.

The third method, changing the palette while LinkWay is running, can yield some interesting effects. Simple animation can be done by making each frame of the animation a single color in the same picture. You can draw frame 1 in color number 1, frame 2 in color number 2, and so on. If you set all of the colors in the palette to black, the picture appears to be blank. To show the animation, set each palette entry to a visible color and then reset it to black. So to see frame 1, set color 1 in the palette to a color other than black. To see the next frame set color 1 back to black and set color 2 to another color.

All of the animation frames are on the screen, but the color of all the pixels is set to the background color.

Program to Change Values of the Palette in Memory

The following program is provided as an example of the third method of customizing a palette. The program functions as an

EXTERN command from within LinkWay and resets the RGB color palette values stored in your computer's memory. The program does not change a palette stored in a file. Also, if you load in a new picture, its palette will replace the palette that this program creates.

Palette Color Groups

The palette that this program creates has 5 groups of colors. The first 18 colors are used by LinkWay to display the menu bar and text. Therefore, they must not be changed. The values for these colors were determined by checking a standard palette file. You shouldn't change these first 18 hues, because the result can exhibit the menu bar and the text it contains with the same color, hiding everything displayed there.

The second group of colors is composed of pastels. A *pastel* is created by adding white to another color. As an example, if the primary color is red, the pastel shade pink is created by adding to the green and blue colors. This has the effect of adding white to the color. This will work as long as the red value is greater than the other two.

The third group of colors is composed of darkened colors created by using lower values for all three colors. Bright colors have high color values; dark shades have low values.

The fourth group of colors is composed of pure colors. These colors are high intensity and contain little white. These are interesting colors; you see them a lot in computer graphics. Used in excess, they are a bit hard on the eyes, because they are too bright.

The last group of colors does not really consist of various colors at all. It is a series of grays ranging from bright white to black. When the red, green, and blue color values are equal, gray is created. Because the color values are in the range 0 to 63, there are 64 possible shades of gray/white. Due to the limitations of most displays, only 20 or so are distinct.

To create these colors, the EXTERN statement uses another color coordinate system called the *hue, saturation, and value (HSV) system.* The three primary colors and three secondary colors are arranged in a circle in the order red, yellow, green, cyan, blue, and magenta. To specify a color, you specify its hue in degrees, its saturation by a fraction in the range 0 to 1, and its brightness value also by a fraction in the range 0 to 1. This is an easier system to use for defining colors than the RGB color coordinate system. If you want a series of colors with the same hue but different brightnesses, just keep the hue and saturation values constant and use a range of brightness values. Such changes can be done in the RGB system, but it isn't easy.

Program Code

Following is the source code to the EXTERN program.

```
\*
 ¦ setpal.c
 ¦
 ¦ Richard A. Harrington
 ¦
 ¦ This program is an EXTERN statement you call from LinkWay.
 ¦ It sets the values of the color palette used by the
 ¦ MCGA 256 color display mode.  If the current mode is not
 ¦ MCGA 256, you exit the program immediately without changing
 ¦ anything.  The palette the code creates is composed of four
 ¦ groups of colors: the standard LinkWay colors, a block of
 ¦ half-saturated colors, a block of half-brightness colors,
 ¦ a block of fully saturated/bright colors, and a block of
 ¦ shades of gray.
 ¦
 ¦ This program uses the BIOS interrupt 0x10 (video interrupt),
 ¦ function 0x10 (set palette registers), subfunction 0x12
 ¦ (update a block of palette registers).
 *\

#include <bios.h>
#include <dos.h>
```

```
#include <fcntl.h>
#include <io.h>
#include <math.h>
#include <stdio.h>
#include <stdlib.h>
#include <string.h>
#include <sys\types.h>
#include <sys\stat.h>

\*
 ¦ hsv stands for hue, saturation, and value.
 ¦ Hue is the shade of the color;
 ¦ the primary hues are red, green, and blue.
 ¦ The secondary hues are cyan, yellow, and magenta.  These are made
 ¦ by combining two primary colors.
 ¦
 ¦ Saturation is the amount of white mixed into the color.  High
 ¦ saturation values create pastel colors.  The value is
 ¦ equivalent to the brightness of the color.
 ¦
 ¦ This function converts a color specified by the HSV system
 ¦ to the corresponding one in the RGB coordinate system.
 ¦
 ¦ The HSV color coordinate system uses a color wheel to specify
 ¦ the color displayed. The colors red, yellow, green, cyan, blue,
 ¦ and magenta are arranged in a circle.
 ¦
 ¦ The hue is specified by an angle in degrees.
 ¦ The dominant colors are
 ¦
 ¦    Red     = 0
 ¦    Yellow  = 60
 ¦    Green   = 120
 ¦    Cyan    = 180
 ¦    Blue    = 240
 ¦    Magenta = 300
```

```
 ¦
 ¦ The angles between the dominants represent
 ¦ combinations of the two colors.
 ¦
 ¦ The saturation value controls the amount of white added to the
 ¦ primary colors.
 ¦
 ¦ The outermost edge of the circle is the brightest value.
 ¦ As the concentric circles get smaller, the brightness gets lower.
 ¦
 ¦ To specify a color, you choose a number between 0 and 359 to select
 ¦ the hue, a number between 0 and 1 to specify the saturation, and
 ¦ between 0 and 1 to specify the brightness value.
 ¦
 ¦ A saturation value of 0 always creates black.
 ¦
 *\
void  hsv_rgb(double h, double s, double v, int *r, int *g, int *b);
void  hsv_rgb(double h, double s, double v, int *r, int *g, int *b)
{
   double   p, q, f, t, i, curr_r, curr_g, curr_b;

   if(s == 0.0) {
      /* A saturation value of 0 automatically creates black */
      curr_r = v;
      curr_g = v;
      curr_b = v;
   } else {
      while(h >= 360.0)
         h -= 360.0;        /* H must be in the range 0 to 360 */
      h = h/60.0;
      i = floor((double)h);    /* Calculate the dominant color */
      f = h - i;               /* Find mix of dominant and next color */
      p = v * (1 - s);         /* Value for third, least important */
```

```
                                  /* color                          */
    q = v * (1 - (s * f));        /* If the dominant color is yellow, */
                                  /* cyan, or magenta, use this value */
                                  /* for secondary color            */
    t = v * (1 - (s * (1 - f))); /* If the dominant color is red,   */
                                  /* green, or blue use this value  */
                                  /* for secondary color            */

   switch((int)i) {
      case 0:                     /* Dominant is red                */
         curr_r = v;
         curr_g = t;
         curr_b = p;
         break;
      case 1:                     /* Dominant is yellow             */
         curr_r = q;
         curr_g = v;
         curr_b = p;
         break;
      case 2:                     /* Dominant is green              */
         curr_r = p;
         curr_g = v;
         curr_b = t;
         break;
      case 3:                     /* Dominant is cyan               */
         curr_r = p;
         curr_g = q;
         curr_b = v;
         break;
      case 4:                     /* Dominant is blue               */
         curr_r = t;
         curr_g = p;
         curr_b = v;
         break;
```

```
        case 5:                     /* Dominant is magenta          */
            curr_r = v;
            curr_g = p;
            curr_b = q;
            break;
        }
    }
    /* Make sure that a number between 0 and 63 is returned */
    *r = 0x3F & (unsigned char)(0x3F * curr_r);
    *g = 0x3F & (unsigned char)(0x3F * curr_g);
    *b = 0x3F & (unsigned char)(0x3F * curr_b);
}
/* The palette is a block of 256 COLOR structs */
typedef struct COLOR {
                unsigned char r, g, b;
            } COLOR;

void main(void);
void main()
{
    COLOR         *p;
    int           r, g, b, old_r, old_g, old_b;
    double        i,
                  d = 360.0 / 100.0,
                  s,
                  t;
    int           j = 0, e = 2;
    union REGS    inregs,outregs;
    struct SREGS  sregs;

    /* Get the current graphics mode with BIOS interrupt 0x10 */
    /* function 0x0F, read current video mode                */
    inregs.h.ah = 0x0F;
    int86(0x10, &inregs, &outregs);
    /* If the current graphics mode is not MCGA 256, exit immediately */
```

```
if(outregs.h.al != 0x13) {
   return;
}

/* Allocate some memory to store the palette */
p = (COLOR *)calloc(256, sizeof(COLOR));
if(p == NULL) {
   return;
}

/* The first 18 colors are used by LinkWay for special purposes    */
/* This section forces the colors to the proper values              */
p[ 0].r =  0; p[ 0].g =  0; p[ 0].b =  0;     /* black           */
p[ 1].r =  0; p[ 1].g =  0; p[ 1].b = 42;     /* medium blue     */
p[ 2].r =  0; p[ 2].g = 42; p[ 2].b =  0;     /* medium green    */
p[ 3].r =  0; p[ 3].g = 42; p[ 3].b = 42;     /* medium cyan     */
p[ 4].r = 42; p[ 4].g =  0; p[ 4].b =  0;     /* medium red      */
p[ 5].r = 42; p[ 5].g =  0; p[ 5].b = 42;     /* medium magenta  */
p[ 6].r = 42; p[ 6].g = 21; p[ 6].b =  0;     /* light yellow    */
p[ 7].r = 42; p[ 7].g = 42; p[ 7].b = 42;     /* medium white    */
p[ 8].r = 21; p[ 8].g = 21; p[ 8].b = 21;     /* light white     */
p[ 9].r = 21; p[ 9].g = 21; p[ 9].b = 63;     /* pale blue       */
p[10].r = 21; p[10].g = 63; p[10].b = 21;     /* pale green      */
p[11].r = 21; p[11].g = 63; p[11].b = 63;     /* light red/pink  */
p[12].r = 63; p[12].g = 21; p[12].b = 21;     /* pale red        */
p[13].r = 63; p[13].g = 21; p[13].b = 63;     /* light green     */
p[14].r = 63; p[14].g = 63; p[14].b = 21;     /* pale blue       */
p[15].r = 63; p[15].g = 63; p[15].b = 63;     /* bright white    */
p[16].r =  0; p[16].g =  0; p[16].b =  0;     /* black           */
p[17].r = 63; p[17].g = 63; p[17].b = 63;     /* bright white    */

/* Each of the following blocks of code creates a range of colors      */
/* The variable j determines the entry in the palette that is being    */
/* set.                                                                */
/* The variable e sets a minimum difference between the current color */
/* and the next color. Unless the brightness and contrast on your      */
/* monitor are turned all the way up in some cases the differences     */
```

```
/* between colors may be unnoticeable. This variable is used in a      */
/* while loop that keeps on trying new hue values until there is a     */
/* difference in the RGB values.                                       */
/* The ranges I used for each for loop are completely empirical.  On   */
/* my monitor there are about 22 visible shades of gray. So, if you    */
/* subtract the first 18 colors and the 22 shades of gray you get 216  */
/* other colors. I divided 216 by three to get 72. Here is a list      */
/* of the color ranges:                                                */
/*                                                                     */
/* 0-17         Predefined colors used by LinkWay                      */
/* 18-90        0.5 saturation, 1.0 value (72 colors)                  */
/* 91-162       1.0 saturation, 0.5 value (72 colors)                  */
/* 163-234      1.0 saturation, 1.0 value (72 colors)                  */
/* 235-255      22 shades of gray                                      */

/* A range of hues at 0.5 saturation and full brightness */
old_r = -1 ; old_g = -1; old_b = -1;
e = 2;

for (i = 0.0, j = 18; j < 90; j++) {
   while((abs(r - old_r) <= e)
   && (abs(g - old_g) <= e)
   && (abs(b - old_b) <= e)) {
      hsv_rgb(i, 0.5, 1.0, &r, &g, &b);
      i += d;
   }
   old_r = r; old_g = g; old_b = b;
   p[j].r = (unsigned char)r;
   p[j].g = (unsigned char)g;
   p[j].b = (unsigned char)b;
}

/* A range of hues at full saturation and 0.5 brightness */
old_r = -1; old_g = -1; old_b = -1;
e = 2;

for (i = 0.0; j < 162; j++) {
```

```
    while((abs(r - old_r) <= e)
    && (abs(g - old_g) <= e)
    && (abs(b - old_b) <= e)) {
      hsv_rgb(i, 1.0, 0.5, &r, &g, &b);
      i += d;
    }
    old_r = r; old_g = g; old_b = b;
    p[j].r = (unsigned char)r;
    p[j].g = (unsigned char)g;
    p[j].b = (unsigned char)b;
}
/* A range of hues at full saturation and full brightness */
old_r = -1; old_g = -1; old_b = -1;
e = 3;
/* Full brightness colors resemble each other, so in this case  */
/* the minimum change in colors is higher                        */

for (i = 0.0; j < 234; j++) {
    while((abs(r - old_r) <= e)
    && (abs(g - old_g) <= e)
    && (abs(b - old_b) <= e)) {
      hsv_rgb(i, 1.0, 1.0, &r, &g, &b);
      i += d;
    }
    old_r = r; old_g = g; old_b = b;
    p[j].r = (unsigned char)r;
    p[j].g = (unsigned char)g;
    p[j].b = (unsigned char)b;
}

/* A series of grays */
old_r = -1; old_g = -1; old_b = -1;
e = 2;
d = 1.0 / (256.0 - (float)j);
for(i = 0.0, s = 0.0; j < 256; j++) {
```

```
        while((abs(r - old_r) <= e)
        && (abs(g - old_g) <= e)
        && (abs(b - old_b) <= e)) {
           hsv_rgb(1.0, s, i, &r, &g, &b);
           i += d;
        }
        old_r = r; old_g = g; old_b = b;
        p[j].r = (unsigned char)r;
        p[j].g = (unsigned char)g;
        p[j].b = (unsigned char)b;
        if(i > 360.0)
           s = modf(s + 0.25, &t);
        i = fmod(i, 360.0);
    }
    inregs.h.ah = 0x10;          /* Set palette registers            */
    inregs.h.al = 0x12;          /* Update a block of palette registers */
    inregs.x.bx = 0;             /* Start at register 0              */
    inregs.x.cx = 0xFF;          /* End at register 256 (0xff)       */
    sregs.es    = FP_SEG(p);     /* Get segment address of our table  */
    inregs.x.dx = FP_OFF(p);     /* Get offset address of our table   */

    /* Use interrupt to reset all palette values */
    int86x(0x10, &inregs, &outregs, &sregs);

    if(p != NULL)                /* Free memory; not needed any more  */
       free(p);
}
```

To compile the program, use the command

```
CL -AL -Zp setpal.c
```

with Microsoft C v5.1.

To use the program, insert the following command in a LinkWay script:

```
extern "setpal",i
```

The program SETPAL.EXE must be in the current directory and the folder must have been created in the MCGA 256 color mode.

CHAPTER 13

LinkWay Sample Applications

This chapter contains two small sample applications. They are complete applications designed to teach you everything about LinkWay. However, they are designed to show the basic concepts.

First Sample Application: Physics Helper

LinkWay is designed around the user interface. It is a program that enables nonprogrammers to create complex applications. LinkWay is a great educational program, too, because it enables teachers to create individual computer-guided tutorials.

The physics helper sample program takes students through a multiple-choice physics tutorial. All questions have associated graphics, with one question per page. The students' answers are recorded so that the teacher can find problem areas.

There are five phases to this example:

1. creating an application from the ground up
2. creating background pictures
3. placing text on pages
4. making some simple buttons
5. creating simple animation

The base page contains two fields: one for the application title and the other for the student's current score. It also contains a button named AUTOEXEC to set the application up when users start it.

Selecting the Graphics Mode

The first decision you make in creating the application is the graphics mode or modes under which the application will run. This sample application uses a lot of text that has to be very legible. The MCGA 256 and CGA modes are very low resolution. Their characters appear blocklike and large. The MCGA Mono and EGA+VGA modes have roughly the same resolution, but the EGA+VGA mode has color. So, the physics helper application uses the EGA+VGA mode.

If you cannot use the EGA+VGA mode, pick the one you can use and substitute its name wherever you see EGA+VGA.

Creating a Work Directory

Next, make a work directory called \PHYSICS. Everything that the teacher creates is placed in this directory. The following DOS commands create the directory:

```
MD \PHYSICS
CD \PHYSICS
```

Creating a New Folder

There are two ways of creating folders: find a folder that uses the correct graphics mode and make a copy of it or use the New command in the Folder pull-down menu. If you copy a folder, you have to erase everything in the duplicate. So, this procedure shows you how to create a new one from scratch.

Start LinkWay in the EGA+VGA mode by typing

```
LINKWAY \E
```

and then select New from the Folder pull-down menu. The physics helper application uses the name PHYSICS for the folder.

Displaying the Menu Bar and Status Line

While you edit folders you may prefer to have the menu bar and status line visible. If they are not displayed, turn them on using the Menu Bar and Status options in the Option pull-down menu.

The status line should now say:

```
PHYSICS(Base)
```

Creating Fields and a Script Button

Select New from the Object menu to create a field. Place it in the top left corner of the screen. Use the biggest font to place the words **Physics Helper** in the field. See Figure 13.1 for an example.

Select New from the Object menu to create a field. Put it in the top right corner across from the first field. This field must have a unique name. It will display the student's current total score for the tutorial. This example gives it the name TOTAL. Leave it empty for now; your scripts will fill it.

Select New from the Object menu to create a script button. Name the button AUTOEXEC. Make the button invisible and place it in some out-of-the-way place. The user should not select this button.

This button is executed every time the folder is opened. It sets the application up and moves to the first page. Its script is very simple:

```
SET TOTAL="0 correct answers";
GO 1;
DO STARTUP;
```

This initializes the field and moves to the first page. Each page will have a button named STARTUP to provide instructions for setting up each page.

Creating the First New Page

It is time to create your first new page, which is shown in its finished state in Figure 13.2. Select New from the Page pull-down menu. The status line should change to

```
PHYSICS(1) Id = 1
```

The STARTUP Button

First, create an invisible button named STARTUP. Each page will have a button with this name. The button creates settings for the

FIGURE 13.1 *The Base Page of Physics Helper Application*

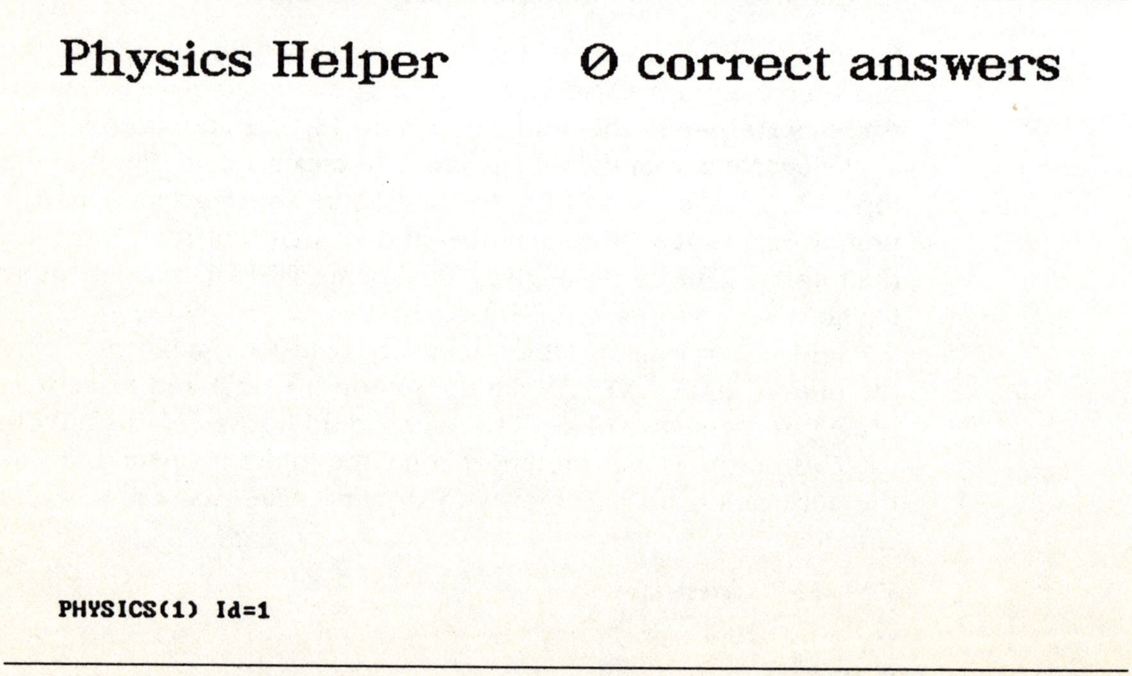

Physics Helper 0 correct answers

PHYSICS(1) Id=1

quiz by creating a variable named TRIES and establishing its value as 0.

The Field Text

Create a field just below the title. Use the medium sized font, the second from the top. Make the field the width of the screen and five lines high. Type the following in this field:

> **The formula s = vt specifies the distance s an object travels when moving at velocity v for time t.**
>
> **If a truck has been traveling at 55 miles per hour for 6 hours how far has it moved?**

FIGURE 13.2 *The First Page*

Physics Helper   0 correct answers

The formula s = vt specifies the distance s an object travels when moving at velocity v for time t.

If a truck has been traveling at 55 miles per hour for 6 hours how far has it moved?

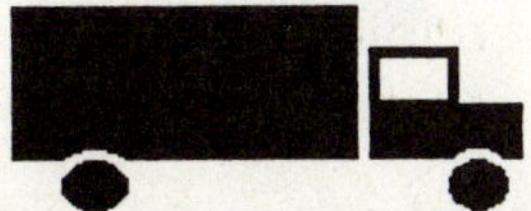

a) 360 miles   c) 330 miles

b) 506 miles   d) 655 miles

PHYSICS(1) Id=1

At the bottom of the screen put 4 fields in two rows. Use the biggest font and different colors for each field. I use the Box/Line command in the Page pull-down menu to line up each field. Create one field. Use the Box/Line command to make a grid at the bottom of the screen, two horizontal and two vertical lines. Use the lines to adjust the position of the fields.

Put the following text in the fields as described:

a) 360 miles In the top left field

b) 506 miles In the bottom left field

c) 330 miles In the top right field

d) 655 miles In the bottom left field

Answer Buttons

Place an invisible script button over each of the answer fields. Use the grid created for the fields to line up the buttons. Make sure that the button covers the field completely. If the student selects any part of a field it should react. Leave the scripts empty for now.

Select the Undraw option from the Page pull-down menu four times to delete the grid.

Insert the following script in the button over the correct answer, 330 miles.

`var PREV(5);` This variable holds the sequence number of the current page. The maximum sequence value is 65535, so the variable is 5 digits.

`set PREV=SEQ;`

`NOSHOW;` You cannot change the contents of the field on the base page unless you are on the base page. However, the student does not have to see this. So, the NOSHOW command stops page updating until the SHOW command is processed.

`go 0;`

`SET TOTAL=TOTAL+1;`	
`SET TOTAL=TRUNC (TOTAL): correct;`	If the TRUNC() function is omitted, there will be multiple spaces between the number and the phrase `correct answers`.
`show;`	Turn page updating back on.
`GO prev+1;`	Go to the next page in the folder.
`do STARTUP;`	

In the other three buttons, the following script is used:

```
IF tries < 3 {
   MSG "  Wrong Answer  ",
      "Try again";
   set tries = tries + 3;
} else {
   msg "The correct answer is",
      "c) 330 miles";
   go seq+1;
   do STARTUP;
}
```

This script displays the message `Wrong Answer, Try again` the first two times a wrong answer is selected. The third time the student enters an incorrect response, the tutorial moves ahead to the next page.

Pictorial Interest

You can select the Paint command from the Option menu to create a picture to dress this page up a bit. To add visual interest to the tutorial, you can place a picture like the truck in Figure 13.2 in the center of the screen between the question and the possible answers.

Creating a Second Page

There is a simple way to create the next page. Select Cut from the Page pull-down menu and store the page in file SCRAP. Then select Paste from the Page menu. A copy of the page is placed after the current page, and this copy becomes the current page. The status line should say

```
PHYSICS(2)  Id=2
```

First, you have to change the contents of the fields. Change the question to

The formula a = (v1 - v0) / t determines the acceleration, a, given the start velocity v0 and end velocity v1 over the period of time t. If a truck traveling at 40 kilometers per hour has to stop in 3 seconds before hitting a wall, what is its rate of deceleration?

Next, change the four fields at the bottom of the page. You will have to move the buttons off of the fields first. Move them to another place on the page temporarily. Remember where you put the button that was over the correct answer; you will be moving it someplace else.

Change the fields to the following:

a) 15 m/s
b) 13.3 m/s
c) 12 m/s
d) 10 m/s

Figure 13.3 shows the problem's text and answer selections as they should appear when you have typed them. The correct answer is b, 13.3 m/s. Place the correct answer button over the corresponding field. Move the other buttons back over the fields. Don't put two buttons over the same field.

Next move the picture of the truck to the right edge. Use the Box/Line command to insert a graphic of a wall just in front of the truck.

Creating the Third Page

The question on the third page should be typed as

> **Using the formula v1*v1 = v0*v0 + 2gs**
> **where v0 = the initial velocity,**
> **v1 = the end velocity,**
> **g = 9.8 m/s/s, the acceleration of gravity,**
> **and s = the distance the object has moved.**
>
> **If you throw a ball into the air with an initial velocity of 12 m/s/s how high**

FIGURE 13.3 *The Second Page*

Physics Helper 0 correct answers

The formula a = (v1 - v0) / t determines the acceleration, a, given the start velocity v0 and end velocity v1 over the period of time t.

If a truck traveling at 40 kilometers per hour has to stop in 3 seconds before hitting a wall, what is its rate of deceleration?

a) 15 m/s c) 12 m/s

b) 13.3 m/s d) 10 m/s

physics(2) Id=2

will it go before it starts to fall back to earth?

Use the Move+Size command to change the size of the question field. Move the bottom edge down to the answer fields and move the right edge closer to the left edge. The right side of the page is reserved for some simple animation. Figure 13.4 shows the third page of the application.

The four answers to type are

a) 5 meters
b) 6 meters
c) 7.3 meters
d) 11.2 meters

FIGURE 13.4 *The Third Page*

Physics Helper   0 correct answers

Using the formula v1*v1 = v0*v0 + 2gs
where v0 = the initial velocity,
v1 = the end velocity,
g = 9.8 m/s/s, the acceleration of gravity
and s = the distance the object has
moved.

If you throw a ball into the air with an
initial velocity of 12 m/s/s how high
will it go before it starts to fall back
to earth?

a) 5 meters   c) 7.3 meters

b) 6 meters   d) 11.2 meters

PHYSICS(3) Id=4

The correct answer is c, 7.3 meters.

If you have the LinkWay Toolkit, you can change the script of the startup button to

```
VAR LST(3000),TRIES(5);
SET TRIES=0;
SET LST=
   "M 550,200; " :
   "E 10,10; ";
EXTERN "LWDRAW",LST;
SET LST=
   "M 550,120; " :
   "E 10,10; ";
EXTERN "LWDRAW",LST;
SET LST=
   "M 550,80; " :
   "E 10,10; ";
EXTERN "LWDRAW",LST;
SET LST=
   "M 550,60; " :
   "E 10,10; ";
EXTERN "LWDRAW",LST;
```

This is a quick-and-dirty way of making some simple animation. To use this script, the LWDRAW.EXE program must be in the current directory. If the program isn't there, nothing happens. When the STARTUP button is executed, a series of four circles approximating the path of a rising object is displayed on the screen.

Creating the Last Page

The last page contains a single field containing the phrase

```
End of tutorial
```

in the largest font in the center of the screen, as shown in Figure 13.5.

The script in the STARTUP button should read

```
VAR name(32);
```

```
INPUT "Enter your name:",name;
noshow;
go 0;
print name : total;
show;
retrace;
mouse;
quit;
```

Preventing Program Corruption

Your last task is to student-proof the application so it cannot be changed or deleted during average use. To do so,

1. Turn off the menu bar and status line.

FIGURE 13.5 *The Last Page*

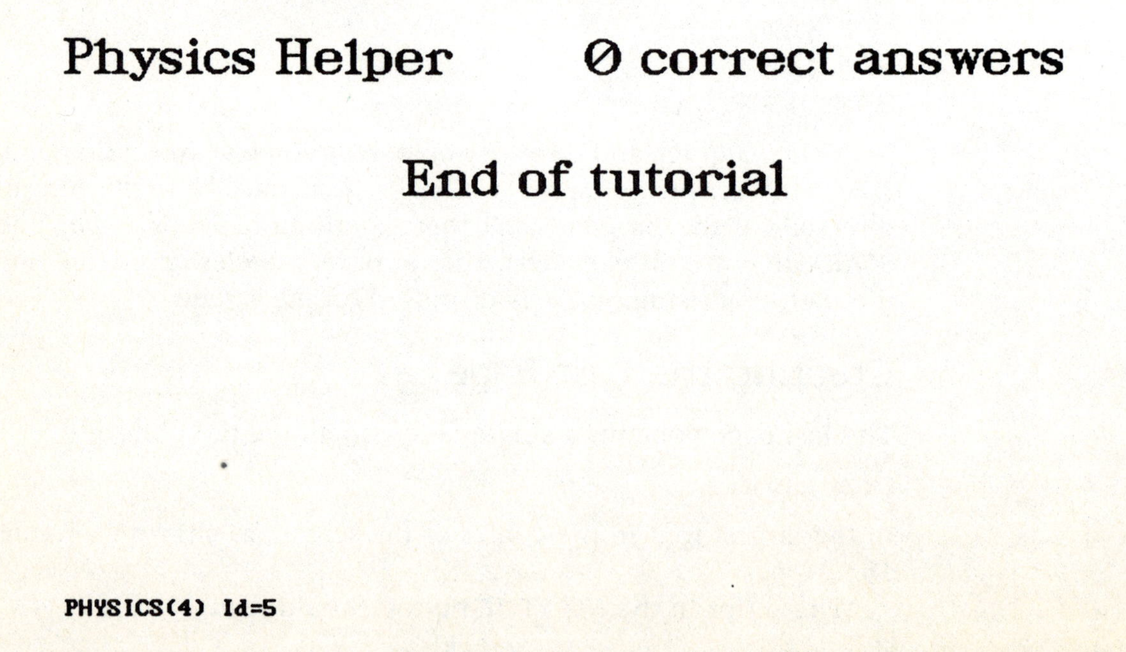

Physics Helper   0 correct answers

End of tutorial

PHYSICS(4) Id=5

2. Lock all of the fields.
3. Set the access level to Read.

Second Sample Application: Buying a Home

LinkWay is a versatile program. Although there are many tasks it cannot do, it can use compiled third-party or custom-developed programs to fill many gaps in its own features.

This sample application provides two types of result. It can calculate the monthly payments on a fixed-rate mortgage given the principal, interest, and term. Also, it can tell you how many years it would take to repay a loan given the principal, interest, and monthly payments.

LinkWay does not include the complex mathematical functions needed to calculate either the monthly payments or the term of a loan. Instead two small programs were written in Microsoft C v5.10 and compiled to perform the calculations.

The Formulas

The formula for calculating the monthly payment is

$$\text{Payments} = \frac{(\text{Principal} * \text{Interest})}{1 - (\text{Interest} + 1)^{-\text{Term}}}$$

The formula for the term is

$$\text{Term} = \frac{\ln\left(1 - \dfrac{\text{Principal} * \text{Interest}}{\text{Payments}}\right)}{\ln(\text{Interest} + 1)}$$

The Source Code

The source code for the first program, stored in the file PAYMENTS.C, follows. Use a text editor such as the LWEDIT program to create the file.

```
/* PRINCIPAL.C                                                      */
/* Created April 27, 1989, by Richard A. Harrington                 */
/* This is a LinkWay EXTERN program. It will not work by itself. */
/* It uses the third and fourth command line arguments, the         */
/* variable address and length, to get the variable's value.       */
/* The variable contains three numbers, the first is the            */
/* principal, the second is the interest rate, and the third is */
/* the term in years. The interest rate is converted to a           */
/* decimal fraction. The term is converted to years.                */

#include <bios.h>
#include <dos.h>
#include <math.h>
#include <memory.h>
#include <stdio.h>
#include <stdlib.h>
#include <string.h>

void main(int argc, char **argv);
void main(int argc, char **argv)
{
   INT      i;
   unsigned varseg, varlen;
   float    principal = (float)0.0,
            interest = (float)0.0,
            term = (float)0.0,
            payments = (float)0.0,
            tmp = (float)0.0;
   char      *var = NULL, *buf = NULL;

   if(argc >= 5) {

      varseg = (unsigned)atoi(argv[3]); /* variable address */
      varlen = (unsigned)atoi(argv[4]); /* variable length */

      var = calloc(1, varlen + 2);
```

```
    /* The extra spaces are for the NULL character used to      */
    /* indicate the end of a string, not strictly necessary     */
    /* here                                                     */

if(var == NULL) {
   goto end;
}

buf = calloc(1, varlen + 2);

if(buf == NULL) {
   goto end;
}
movedata(varset, 0, FP_SEG(var), FP_OFF(var), varlen);
/* Move the data from the string to a variable */
sscanf(var, "%f %f %f", &principal, &interest, &term);
/* Get the values out of the variable */

interest = interest / (100.0 * 12.0);
/* Convert the interest from percentile to hundredths and   */
/* divide by 12 to get monthly interest                     */
term = term * 12.0;
/* Convert term from years to months */
tmp = (float)(1.0 - pow((1.0 + interest), -term));
/* Calculate denominator of equation first */
if(tmp != (float)0.0) {
   /* Make sure that you aren't dividing by zero! */
   payments = principal * interest / tmp;
   sprintf(buf, %7.2f ", payments);
} else {
   sprintf(buf, "ERROR");
}
for(i = 0; i < strlen(buf); i++)
   var[i] = buf[i];
   /* Copy the new string into the variable.  Don't         */
   /* use the strcpy function, because it places a          */
```

```
         /* null character at the end of the string.                */
      while(i < varlen)
         var[i++] = ' ';
         /* Make sure that the entire string is replaced with       */
         /* spaces                                                  */
      movedata(FP_SEG(var), FP_OFF(var), varseg, 0, varlen);

   }
end:
   if(var)
      free(var);
   if(buf)
      free(buf);
}
```

To compile the program, type the following command at the DOS prompt:

CL -AL payments.c

Creating Folders, Fields, and Script Buttons

Create a new folder. The graphics mode doesn't really matter, because this is a short sample application. The MCGA 256 mode was used here.

Create four fields named PRINCFLD, INTERFLD, TERMFLD, and PAYFLD to correspond to the fields displayed in Figure 13.6. Because the display isn't text intensive, you can place them along the right edge of the screen in a large font. However, it really doesn't matter where you put them as long as they are on the same page. To the left of each field, create the field that describes its contents (along the left in the figure).

Create a script button named PAYMENTS and pick the sign as its appearance. Place the following script inside the button. You don't have to use the remarks, but they provide helpful documentation.

```
VAR s(3000);
set s=trunc(PRINCFLD) : " " :
      trunc(INTERFLD) : " " :
      trunc(TERMFLD);
/*
This SET command takes the
values out of the fields and
creates a single string out
of them which is then passed
to the external program

*/
EXTERN "payments",s;
set payfld=s;
```

FIGURE 13.6 *Buying a Home Application*

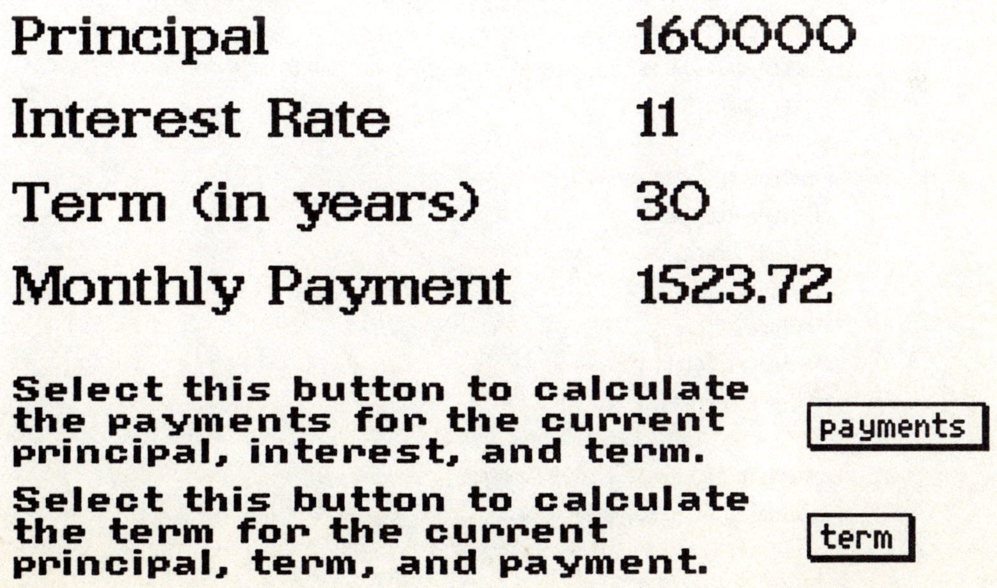

Principal	160000
Interest Rate	11
Term (in years)	30
Monthly Payment	1523.72

Select this button to calculate the payments for the current principal, interest, and term. [payments]

Select this button to calculate the term for the current principal, term, and payment. [term]

```
/*
The contents of the
variables are put into the
field payfld
*/
```

Place the values you want to use in the principal, interest, and term fields and then select the payments button. The payments field will be replaced with the monthly payments needed to repay the mortgage.

The source code for the second program, TERM.C, follows. This program calculates the number of years required to pay a loan given the principal, interest, and monthly payments.

```
/* TERM.C                                                        */
/* Created April 27, 1989, by Richard A. Harrington              */
/* This program is for use with the LinkWay EXTERN command. It   */
/* will not work by itself. It uses the third and fourth         */
/* parameters, the variable and the length, to copy the data     */
/* in the variable to a buffer. It gets three values out of the */
/* buffer, the principal, interest, and monthly payments. It     */
/* then calculates the number of years required to pay the       */
/* mortgage.                                                     */

#include <bios.h>
#include <dos.h>
#include <math.h>
#include <memory.h>
#include <stdio.h>
#include <stdlib.h>
#include <string.h>

void main(int argc, char **argv);
void main(int argc, char **argv)
{
   int      i;
   unsigned varseg, varlen;
```

```
   float    principal   = (float)0.0,
            interest    = (float)0.0,
            term        = (float)0.0,
            payments    = (float)0.0,
            tmp1        = (float)0.0,
            tmp2        = (float)0.0;
   char     *var = NULL,
            *buf = NULL;
if(argc >= 5) {
   varseg = (unsigned)atoi(argv[3]);
   varlen = (unsigned)atoi(argv[4]);

   var = calloc(1, varlen + 2);
   if(var == NULL) {
      goto end;
   }
   buf = calloc(1, varlen + 2);

   if(buf == NULL) {
      goto end;
   }

   movedata(varseg, 0, FP_SEG(var), FP_OFF(var), varlen);

   sscanf(var, "%f %f %f ", &principal, &interest, &payments);

   interest = interest / 1200.0
      /* Divide by 100 to get decimal fraction rather than       */
      /* percentile points, and divide by 12 to get monthly      */
      /* rate instead of yearly rate                             */

   if((payments != (float)0.0) && ((principal * interest) < payments)) {
      /* The log function cannot handle negative numbers and     */
      /* division by zero is an error so I check for both        */
      /* conditions before continuing.                           */
      tmp1 = (float)log(1 - (principal * interest / payments));
```

```
        tmp2 = (float)log(interest + 1);
    }

    if(tmp1 != (float)0.0) {
        /* Check for division by zero again  */
        term = (float)(-1.0 * tmp1 / (tmp2 * 12));
        /* result is in months so divide by  */
        /* 12 to get years                   */

        sprintf(buf, "%-8.2f ", (float)term);
        /* make sure that text is flush right */
    } else {
        sprintf(buf, "ERROR");
    }
    for(i = 0; i < strlen(buf); i++)
        var[i] = buf[i];
        /* move new text into buffer */

    while(i < varlen)
        var[i++] = ' ';

    movedata(FP_SEG(var), FP_OFF(var),varseg, 0, varlen);
}
end:

    if(var)
        free(var);
    if(buf)
        free(buf);
}
```

Compile the program with the following command:

CL -AL term.c

Go back to your LinkWay and add another script button. Name it TERM and use the sign as its appearance. Insert this script in it:

```
VAR s(3000);
set s=trunc(PRINCFLD) : " " :
      trunc(INTERFLD) : " " :
      trunc(PAYFLD);
EXTERN "term",s;
SET termfld=s;
```

This script is almost identical to the PAYMENTS script given earlier. Select the PAYMENTS button to calculate the number of years needed to fully amortize a mortgage of the given principal, interest, and monthly payment.

Now that you know the basics, take the time to dress up the application a bit. Place fields with instructions beside each button and insert a text pop-up HELP button on the page with full instructions.

Glossary

ACCESS LEVEL: Access is the ability to use or change something. The access level determines the user's ability to use and change the contents of a LinkWay folder.

ACTIVE OBJECT: The object that reacts to being selected.

ASCII: (American Standard Code for Information Interchange) The organization that developed the ASCII coding standard used to store and exchange textual information in computer files. The standard defines 128 characters. Characters 0 to 31 are control codes. They control the operation of peripheral devices like printers and modems. Characters 32 through 127 are represented by common symbols including the English alphabet and numeric symbols.

ASPECT RATIO: The ratio of a screen's width to its height or the ratio of a pixel's width to its height. The standard IBM color display has an aspect ratio of 4:3 or 1.333. This means that the horizontal dimension of the picture is 1.333 times the vertical dimension. The aspect ratio of a display cannot change, but the pixel aspect ratio can change. Use the following formula to calculate the aspect ratio of a pixel on a standard IBM color display:

$$\frac{\text{height in pixels}}{\text{width in pixels}} * \frac{3}{4}$$

The MCGA 256 color mode has 320 horizontal pixels and 200 vertical pixels so the aspect ratio of a pixel is 1.2. The MCGA Mono mode has 640 horizontal and 480 vertical pixels. Its aspect ratio is 1; the height and width of each pixel are the same.

BACKUP: A duplicate copy of files, directories, or an entire diskette or hard disk. No matter how secure you think your computer files are, you may lose or damage some or all of them. The only way to ensure that your files are not lost is to keep backup copies of the files in a safe place. The more you use a computer, the greater the chance of a problem. If you do lose a file, restore it from the backup copy.

BUTTON: In its most basic sense, something that causes an action when you press it. Buttons on your computer keyboard are usually called keys. Inside LinkWay the button objects are displayed on the screen. You don't even touch them with your finger; you use the mouse cursor to push them. In fact, you press buttons on the screen by pressing the buttons on your mouse.

CGA: (Color Graphics Adapter) This is the name of the first display adapter developed to handle color graphics on the IBM PC. It has a resolution of 320 pixels horizontally and 200 pixels vertically. Each pixel displays one of four colors: black, white, cyan, or magenta.

CLASS: A category of objects that have some property in common. Apples and oranges are both fruit, because they belong to the class of fruit. LinkWay has five major classes of objects: folders, pages, buttons, pictures, and fields. A class that shares some, but not all, of the properties of another class is called a subclass. Just as pippin apples are a subclass of apples, and apples are a subclass of fruit, buttons and fields are subclasses of pages, and pages are subclasses of folders.

CLOSE: A term used in the sense of closing a deal rather than closing a door. You close a deal when you are satisfied with the conditions. You close a dialog box when you are satisfied with its contents. To close a dialog box, either select the circle in the top left corner of the box with the mouse or press the mouse button while the mouse cursor is outside of the box.

COMMAND LINE ARGUMENT: A word or phrase typed after the command name at the DOS command line. To start a program, for example, you type its name at the DOS command line followed by its arguments, which are separated by spaces. As an example, to start LinkWay in EGA+VGA mode, you type **LINKWAY \E**, where LINKWAY is the command and \E is the command line argument.

CONTROL CODE: The ASCII standard assigns numbers to 128 symbols and characters. The first 32 characters are control codes. They control the printing of the other 96 characters.

CURSOR: A symbol representing the current location. The text cursor represents the location where text will be inserted or changed in a block of text. The graphics cursor represents the location where graphics will be drawn or changed.

DIALOG BOX: A means provided by a program for the exchange of information. A dialog box is a displayed construct that exchanges information with the user. It is called a box because it is displayed in a rectangle or square drawn over the current display. When you close a dialog box, the screen display behind it is restored. LinkWay uses several types of dialog boxes.

DISPLAY: Also known as a screen, cathode ray tube, CRT, or monitor, the piece of machinery that displays the visual output of the computer.

DISPLAY ADAPTER: A piece of hardware inside your computer that generates the picture shown on your display. Some adapters have more than one graphics mode.

DOS: (Disk Operating System) The program or programs that you use to control your computer's disk system. Application programs such as LinkWay or your custom applications run in conjunction with DOS. To control the disks, DOS must also control the hardware.

EGA: (Enhanced Graphics Adapter) The successor of the CGA, the EGA added several graphics and text modes to those available with the CGA.

ENVIRONMENT VARIABLE: A named area of the COMMAND.COM program that stores data. When you start your computer, DOS is loaded into memory. Part of DOS is the COMMAND.COM program, which interprets the commands you type in and defines your environment. Part of the COMMAND.COM program can store data, keeping it available to all of the program that it executes. Values are assigned to environment variables with the DOS command SET.

ESCAPE CODE: The ASCII character number 27, called the ESCAPE character, followed by one or more characters. Because there weren't enough ASCII control codes to create all of the effects needed by computer displays and printers, escape codes were added to fill the gap. Just about every company that makes printers uses a different set of escape codes.

EXPRESSION: A statement composed of operands and operators that yields a result. The phrase 2+3 is an expression. The operands are the numbers 2 and 3. The operator is the addition symbol, +. The result of the expression is the value 5. Operators perform actions on the operands. Expressions can be used as operands. Simple expressions have a single operator. Complex expressions have expressions as operands. The phrase 7 * (2 + 3) is a complex expression composed of two simple expressions.

FIELD: An area in which something is drawn or displayed. In LinkWay, a field is an area where text is displayed. Most fields in LinkWay contain text that you can change.

FILE: One long sequence of bytes stored on a computer disk. The basic unit of a file is a byte, a number between 0 and 255. The size of a file is measured in bytes. See the definition of ASCII for more information on converting bytes to characters.

FILE EXTENSION: The optional part of a file name that occurs after the period. All files are named with characters divided into two parts—the name and the extension. A file extension is an optional string of 1 to 3 characters separated from the primary name by a period. Extensions are usually used to indicate the file type. The file name and extension are completely independent of the file contents.

FOLDER: One of the five basic objects in LinkWay. A folder is stored one per file. The file extension of the folder name determines its graphics mode.

FONT: A collection of symbols—alphabetic and numeric—in a similar style and size. Some styles date back to the beginnings of the printing press.

ICON: A symbol that represents a concept. As an analogy, the red octagonal stop sign is familiar to all and tells the driver to stop. The text on the sign is almost unnecessary, because everyone knows what the shape and color of the sign icon represents. In LinkWay such icons are used to represent common actions.

ID NUMBER: A sequentially assigned digit created by LinkWay when you create a page. ID numbers are unique within folders. No two pages have the same ID number in the same folder. Pages in other folders may, however, have the same ID number. They are unique within folders only.

LAN: (Local Area Network) A collection of hardware and software that allows computers to communicate among themselves directly. Files and programs can be transmitted between computers attached to a LAN. Some LANs provide transparent access to other computers, the appearance that the other computer's files are on your computer.

MCGA: (Multicolor Graphics Array) A successor to the EGA display adapter. Originally created for the IBM PS/2 Model 25 and Model 30 computers, MCGA is equivalent to the VGA display adapter found on the other IBM PS/2 models.

MENU BAR: A line along the top of the screen that displays options you can select. The bar is divided into menus, and each menu has a title. Selecting a menu or option causes one or more rows of text to be displayed below the menu bar. Each row represents a choice. When the mouse cursor moves over a row, the choice changes color. When you press the mouse button, the current choice is activated.

MENU: A list of choices displayed on the screen.

OBJECT: The basic unit of LinkWay. Objects have properties such as appearance, size, position, color, value, and purpose. Folders have a background color, a set of fonts, and a collection of pages. Pages contain buttons, pictures, and fields.

PAGE: A collection of buttons, pictures, and fields stored in a folder.

PALETTE: A subset of the available colors. The MCGA 256 color mode can display 256 colors simultaneously, but it can display up to 262,144 colors. The palette defines which of the 256 out of 262,144 colors are visible.

PEL or PIXEL: An abbreviation for the phrase *picture element.* The computer display is divided up into tiny discrete dots, each of which is a pixel.

RAM: (Random Access Memory) The portion of the memory of your computer that is volatile, in which data can be changed. If the computer loses power, the data in RAM is lost. Any section of random access memory may be read from or written to in any order.

ROM: (Read Only Memory) Unlike RAM, this is the part of memory that retains its contents when the computer is turned off. ROM holds important codes that perform the routine duties of the computer.

SCRIPT: A sequence of commands.

SEQUENCE NUMBER: The number assigned to each page in a LinkWay folder. The base page is sequence number 0, the first page is 1, and so on. They are not permanent. If you change the order of the pages in a folder, the sequence numbers change.

SYSTEM VARIABLE: A named object that contains a value but has no visible appearance. Unlike regular variables, system variables are created and controlled by LinkWay.

VARIABLE: A named object that contains a value but has no visible appearance. The programmer creates and controls variables.

VGA: (Video Graphics Array) The newest display adapter in the IBM line. It can simulate all of the CGA, EGA, and MCGA modes.

WORM DISK: (Write Once Read Many) A new type of disk drive that is perfect for backups. Once a file is written to a WORM disk, it is there forever; you cannot erase it. WORM disks have a large capacity and can hold a large number of files.

XOR: (Exclusive-Or) A boolean (logical) operator that returns a true value if its two operands are not equal to each other. The phrase, *either one or the other but not both* is an equivalent way of saying exclusive-or. If a pixel of color A is XORed with the color value B a third color C is created. If the color C is XORed with B, the result is the color A. Thus, if the same pixel is XORed with the same color twice, its original color is restored. This property is used to draw buttons. If two identical buttons are drawn in the same position, they become invisible. Each pixel in the first button is XORed with its corresponding pixel in the second button.

APPENDIX A

Starting LinkWay

If you haven't already installed LinkWay, please refer to your LinkWay documentation for instructions on doing so.

Environment Variables

The following environment variables affect LinkWay's operation:

PATH DOS uses this variable to find executable programs. The directory that contains the LINKWAY.EXE program must be listed in the PATH.

LWPATH When LinkWay tries to use a font, icon, or folder file it searches the current directory first and then the directory specified by this environment variable. Its default value is \LINKWAY.

LWDOC When a document button is selected the LWEDIT program adds the contents of this environment variable to the beginning of the text file name. This becomes the path of the text file. There is no default value for this variable; documents are assumed to be in the current directory.

If the value of the LWDOC environment variable is \LINKWAY\DOC\ and the document file name is MANUAL.TXT, the LWEDIT program will try to open the file \LINKWAY\DOC\MANUAL.TXT.

The variable is added directly to the file name. No characters are added. Unlike the LWPATH or PATH variables, the value of this variable should end with a backslash character.

LWPIC If a picture file cannot be found in the current directory, the directory specified by this environment variable is searched.

The DOS command SET is used to work with environment variables. To see the values of all variables currently set type the command SET at the DOS prompt. You should see a list similar to the following:

```
COMSPEC=C:\COMMAND.COM
LWPATH=C:\LINKWAY
LWDOC=C:\LINKWAY\DOC\
PROMPT=$P$G
```

The variables are listed in the order they were created. The name of the variable is followed by an equals sign and the value.

To assign a value to an environment variable, type the command **SET** followed by the variable name, an equal sign, and the value.

The statement

```
SET LWDOC=C:\LINKWAY\DOC\
```

assigns the value C:\LINKWAY\DOC\ to the variable LWDOC.

Command Line Arguments

You start a program by typing its name at the DOS prompt, also called the command line. Most programs have command line arguments, which are a series of characters directly after the command name that affects the operation of the program. Arguments are separated from each other by spaces.

LinkWay recognizes two types of command line arguments: flags and folder names.

The first folder name on the command line is opened instead of the main folder. It becomes the default folder. See the MODE command for more information about the default folder.

Flags are one or two characters following a slash character. These arguments tell LinkWay how to behave. Some flags have values. The value is typed directly after the flag. Spaces are not allowed in the value.

/C Force the screen to CGA 320 X 200 4-color mode if it is supported; otherwise, choose the highest resolution mode available.

/E Force the screen to EGA 640 X 350 16-color mode.

/H Force the screen to MCGA 640 X 480 2-color mode if it is supported; otherwise, choose the highest resolution mode available.

/LWDOC=str

/LWPATH=str

/LWPIC=str These three command line arguments take precedence over the environment variables just listed, but their behavior is the same.

/M Force the screen to MCGA 320 X 200 256-color mode if it is supported; otherwise, choose the highest resolution mode available.

/N Enable National Language Support and double-capacity fonts. This option requires an extra 36K of memory.

/P Inform LinkWay that the system printer is not attached normally; printer output has been redirected to a DOS device or network printer. It is the user's responsibility to make sure that the printer is ready. If it isn't, the program may stall indefinitely or display the DOS messages over the current screen.

/Snnn Set the size of the buffer used for folders to nnn. The default is 50K, the range is 4K to 250K. The buffer must be big enough to hold the largest folder you will use.

/V A VGA display card has been added to the computer. This option must be used if the computer does not normally have a VGA display. The IBM PS/2 Model 25 and 30 contain MCGA adapters; therefore, this option must be used with them.

/X Prevent the use of the EGA 640 × 350 16-color mode. This will save approximately 50K of memory.

/Z Only permit the CGA 320 × 200 4-color mode display. This will save approximately 50K to 100K of memory.

Following are some examples:

LINKWAY /E MYFOLDER	Starts LinkWay in EGA+VGA if that mode is supported and opens the folder MYFOLDER.
LINKWAY /S110 DEMO	Sets the size of the folder buffer to 110K and opens the DEMO folder.
LINKWAY /LWPATH=C:\BIN	Opens the folder MAIN as normal, but files not found in the current directory must be in the C:\BIN directory.

APPENDIX B

File Extensions

Table B.1 lists the file extensions used by the LinkWay program and support programs.

TABLE B.1 *File Extensions*

Extension	Description
.BIN	Binary executable, used by BCALL script command
.EXX	Intermediate file created by Toolkit program MSGPUT
.FMF	Font or icon file
.LWC	Folder in CGA mode
.LWE	Folder in EGA+VGA mode

.LWH	Folder in MCGA 2 color mode
.LWM	Folder in MCGA 256 color mode
.MSG	Source message file used by Toolkit program MSGPUT
.OB	Object cut/paste file
.P13	MCGA 256 palette files
.PCC	CGA picture
.PCE	EGA+VGA picture
.PCH	MCGA 2 color picture
.PCM	MCGA 256 color picture
.PG	Page cut/paste file
.PIC	IBM PC/Storyboard™ picture file

APPENDIX C

Converting Folder Display Modes

The file extension of a folder's file name determines its graphics mode. To change a folder's graphics mode change its extension.

Use the DOS COPY or RENAME command to change the name of a file. The COPY command will always work, but if a file already exists with the new name it will be replaced without warning. The RENAME command will stop and display a warning if the new name is used by another file.

The extensions are listed in Table C.1.

Following are some examples:

`COPY MAIN.LWC MAIN.LWE`	Convert the main folder from CGA to EGA+VGA.
`RENAME NEW.LWH NEW.LWM`	If the file NEW.LWM does not exist the file NEW.LWH will be renamed to NEW.LWM.

`COPY BOOKS.LWC MAGAZINE.LWE`	Create a new folder called MAGAZINE in EGA+VGA mode from a folder called BOOKS in CGA mode.

When you open these modified files for the first time a message box will say

```
Wrong display mode    Will adjust
```

The name of the folder may have changed, but its internals do not change until LinkWay tries to open it.

Because each graphics mode has a different resolution and aspect ratio, the locations and sizes of the objects in the folder must be adjusted. The objects in a converted folder will be approximately the same size and position as those in the original folder.

TABLE C.1 *IBM LinkWay Folder Extensions*

Extension	Description
.LWC	CGA 320 × 200 4-color
.LWM	MCGA 320 × 200 256-color
.LWE	EGA+VGA 640 × 350 16-color
.LWH	MCGA 640 × 480 2-color

APPENDIX D

LinkWay File Formats

The following abbreviations are used in this appendix:

- **CHAR** An ASCII character string of one or more characters
- **BYTE** An 8-bit unsigned number
- **BIN** A 16-bit unsigned number

Folders

Folder files have one of these extensions: .LWC, .LWE, .LWH, or .LWM. Each file consists of a 40-byte folder prefix followed by the base page and the regular pages. Table D.1 lists and describes the folder prefixes.

TABLE D.1 *The Folder File Format*

Name	Offset	Type	Description
CHECK BYTES	0–2	CHAR	Sometimes called a magic number, these three bytes contain either the letters STK or LWF. This is an internal way of confirming that the file is a folder. New folders should have the letters LWF here
ACCESS LEVEL	3	BYTE	Used as a bit field: Bit 7 Status ON/OFF 0 = OFF 1 = ON Bits 6–3 Unused Bits 2–0 Access Level 000 = READ 001 = UPDATE 010 = INSERT 011 = DELETE 100 = FORMAT
PASSWORD	4–5	BIN	Encrypted password; 0 = no password. Change this value to 0 to access folders with lost passwords
PAGECOUNT	6–7	BIN	Number of pages, excluding base page
NPAGEID	8–9	BIN	Next page ID to assign
FONT1	10–17	CHAR	Name of font 1, small
FONT2	18–25	CHAR	Name of font 2, medium
FONT3	26–33	CHAR	Name of font 3, large
BGCOLOR	34	BYTE	Current background color

TABLE D.1 *The Folder File Format (continued)*

Name	Offset	Type	Description
DISPMODE	5	BYTE	Current display mode: 4 = CGA 16 = EGA+VGA 17 = MCGA 2 color 19 = MCGA 256 color
BASESIZE	36–37	BIN	Size of base page in bytes
FOLDSIZE	38–39	BIN	Total size of all regular pages in 16-byte pages (multiply by 16 to get number of bytes)

Page Format

A *page* consists of an 8-byte prefix followed by the object data. The object data may be up to 8000 bytes. Table D.2 lists and describes the page formats.

TABLE D.2 *The Page Format*

Name	Offset	Type	Description
CHECK BYTES	0–1	CHAR	New files contain the letters PG; some older files contain CD
PAGE ID	2–3	BIN	A unique number assigned to each page when it is created. The base page is always 0. The maximum value is 65535
PAGE SIZE	4–5	BIN	Total number of paragraphs (16-byte blocks) in the current page, including the 8-byte prefix. To get the number of bytes in a page, multiply this number by 16

TABLE D.2 *The Page Format (continued)*

Name	Offset	Type	Description
OBJECT SIZE	6–7	BIN	Total number of bytes used for objects on the current page. The PAGE SIZE value is measured in paragraphs, 16-byte blocks, this value is measured in bytes

Object Format

Objects are composed of a fixed 22-byte prefix followed by a variable-length body of up to 3000 bytes. The value OVLENGTH in the prefix contains the length of the variable part. Some types of objects have no variable part, so OVLENGTH is equal to 0.

The four types of objects are fields, pictures, buttons, and draw lists. There is only one draw list per page. To create it, select the Box/Line option on the Page pull-down menu. Each new draw command is added to the end of the list. Table D.3 lists and describes the object formats.

The objects on a page are stored in a list in the order in which you create them, except for the draw list, which is always first.

The variable part of an object consists of one of the objects listed and described in Table D.4.

TABLE D.3 *The Object Format*

Name	Offset	Type	Description
OTYPE	0	CHAR	B = Button D = Draw F = Field P = Picture

TABLE D.3 *The Object Format (continued)*

Name	Offset	Type	Description
OFLAG	1	CHAR	Depends on OTYPE: Buttons D = Document G = Go to L = Link P = Picture pop-up T = Text pop-up Draw Lists unused Fields Font Number Picture Always C
OLENGTH	2–3	BIN	Length of object in bytes
ONAME	4–11	CHAR	Name of object, padded with spaces
OLEFT	12	BYTE	Left column of bounding box
OTOP	13	BYTE	Top row of bounding box
ORIGHT	14	BYTE	Right column of box
OBOTTOM	15	BYTE	Bottom row of bounding box
OROW	16	BYTE	Fields Number of text rows The number of columns in a field is calculated by dividing OVLENGTH by OROW Go to buttons 1 = Base page 2 = First page 3 = Last page 4 = Next page 5 = Previous page Picture pop-up button top row of window Picture top row of window

TABLE D.3 *The Object Format (continued)*

Name	Offset	Type	Description
OCOL	17	BYTE	Field 0 = unlocked 1 = locked Picture pop-up button left edge of window Picture left edge of window
OIVALUE	18–19	BIN	Field text color number Button Icon number, 99 = sign
OVLENGTH	20–21	BIN	Length in bytes of variable part of object, 0 = none, max 3000

TABLE D.4 *The Variable Part of an Object*

Type of Object	Length	Description
BUTTON, Document	16 bytes	The name of the text file
BUTTON, Find	32 bytes	The first 8 characters contain the folder name, the next 8 contain the field name, and the last 16 contain the search string
BUTTON, Link	13 bytes	The first 8 characters contain the folder name, the next 5 contain the page ID
BUTTON, Picture Pop-Up	16 bytes	The name of the picture file
BUTTON, Script	variable	The contents of the script

TABLE D.4 *The Variable Part of an Object (continued)*

Type of Object	Length	Description
BUTTON, Text Pop-Up	variable	The contents of the text pop-up
DRAW	variable	A list of draw commands, not related to the LWDRAW Toolkit option
FIELD	variable	Contents of the field
PICTURE	16 bytes	The name of the picture file

Picture File Format

The LinkWay picture file format is the same as Zsoft Corporation's PC Paintbrush™ .PCX format. You can use PC Paintbrush pictures inside LinkWay by changing their file extensions. They are listed and described in Table D.5.

Each picture file consists of a 128-byte prefix and the picture data.

TABLE D.5 *Picture Filename Extensions*

Extension	Type of Adapter Using the File
.PCC	CGA
.PCE	EGA+VGA
.PCH	MCGA/VGA Mono
.PCM	MCGA 256 Color

Picture Prefix

Table D.6 lists and gives the values for the picture file formats.

TABLE D.6 *The Picture File Format*

Name	Offset	Type	Value	
Manufacturer code	0	BYTE	10	
Version	1	BYTE	5	
Encoding scheme	2	BYTE	1	
Bits per pixel	3	BYTE	CGA	2
			EGA	1
			MCGA 256	8
			MCGA Mono	1
Window size	4–11	BIN	CGA	0,0,399,199
			EGA	0,0,639,349
			MCGA 256	0,0,319,199
			MCGA Mono	0,0,639,479
Horizontal size	12–13	BIN	CGA	320
			EGA	640
			MCGA 256	320
			MCGA Mono	640
Vertical size	14–15	BIN	CGA	200
			EGA	350
			MCGA 256	200
			MCGA Mono	480

TABLE D.6 *The Picture File Format (continued)*

Name	Offset	Type	Value
Color Maps	16–63	BYTE	CGA 0x00,0x00,0x00, 0xF0,0xF0,0xF0, 0x00,0x00,0x00, 0xF0,0xF0,0xF0, 0x00,0x00,0x00, 0xF0,0xF0,0xF0, 0x00,0x00,0x00, 0xF0,0xF0,0xF0, 0x00,0x00,0x00, 0xF0,0xF0,0xF0, 0x00,0x00,0x00, 0xF0,0xF0,0xF0, 0x00,0x00,0x00, 0xF0,0xF0,0xF0, 0x00,0x00,0x00, 0xF0,0xF0,0xF0 EGA 0x00,0x00,0x00,0x00, 0x00,0xAA,0x00,0xAA, 0x00,0x00,0xAA,0xAA, 0xAA,0x00,0x00,0xAA, 0x00,0xAA,0xAA,0xAA, 0x00,0xAA,0xAA,0xAA, 0x55,0x55,0x55,0x55, 0x55,0xFF,0x55,0xFF, 0x55,0x55,0xFF,0xFF, 0xFF,0x55,0x55,0xFF, 0x55,0xFF,0xFF,0xFF, 0x55,0xFF,0xFF,0xFF MCGA Mono 0x00,0x00,0x00, 0xFC,0xFC,0xFC, 0x00,0xA8,0x00,

TABLE D.6 *The Picture File Format (continued)*

Name	Offset	Type	Value	
			0xFC,0xFC,0xFC, 0xA8,0x00,0x00, 0xFC,0xFC,0xFC, 0xA8,0x54,0x00, 0xFC,0xFC,0xFC, 0x54,0x54,0x54, 0xFC,0xFC,0xFC, 0x54,0x0F,0x54, 0xFC,0xFC,0xFC, 0xFC,0x54,0x54, 0xFC,0xFC,0xFC, 0xFC,0xFC,0x54, 0xFC,0xFC,0xFC	
			MCGA 256 0x70,0x50,0x00,0x70,0x00,0x00, 0x8C,0x00,0x00,0xA8,0x00,0x00, 0xC4,0x00,0x00,0xE0,0x00,0x00, 0xFC,0x00,0x00,0x00,0x90,0x00, 0x70,0x90,0x00,0x8C,0x90,0x00, 0xA8,0x90,0x00,0xC4,0x90,0x00, 0xE0,0x90,0x00,0xFC,0x90,0x00, 0x00,0xAC,0x00,0x70,0xAC,0x00	
Reserved	64	BYTE	0 (Unused)	
Number of planes	65	BYTE	CGA EGA MCGA 256 MCGA Mono	1 4 1 1
Bytes per scan line	66–67	BIN	CGA EGA MCGA 256 MCGA Mono	80 80 320 80
Filler	68–127		Unused	

Picture Data

The data for pictures is stored immediately following the prefix using a run-length encoding scheme. A series of pixels of the same color is called a run. Instead of storing each pixel individually, the run is stored as a number representing the length of the run followed by the color of the run. One horizontal line on the screen is called a *scan line.* Pixel runs are stored in blocks of scan lines, so a run cannot continue from one scan line to the next. The picture is composed of a series of sequential scan lines starting from the top of the picture.

The EGA graphics modes has four bit planes. Conceptually, each plane is one whole monochrome screen. Each pixel is represented by one bit on each plane. The pixel's color is the combination of all four planes. Each horizontal line in an EGA screen is stored as four scan lines, one for each bit plane.

The run-length encoding scheme is very simple. If the upper 2 bits of the current byte are 0, the lower 6 bits represent the color of the current pixel. If the upper 2 bits are nonzero, the lower 6 bits represent the length of the run. The color of the run is stored in the next byte of the file. So, there are two possibilities here: set one pixel or set more than one.

Palettes

In the MCGA 256 color mode there are 8 bits per pixel allowing 256 colors simultaneously. The value stored in each pixel is not a color but an index into a table of colors. This table of colors is called a *palette.* MCGA 256 pictures may have palette files associated with them. The palette file has the same name as the picture file, but the palette file uses the extension .P13. When a picture is loaded, its palette replaces the current palette. If more than one picture is shown on a page, the last palette will be used. When a new page is displayed the palette is reset to the default palette.

A palette file consists of 256 sets of 3-byte color values, for a total of 768 bytes. The first byte in each set is the red color value, the second is green, and the third is blue.

Your television set creates colors by combining the colors red, green, and blue in varying intensities. To get white or gray, you use equal intensities of the three.

These colors follow the rules for transmitted light, not pigments.

Font/Icon Files

Font and icon files have the same extension: .FMF. Each file starts with a 32-byte prefix followed by the character data. The font prefix and values for font and icon files are listed in Table D.7.

TABLE D.7 *The Font File Format*

Name	Offset	Type	Value
CHECK BYTES	0–1	CHAR	FT
CELL WIDTH	2	BYTE	Bit width of average character (not used)
CELL HEIGHT	3	BYTE	Number of pixels between lines of characters
PATTERN WIDTH	4	BYTE	Bytes per row in characters data
PATTERN HEIGHT	5	BYTE	Number of rows in each character
TYPE FLAG	6	BYTE	D if double-sized font
	7–31	BYTE	Unused

Character Data

If the TYPE FLAG is D, there are 192 characters following the prefix; otherwise, there are 96. The first character is ASCII index 32, the space character.

The first byte for each character is its width, the number of pixels to move ahead for the next character.

The character data is composed of PATTERN HEIGHT rows of PATTERN WIDTH bytes each. Each pixel is stored as 2 bits, with four pixels per byte. Each pixel may be one of four colors, and color 0 is the background color.

In a text field, color 3 is replaced by the color selected for the field.

APPENDIX E

Memory Usage

LinkWay is a large program; it uses a lot of memory. Because LinkWay can only use the first 640K of memory, creating a large application can be a series of trade-offs.

LinkWay requires 225K just to start the program. This is a non-negotiable number; you cannot change it.

A buffer must be allocated for the folders. The default size of this buffer is 50K. You may use the /S command line argument to change the size of the buffer to any size from 4K to 250K. The buffer must be at least as big as the biggest folder. You cannot load a folder bigger than the buffer.

Another buffer for the display must be allocated. The display buffer must be big enough to show the highest resolution mode permitted. You may specify which modes are available with command line arguments when LinkWay is started. The display buffer sizes are

16K Only CGA mode is permitted, use /Z command line argument

64K EGA+VGA mode not permitted, use /X command line argument

112K EGA+VGA mode is permitted

Using the National Language Support for memory usage, which is represented by the /N command line argument, increases the font buffer by 36K, because double-length fonts may be used.

The programs that you can call from within LinkWay also need memory.

The LWEDIT program needs 80K for the code and up to 25K for the data. The LWPAINT needs 120K, and LWPrint needs 16K. LWCAPTUR is a terminate-and-stay-resident (TSR) program. When you execute the program from the DOS command line, LWEDIT stakes out its own area of memory and stays there until you reset the computer or execute the LWRemove program. The LWCAPTUR program takes 11K of memory.

When you execute a DOS command from within LinkWay, there must be enough memory for the COMMAND.COM program and the program you want to execute.

Variables are allocated from the pool of empty memory. The length of the variable determines the amount of memory needed. The memory is allocated in paragraphs (blocks of 16 bytes). You can allow up to 15 unused bytes per variable.

Use the CHKDSK command to find out the amount of memory available. After the disk statistics are printed, the total memory and the free memory totals are printed. If you are at the DOS command line, the difference between the two is caused by device drivers and TSR programs.

Device drivers are special programs loaded into the computer's memory when the computer is reset or turned on. They are listed in a text file called CONFIG.SYS. Each line of the file that starts with the word DEVICE loads in another device driver. Some device drivers can be large memory hogs.

TSR programs are generally executed when the computer is started by calling them from the AUTOEXEC.BAT file. Most can also be started from the DOS command line. Borland's SideKick® and Turbo Lightning® are two famous TSR programs. Most networks have TSR drivers.

A program will not run if your system lacks enough memory for it. If you want to run the LWPAINT program in EGA mode, you need at least 512K of memory. If you use the DOS Cmd option of the Option pull-down menu to execute a program, it must fit in the memory left over from LinkWay and its buffers.

If an option does not work, or if even LinkWay will not run, you must eliminate as many device drivers and TSR programs as possible from memory. Make sure you read the appropriate manuals before you alter the CONFIG.SYS or AUTOEXEC.BAT files. Your DOS manual describes the structure of these files, and some of the device drivers. Some devices require special drivers to work, so you should consult their manuals also.

APPENDIX F

Apple Hypercard and IBM LinkWay

LinkWay and Hypercard

This appendix is provided for a number of reasons. First, it gives those familiar with Apple® Hypercard® a quick reorientation for LinkWay. Here you will see terminology familiar from Hypercard translated to corresponding terminology for LinkWay. Second, the appendix is intended to give those familiar with LinkWay a glimpse of the program that inspired it. And finally, you will find here some hints for porting an existing Hypercard stack to LinkWay. The appendix examines LinkWay and Hypercard first from the viewpoint of the casual user, then explores the products from the author's or programmer's point of view.

Any discussion of LinkWay and Hypercard requires some understanding of both the PC and Macintosh computing environments. Here, PC means any machine running MS-DOS, and Macintosh means an Apple Macintosh. This appendix assumes no knowledge of either system, so if you know one of the machines, you'll only be bored half the time!

The Kiosk Level View

A *casual user* is someone who interacts with a program at the kiosk level. Such a user might not even be aware of using LinkWay or Hypercard. He or she might encounter LinkWay or Hypercard at a shopping mall's information kiosk, when the only concern with the program is as means to achieve an immediate end, such as finding a particular store. At this level, LinkWay and Hypercard seem quite similar. Both have a point-and-click interface. Both have buttons to select to perform actions. Both can display pictures and text. Both can play sounds. For the most part, anyone who can navigate the screen in LinkWay can get around in Hypercard. A well-designed application in either LinkWay or Hypercard is intuitive and obvious. Buttons are clearly labeled and their actions are predictable. The user of such an application feels comfortable and in control.

There are two differences between the two packages that a casual user might notice. One is that LinkWay pages can have color text and pictures. Currently, Hypercard is pretty much a black-and-white affair, although existing extensions to Hypercard allow the display of colored text and pictures in windows.

The second noticeable difference is that Hypercard buttons light up when they're pushed. This may seem like an insignificant feature, but to the novice user this kind of immediate feedback is very important. The user may feel uncertain of whether the mouse click was noticed by the program until something happens. A delay of even half a second can be quite disconcerting.

The Author-Level View

Hypermedia in general blurs the distinction between users (or readers, listeners, or viewers) and programmers (or authors, performers, or artists). As you cross this blurry line, differences between LinkWay and Hypercard become more pronounced, but similarities still predominate. Table F.1's translating dictionary shows how pervasive the similarities are.

Actually, none of these translations is exact and each deserves some comment.

MS-DOS/Macintosh OS + Toolbox + Finder

MS-DOS is a disk operating system with a command line interface. Some of the MS-DOS operating system is stored permanently inside

TABLE F.1 *LinkWay and Hypercard Translating Dictionary*

MS-DOS	**Macintosh OS + Toolbox + Finder**
Directory	Folder
Executable File (.EXE or .COM)	Application
Data File	Document
LinkWay	**Hypercard**
Folder	Stack
BasePage	Background
Page	Card
Field	Field
Button	Button
Script	Script
Menu	Menu
Document	TextFile
Machine Language Subroutine	XCMD and XFCN

the machine in read only memory (ROM BIOS), whereas some is read from the boot disk when the machine is started up. The user interface is provided by a program called COMMAND.COM. The user communicates with the operating system through COMMAND.COM by typing a command followed by some (usually optional) program-specific command line arguments. The Macintosh OS, together with a bunch of routines called the Toolbox and a program called Finder, make up a disk operating system with a graphical user interface.

The Macintosh OS and Toolbox are stored mostly in ROM, whereas the Finder is read from the boot disk. Files are represented by small pictures called *icons.* To run a program, the user points with the mouse to the icon representing the program and clicks twice.

Directory/Folder

MS-DOS directories and Macintosh folders are almost identical. You must be careful, though, not to confuse the LinkWay folder with the Macintosh folder. The name clash is unfortunate, but the context should clarify which is meant.

Executable File/Application

In the MS-DOS world, files come in only one flavor. In order to differentiate executable (program) files from data files, the names of executable files end with the .EXE or .COM extension. To run a program, the user types the name of the file without the trailing .EXE or .COM. In the Macintosh world, files come in many flavors. Each file has a type. Executable files have type APPL. Their names can be any string of up to 32 characters.

Data File/Document

As just noted, MS-DOS files come in one flavor and are distinguished by their names. In the Macintosh environment, in addition to having a type, each file has a creator. Clicking twice on a document causes the Finder to run the program identified as the document's creator. To see the type and creator of a file, you must use a program like Apple's ResEdit™.

LinkWay/Hypercard

Both LinkWay and Hypercard could be called integrated authoring tools for hypermedia. Each provides for the creation of objects of certain types. In the usual language of object oriented programming (OOP), object types are called *classes.* A general object oriented programming language provides for the creation of classes. You might think of LinkWay or Hypercard as a specialized OOP system with a fixed number of predefined classes. Some of these classes are user instantiable. That is, we can freely create new instances of these classes. LinkWay user-instantiable classes are the folder, page, button, field, and picture. Hypercard user-instantiable classes are stack, background, card, button, and field.

Objects from these classes (called instances of the classes) have some fairly sophisticated properties, causing the objects to show themselves on the screen, respond appropriately to user input, and so on. In this view, the text in a field is a property of the field, as is its bounding rectangle. Some objects have a property called a *script.* The script of an object enables the author or programmer to specify the behavior of an object under certain conditions. Scripts are described further later in this appendix.

Folder/Stack

Folders have only one base page, and because a base page corresponds to a background, folders are like stacks with a single background. For LinkWay users, a Hypercard stack is like a folder with multiple base pages. Another more subtle but limiting difference is that stacks are file-based objects and folders are memory based. This distinction is discussed further under Porting a Hypercard Stack to LinkWay later in the appendix.

Base Page/Background

You could argue that a Hypercard background really corresponds to a LinkWay folder and that a stack corresponds to a directory in that a stack can contain multiple backgrounds and a directory can contain multiple folders (files). In this view, the base page is what you get when you select background from the Hypercard Edit menu. The fact that directories are not LinkWay objects but MS-DOS objects complicates this picture somewhat. However, this comparison may help you to understand the situation. There is no correct translation—only ones that are inaccurate in different ways.

Page/Card

Pages and cards are the individually viewable units in a folder or stack. You always see exactly one page or card from the current folder or stack.

Fields

For someone used to Macintosh text editing and scrolling text fields, LinkWay fields will seem somewhat strange at first. (For those unfamiliar with Macintosh text editing, note that on a Macintosh, text editing is the same in every program. As a result, Macintosh users have strong expectations about how text editing should work in an unfamiliar program.) Perhaps the biggest surprise for Hypercard users is that in LinkWay, text editing is not uniform. In LinkWay, fewer editing commands are available when you edit text in a field than when you edit text in a document. Specific differences are discussed under documents.

Scrolling is different too. There are no scroll bars or thumbs. (Scroll bars and thumbs let you visually adjust the scroll of a field by dragging a small marker along a vertical axis. They provide a coarse adjustment for the amount of scrolling, whereas the up and down arrows give fine tuning.) In LinkWay, the text insertion point moves as a result of scrolling a field. This never happens in normal

Macintosh text editing. The action of LinkWay's up and down scroll arrows is somewhat like that of the up and down arrow keys on a Macintosh. The insertion point (text cursor in LinkWay) moves up or down successive lines until it reaches the top or bottom of the field; only then does scrolling begin.

Buttons

Actually, LinkWay has seven classes of buttons. In usual OOP terminology, the button is an abstract class in LinkWay. You cannot create instances of buttons per se. Instead, you create instances of subclasses of the Button class. Instances of the subclasses all share common button features (like icons) but have other distinguishing features (the button actions). The subclasses are Go, Link, Find, Text Pop-Up, Script, Picture Pop-Up, and Document.

Hypercard has only one button class, but it is easy to create a button that acts like an instance of any LinkWay button subclass. For example, the LinkWay Go button can be emulated with a one-line script (go to next card, go to first card, and so on). The LinkWay Text Pop-Up button can be emulated if you create a field and write a button script that shows the field when the button is pressed. A one-line field script can then hide the field when the user clicks inside the field.

Scripts

The LinkWay script language has about 40 built-in commands and functions. In certain ways it is similar to BASIC or Fortran. Program flow control is achieved through the if . . . else statement or the jump statement. Hence the LinkWay script language is not a structured language. Many programmers see this as a drawback.

Hypertalk™, the Hypercard script language, has more than 80 built-in commands and functions. Hypertalk flow control commands include if . . . then . . . else . . . end if, and repeat . . . end repeat. Each of these commands has several variant forms. Hypertalk is a structured language. In this way, Hypertalk is like more modern high-level languages, such as Pascal or C.

The only LinkWay object with a script is the scripted button. All Hypercard objects have scripts. Hypercard scripts are composed of message handlers. A *message handler* is a small program in Hypertalk that is executed when the object receives the message in question. User actions cause Hypercard to send messages to objects. For example, the messages that Hypercard sends to a button include mouseDown, mouseUp, mouseEnter, and mouseLeave. A script can include handlers for any number of messages. Authors developing material for use in both LinkWay and Hypercard generally prefer to limit Hypercard scripting to mouseUp and openStack handlers. The mouseUp message corresponds to the conditions for executing a LinkWay button script or action. The openStack message corresponds to the conditions for executing the LinkWay AUTOEXEC button script.

Menus

The main difference between LinkWay and Hypercard menus is that only some of the LinkWay pull-down menu commands can be executed from a script, whereas all Hypercard pull-down menu commands can be executed from a script. In particular, the Object menu commands in LinkWay are inaccessible from a script. This means that you cannot create buttons or fields from a script. Hypertalk, on the other hand, enables programmers to redefine menu commands upon request. Again, authors developing materials for both LinkWay and Hypercard should avoid the use of Hypercard features not available in LinkWay. You can use the open command to start other applications—in this case, a text editor.

Documents/Text Files

Documents and text files are both ASCII files. Neither Hypercard nor LinkWay directly edits or even displays ASCII files. Both provide a general means for opening a file with another program. LinkWay provides special means (Document Buttons) for opening text files with one particular program (LWEDIT.) LWEDIT is small enough that it will run under LinkWay in 384K of memory. Hypercard plays no favorites. You can use the open command to start other applications—in this case, a text editor.

LWEDIT guarantees that LinkWay users have a means of editing text files without shutting down the program. But the fact that LWEDIT must run in 384K while LinkWay is memory resident imposes severe size constraints on the program resulting in somewhat limited functionality.

Machine Language Subroutines/XCMD and XFCN

LinkWay enables programmers to extend the existing services available with machine language subroutines that can be executed via the BCALL command. Hypercard provides a similar facility through XCMDs. The basic idea is the same. If you want to do something that LinkWay or Hypercard doesn't handle already, you can extend the program by calling a subroutine that you create to do the task. XCMDs and XFCNs provide a callback mechanism that allows your custom code to send messages to Hypercard and access other Hypercard facilities (such as evaluating an expression).

Porting a Stack to LinkWay

Moving an existing Hypercard stack to LinkWay presents a number of challenges, but the basic problem is one of moving data from the Macintosh environment to the PC environment. Several avenues are available.

Via Communications Software

Files can be transferred serially using a communications program at each end. The communications programs talk to each other using the serial ports on the PC and Macintosh. Text files can be transferred directly, but it is usually preferable to use the XMODEM or KERMIT protocol for all file transfers. Both these protocols are widely available in communications programs and are quite reliable. They make provisions for correcting errors in transmission due to noise or other glitches.

One problem with transferring text files this way is that PC text editing programs expect lines to end with a carriage return character and a line feed character. Lines in a Macintosh text file end with a carriage return only. Depending on your text editor, this can make text from a Macintosh unreadable on a PC. Another drawback to this approach is speed. The maximum transfer rate is usually 9600 baud, approximately 1000 characters per second. Moving large quantities of text or large numbers of pictures can be quite time consuming. Many communications programs also offer YMODEM protocol, which allows you to transfer many files automatically. YMODEM provides error correction and eliminates much of the repetitive work in transferring files one at a time.

Via a Network

Files can be transferred using a network. A number of products exist for linking PCs and Macs over a shared network. In this approach, you can publish a folder on the Macintosh and mount it on the PC. Files can then be copied from the mounted folder as if it were on disk on the PC. Or you can publish a directory on the PC and mount it on the Macintosh. Files can then be dragged from Macintosh folders into the PC directory. Networks are faster than communications programs and often provide for text file conversion to eliminate the carriage return/line feed problem mentioned in connection with communications programs. In many ways a network is the best route currently available for transferring data between PC and Macs.

Via MS-DOS Readable Disks on a Macintosh

A third approach is to use software to write MS-DOS readable disks on the Macintosh. Apple provides such software under the name

Apple File Exchange. The main limitation here is that the amount of data that can be transferred at one time is limited by the size of the disk (1.44MB). This might seem like a lot, but picture and sound files tend to be big, and it's amazing how quickly they can fill a disk.

Phases of Porting the Stack

Regardless of the method used to move the data, the task of porting a Hypercard stack to LinkWay consists of three phases: Getting the data out of the Hypercard stack (or stacks), moving the data to the PC, and getting the data into a LinkWay folder (or folders).

Pictures can be exported from an existing stack with the Hypercard pull-down menu option Export Paint. . . . Your main concern here is that each picture file must be named individually. Even if a script is used to partially automate the process, files still have to be named one by one. You can create a Hypercard XCMD to write a picture in the clipboard to a MacPaint format file. The name of the file to be created is passed to the XCMD as a parameter. Writing an XCMD requires the use of a programming language such as Pascal or C. Once such an XCMD is available, card or background pictures can be copied to the clipboard via a script, and the XCMD can be called with a filename as a parameter. Using such a mechanism, the pictures from a given stack or background can be quickly exported.

Text to be moved to the PC can be exported much more conveniently. Scripts can easily be written to create files from the text contained in fields. Buttons that export text are available in the public domain and can usually be found on Macintosh oriented bulletin boards.

Hypercard sounds are stored as resources in the stack. Getting these resources to a PC is somewhat tricky, because MS-DOS files have no resource fork. One reasonable approach to the problem is to first record the sounds onto tape. The sounds on the tape can then be digitized into either the Macintosh or the PC. If your Hypercard stack has already been created and the sounds were digitized directly into the Macintosh, you can try playing the sounds from the Macintosh and redigitizing them into the PC.

Because sounds on the Macintosh are 8-bit samples, the fidelity is not the best, and redigitizing may cause enough degradation to make the result unusable. Another approach is to convert the Macintosh sound resources into data files. Sound conversion utilities exist for several data formats. The resulting data files are specific to a particular sound manipulation program and can be moved to the PC like any other file. Depending on your PC sound software, you may be able to find an available program to convert these files to something you can use, or you may need to write a conversion program. If a conversion program needs to be written, you should weigh the cost of paying a programmer to do it against the cost of simply creating the sounds anew on the PC.

Once the data exists on the PC, it requires further attention. Picture files need to be converted to LWPAINT format, and text must be imported into LinkWay fields.

Picture conversion can be accomplished using the LWCAPTUR utility. One scenario is to convert the Macintosh pictures first into GIF format. GIF stands for Graphics Interchange Format. Public domain programs to convert Macpaint files to GIF are available free on many bulletin boards. LWCAPTUR will grab the displayed picture from the PC screen and save it in LWPAINT format. LWPAINT can then be used to color or otherwise touch up the pictures.

One problem that can arise is caused by different screen resolutions. The standard Macintosh screen is 512 pixels × 340 pixels. This is the size of Hypercard pictures. If you are using CGA or MCGA Mode in LinkWay, the screen size is 320 × 200. This means that only part of the picture will be visible unless the picture is resized. Such resizing results in picture quality degradation that may require extensive cleanup. In EGA, VGA, or MCGA Mono modes, the resolution is 640 × 480. In this case, the Macintosh pictures will be too small to fill the screen. Usually this is easier to live with, but it can be a problem. Be forewarned.

You can import text with scripted buttons in LinkWay. Remember that LinkWay fields can hold only 3000 characters. If your text chunks are bigger than this, consider keeping the text in files and presenting it via Document buttons. Unfortunately, there is no mechanism to read a file directly into a field; the trick in creating an import button is to read a text file into a variable using the LOAD command and then to place the text in the field with the SET command.

Perhaps the most difficult element to port to LinkWay is the functionality of the Hypercard stack. The LinkWay objects and script language differ enough from Hypercard objects and Hypertalk that an automatic script translator is not really practical.

Linked buttons (ones that take you to another card or stack) are easy to do. Unfortunately, they have to be created individually, because LinkWay does not create buttons from a script. It is theoretically possible to write a machine language subroutine to create buttons and to invoke it with the BCALL command, but such a project involves restructuring the data in the LinkWay folder file and should not be undertaken lightly.

Other Hypercard button scripts can be more difficult to simulate in LinkWay. For example, buttons that change their names or appearances as the result of user actions cannot be easily created in LinkWay, although again the BCALL mechanism may be of some help. For the most part, scripts for buttons other than linked buttons have to be rewritten.

Stacks with multiple backgrounds need to be implemented as separate LinkWay folders, one for each background.

Generally speaking, you're much better off if you can design your Hypercard stack with LinkWay in mind, so that key functionality is not tied to services unavailable in LinkWay. Stacks that are largely text oriented will be easier to port than stacks that rely heavily on graphics and sounds. As you move from Hypercard to LinkWay, the number of files you need to keep tabs on increases dramatically. A Hypercard stack is one file. A LinkWay folder has separate files for the folder itself and each picture in the file. Further, unless you want to write special machine language code to be called with BCALL, you have separate files for each 3000 bytes of text.

Although it's not a smooth road from Hypercard to LinkWay, the transition can be made. At the end of the translation road lies the huge (by Macintosh standards) installed base of PC owners that is hungry for hypermedia. It's a move that can be well worth your while.

APPENDIX G

Troubleshooting LinkWay Problems

A computer is a complex piece of machinery, and LinkWay is a complex piece of software. If the two are not synchronized, problems arise. The following sections describe symptoms, possible causes, and possible cures for common errors with LinkWay.

DOS Cannot Find the Program

If the message, `Bad command or file name` is printed when you try to start LinkWay, check whether the PATH environment variable lists the directory that contains the LINKWAY.EXE program. To see the contents of the variable, enter the PATH command at the DOS prompt. The path will look something like

```
PATH=C:\DOS;C:\BIN;C:\LINKWAY
```

Your PATH environment variable most likely is different from this sample. The directory \LINKWAY, or the directory where your

LinkWay files are stored, should be listed in the path. If the directory is not listed in the path you must add it.

There are three formats of setting the path. The following commands show three ways to establish the same path:

```
PATH=C:\DOS;C:\BIN;C:\LINKWAY
PATH C:\DOS;C:\BIN;C:\LINKWAY
SET PATH=C:\DOS;C:\BIN;C:\LINKWAY
```

These are examples, so your path probably is different. Note that the directories in the path are separated by semicolons.

It is better to change the PATH permanently in the file \AUTOEXEC.BAT. That way it is set every time your computer is turned on or reset.

LinkWay Cannot Find the Files It Needs

If you get one of the messages `Cannot find folder`, `Cannot load a system file`, or `Cannot open file inside LinkWay`, either of two problems may be responsible: The LWPATH, LWDOC, or LWPIC environment variable is not set properly, or you have inadvertently changed directories.

See Chapter 5 for more information about environment variables.

LinkWay looks in the current directory for folders and other files first. If you change directories with the DOS command, LinkWay will look in the new directory for the files it needs. If you must change directories, either make sure that the appropriate files are in the new directory or change back to the previous directory before another file is needed.

Memory Problems

If you see one of the messages, `Memory is full`, `Processing cannot continue`, or `Insufficient memory`, you have obviously run out of memory. This can happen in several ways: terminate-and-stay-resident

(TSR) programs may be consuming memory, LinkWay options may be using much of your RAM, or your graphics mode may be using more memory than is required to give you the resolution the adapter can handle. See Appendix E for more details.

If your computer does not have much memory, LinkWay may not be able to start at all, although this is extremely unlikely.

There are several remedies to increase the memory available and decrease the memory needed by LinkWay.

First, you may have to reduce the number of device drivers and TSR programs in memory. Device drivers are loaded when the computer is started. They are listed in the file CONFIG.SYS in the root directory. Some drivers are very necessary, like those needed to use a fixed disk partition. Some may be temporarily left out, like those for write once read many (WORM) drives that are only used occasionally.

TSR programs, such as Borland's SideKick and Turbo Lightning, stay in memory until you remove them or reset the machine. If these programs are executed by the \AUTOEXEC.BAT file, you should edit the file and either delete the lines that execute the programs or make them into remarks. See your DOS manual for more information about batch files.

Second, LinkWay has many options that affect the amount of memory the program needs:

- Do not specify National Language Support with the command line argument /N unless you must; it consumes 36K.
- The /Z command line argument permits the CGA display mode, saving 100K over the EGA mode and 50K over the MCGA modes.
- The /X option saves 50K by preventing the EGA mode from being used.
- The /S option determines the size of the folder buffer. The folder buffer must be at least as large as the biggest folder. If it isn't the folder cannot be opened. If you have small folders you may make the folder buffer smaller.

Problems with the Display

LinkWay supports 4 graphics modes, CGA, EGA+VGA, MCGA 256 color, and MCGA Mono. Your graphics adapter and graphics display must support a subset of these modes. If your adapter card does not support any of the four modes, you cannot run LinkWay. If you try to use a display mode that your adapter does not support, the highest resolution mode available will be used instead.

Your graphics display and graphics adapter have at least one mode in common; otherwise, they wouldn't work. Problems may arise if your adapter supports modes that your display doesn't handle. LinkWay has no way of knowing which modes your display doesn't support. If LinkWay chooses the wrong mode, you either get a blank or an extremely distorted picture.

If this happens, switch modes quickly, because your display may be damaged by using the wrong mode. If the display is too distorted to reset the mode, reset the computer and start over. Use the command line arguments listed in the section about starting LinkWay to prevent the unsupported modes from being used.

The Mouse Doesn't Work

Check your mouse instruction manual to ensure that both the hardware and software are set up properly. Most mice need a program called MOUSE.COM to be executed before the mouse can work.

APPENDIX H

The ASCII Character Set

Computers understand only numbers. The ASCII character set was defined to store textual data as a series of numbers. ASCII stands for American Standard Code for Information Interchange. Each of the 128 characters in the standard ASCII character set has a number assigned to it.

Table H.1 lists the standard ASCII character set. The first 32 characters are control codes; they have no symbol.

TABLE H.1 *The ASCII Character Set*

Decimal values through 127 are the standard low bit character set. Decimal values above 127 are the IBM extended high bit character set.

00 NUL CTRL@ 0	10 ► DLE CTRL P 16	20 SP 32	30 0 48	40 @ 64	50 P 80	60 ` 96	70 p 112
01 ☺ SOH CTRL A 1	11 ◄ DC1 CTRL Q 17	21 ! 33	31 1 49	41 A 65	51 Q 81	61 a 97	71 q 113
02 ☻ STX CTRL B 2	12 ↕ DC2 CTRL R 18	22 " 34	32 2 50	42 B 66	52 R 82	62 b 98	72 r 114
03 ♥ ETX CTRL C 3	13 ‼ DC3 CTRL S 19	23 # 35	33 3 51	43 C 67	53 S 83	63 c 99	73 s 115
04 ♦ EOT CTRL D 4	14 ¶ DC4 CTRL T 20	24 $ 36	34 4 52	44 D 68	54 T 84	64 d 100	74 t 116
05 ♣ ENQ CTRL E 5	15 § NAK CTRL U 21	25 % 37	35 5 53	45 E 69	55 U 85	65 e 101	75 u 117
06 ♠ ACK CTRL F 6	16 ▬ SYN CTRL V 22	26 & 38	36 6 54	46 F 70	56 V 86	66 f 102	76 v 118
07 • BEL CTRL G 7	17 ↨ ETB CTRL W 23	27 ' 39	37 7 55	47 G 71	57 W 87	67 g 103	77 w 119
08 ◘ BS CTRL H 8	18 ↑ CAN CTRL X 24	28 (40	38 8 56	48 H 72	58 X 88	68 h 104	78 x 120
09 ○ HT CTRL I 9	19 ↓ EM CTRL Y 25	29) 41	39 9 57	49 I 73	59 Y 89	69 i 105	79 y 121
0A ◙ LF CTRL J 10	1A → SUB CTRL Z 26	2A * 42	3A : 58	4A J 74	5A Z 90	6A j 106	7A z 122
0B ♂ VT CTRL K 11	1B ← ESC CTRL [27	2B + 43	3B ; 59	4B K 75	5B [91	6B k 107	7B { 123
0C ♀ FF CTRL L 12	1C ∟ FS CTRL \ 28	2C , 44	3C < 60	4C L 76	5C \ 92	6C l 108	7C ¦ 124
0D ♪ CR CTRL M 13	1D ↔ GS CTRL] 29	2D - 45	3D = 61	4D M 77	5D] 93	6D m 109	7D } 125
0E ♫ SO CTRL N 14	1E ▲ RS CTRL ∧ 30	2E . 46	3E > 62	4E N 78	5E ∧ 94	6E n 110	7E ~ 126
0F ☼ SI CTRL O 15	1F ▼ US CTRL _ 31	2F / 47	3F ? 63	4F O 79	5F — 95	6F o 111	7F DEL △ 127

LEGEND

Hex	0D ♪ CR	ASCII Name
		Display Character
Key	CTRL M 13	Decimal

TABLE H.1 *The ASCII Character Set (continued)*

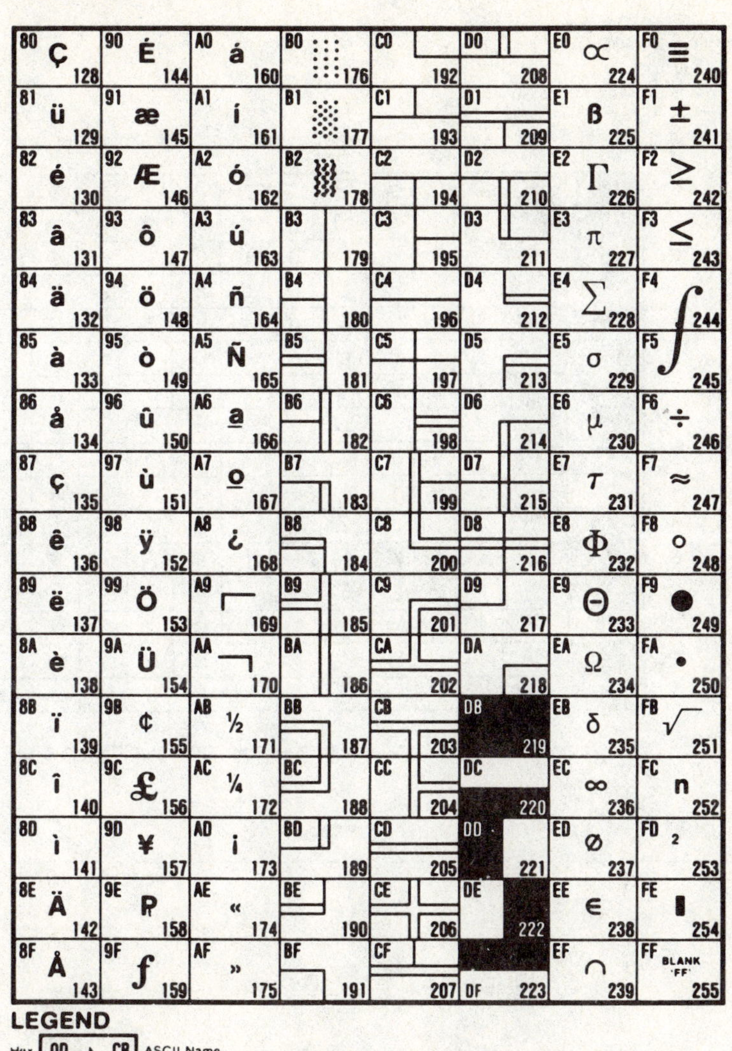

80 Ç 128	90 É 144	A0 á 160	B0 ░ 176	C0 └ 192	D0 ╨ 208	E0 ∝ 224	F0 ≡ 240
81 ü 129	91 æ 145	A1 í 161	B1 ▒ 177	C1 ┴ 193	D1 ╤ 209	E1 ß 225	F1 ± 241
82 é 130	92 Æ 146	A2 ó 162	B2 ▓ 178	C2 ┬ 194	D2 ╥ 210	E2 Γ 226	F2 ≥ 242
83 â 131	93 ô 147	A3 ú 163	B3 │ 179	C3 ├ 195	D3 ╙ 211	E3 π 227	F3 ≤ 243
84 ä 132	94 ö 148	A4 ñ 164	B4 ┤ 180	C4 ─ 196	D4 ╘ 212	E4 Σ 228	F4 ⌠ 244
85 à 133	95 ò 149	A5 Ñ 165	B5 ╡ 181	C5 ┼ 197	D5 ╒ 213	E5 σ 229	F5 ⌡ 245
86 å 134	96 û 150	A6 ª 166	B6 ╢ 182	C6 ╞ 198	D6 ╓ 214	E6 µ 230	F6 ÷ 246
87 ç 135	97 ù 151	A7 º 167	B7 ╖ 183	C7 ╟ 199	D7 ╫ 215	E7 τ 231	F7 ≈ 247
88 ê 136	98 ÿ 152	A8 ¿ 168	B8 ╕ 184	C8 ╚ 200	D8 ╪ 216	E8 Φ 232	F8 ° 248
89 ë 137	99 Ö 153	A9 ⌐ 169	B9 ╣ 185	C9 ╔ 201	D9 ┘ 217	E9 Θ 233	F9 ● 249
8A è 138	9A Ü 154	AA ¬ 170	BA ║ 186	CA ╩ 202	DA ┌ 218	EA Ω 234	FA • 250
8B ï 139	9B ¢ 155	AB ½ 171	BB ╗ 187	CB ╦ 203	DB █ 219	EB δ 235	FB √ 251
8C î 140	9C £ 156	AC ¼ 172	BC ╝ 188	CC ╠ 204	DC ▄ 220	EC ∞ 236	FC ⁿ 252
8D ì 141	9D ¥ 157	AD ¡ 173	BD ╜ 189	CD ═ 205	DD ▌ 221	ED Ø 237	FD ² 253
8E Ä 142	9E ₧ 158	AE « 174	BE ╛ 190	CE ╬ 206	DE ▐ 222	EE ∈ 238	FE ■ 254
8F Å 143	9F ƒ 159	AF » 175	BF ┐ 191	CF ╧ 207	DF ▀ 223	EF ∩ 239	FF BLANK 'FF' 255

LEGEND

Hex: 0D — ASCII Name: CR — Display Character: ♪ — Key: CTRL M — Decimal: 13

TABLE H.1 *The ASCII Character Set (continued)*

Second digit ↓ / First digit →

	0	1	2	3	4	5	6	7	8	9	A	B	C	D	E	F
0	NUL	DLE	space	0	@	P	`	p	Ä	ê	†	∞	¿	–		
1	SCH	DC1	!	1	A	Q	a	q	Å	ë	°	æ	¡	—		
2	STX	DC2	"	2	B	R	b	r	Ç	í	¢	≤	¬	”		
3	ETX	DC3	#	3	C	S	c	s	É	ì	£	≥	√	"		
4	EOT	DC4	$	4	D	T	d	t	Ñ	î	§	¥	ƒ	‘		
5	ENQ	NAK	%	5	E	U	e	u	Ö	ï	•	µ	≈	’		
6	ACK	SYN	&	6	F	V	f	v	Ü	ñ	¶	∂	∆	÷		
7	BEL	ETB	'	7	G	W	g	w	á	ó	ß	Σ	«	◊		
8	BS	CAN	(	8	H	X	h	x	à	ò	®	Π	»	ÿ		
9	HT	EM	)	9	I	Y	i	y	â	ô	©	Π	…			
A	LF	SUB	*	:	J	Z	j	z	ä	ö	™	∫	␣			
B	VT	ESC	+	;	K	[	k	{	ã	õ	´	º	À			
C	FF	FS	,	<	L	\	l	|	å	ù	¨	º	Ã			
D	CR	GS	–	=	M	]	m	}	ç	ú	≠	Ω	Õ			
E	SO	RS	.	>	N	^	n	~	é	û	Æ	æ	Œ			
F	SI	US	/	?	O	_	o	DEL	è	ü	Ø	ø	œ			

␣ stands for a nonbreaking space, the same width as a digit.

APPENDIX I

The Origins of IBM LinkWay

Kheriaty's Challenge

Several years ago, Larry Kheriaty got bothered. A friendly Macintosh® enthusiast had just obtained a copy of Hypercard®, was amazed at what it could do, and made a point of telling Larry Kheriaty all about it. The Mac user declared, "You can't do that on a PC!"

This, of course, was not the first time that a PC enthusiast had felt like a second class citizen for devotion to the reliable old PC. For Kheriaty, it was especially galling. The campus of the University of Western Washington, where he was employed as a member of the staff of Western Educational Software Tools Center, was chock full of PCs. IBM used the place as an academic test and development bed, and Larry had actually worked on some fancy IBM software products for interactive video.

Kheriaty, a capable programmer, concluded that little stood in the way of producing a product like Hypercard for the PC. Moreover, he was convinced that the greatest single impediment to the success of software was the level of sophistication required to use it. Most PC software was too hard.

Kheriaty figured that there was more than enough life left in DOS to create a program that helped people organize data—even multimedia—on their office desks. He was also aware that Hypercard had not sprung full blown from the void—that there were several decades of anticipatory thinking behind it. He further knew that the seminal hopes and dreams of some of those early thinkers—to duplicate the look and feel of human thought—had not been fully realized in Hypercard.

In the fall of 1987, Kheriaty set about making hypermedia happen on the PC. He worked three months, then in March 1988 showed the results of his work to people at IBM's Educational Systems Division in Atlanta. The folks at IBM were already confident of Kheriaty because of his past work on interactive video software, and they promptly sought to license Kheriaty's early work. Under the code name of Marlin, IBM set in motion a high-speed development program for what would ultimately become IBM LinkWay.

A small group of people at IBM in Atlanta and Boca Raton focused on getting the product defined, finessed, and out the door. Often new specs would be sent to Kheriaty, and the improvements would be back for testing within two weeks. By the fall of 1988, software developers were being invited to private seminars about LinkWay.

One of Christina Onassis's early husbands was once quoted as saying, "When a billion dollars leans on you, you feel it." Perhaps such a thought passed though Kheriaty's mind as he welcomed the array of marketing, technical, and product management types who came to test, challenge, and generally pick apart what he had accomplished. LinkWay was designated a strategic IBM product. For IBM, that meant that it would live for at least three years, and support and funding would sustain it through at least two annual product revisions after its introduction.

For Tony Peacock, the man at IBM tasked with making LinkWay a reality, three years represented a healthy chunk of his career. And as with all such projects, it could be a great success, or the organizational equivalent of concrete shoes. For him and his team, LinkWay proved to be more than simply a challenging new marketing task, because LinkWay was beginning to be perceived as an avenue of access into the future of computing.

Atkinson's Lament

That future seemed out of IBM's reach, usurped by the aggressively visionary approach of the people at Apple. With a base software technology called Hypercard, a marketing thrust being built around the use of multiple media on a microcomputer, and John Sculley's vision of the future in the form of the Knowledge Navigator®, Apple seemed to be several strides ahead. None of that had been accomplished overnight.

When Atari imploded in 1985, Apple hired an array of its capable people. Alan Kay, a highly regarded professional visionary who had earlier been a leading member of the much vaunted staff of Xerox's Palo Alto Research Center (PARC), was made an Apple Fellow. He continued to be paid well and to have an immense research budget. Christina Hooper and Mike Leihbold moved to Cupertino, too. Both were videodisk enthusiasts and held their own visions of microcomputers that taught and electronic encyclopedias.

Just as this high-powered talent arrived, Steve Jobs and John Sculley parted company at Apple's helm. Hidden behind that melodrama was the first work done on an secret project called Jonathan. The Jonathan project was dedicated to delivering all the neat features the Macintosh lacked—color graphics, video, HiFi sound, and the operating system enhancements to make good use of those core capabilities.

The project manager for Jonathan, Wayne Rosing, traveled back and forth to Japan, reviewing the latest in CD-ROM technology and entertaining thoughts of the Jonathan replete with a library of multimedia information. The Jonathan would have an open architecture, so additional capabilities could be added simply by adding new cards filled with as yet unimagined technologies. In this heady but secret atmosphere, Bill Atkinson was struggling to overcome a feeling of lost purpose.

Atkinson was part of the team that made the Mac. He was the author of the program that had made the simplicity and responsiveness of the Mac manifest to even the most computerphobic user. Atkinson was also responsible for masses of Macintosh sales through his showy graphics program, MacPaint®.

For Atkinson, MacPaint was the essence of good works, a distillation of the best ideas in interactive graphics, all elegantly presented and included for free with every Mac. MacPaint owed an enormous debt of gratitude to its predecessors, beginning with Ivan Sutherland's early PhD work on Sketchpad, stretching through Dick Shoup's Superpaint program spawned at Xerox PARC in the early seventies, and by the early eighties one of the staples of high class broadcast TV production work, and finally inclusive of the more recent simplex paint programs for the IBM PC.

For Atkinson, the thrill of discovery and accomplishment was gone after the Mac was launched and MacPaint was a reality. Just a little past 30 years old, Atkinson contemplated his career on a slide into inconsequential projects. Other people were working on Jonathan, which later became the Mac II. Atkinson undoubtedly noticed that one particular name, Vannevar Bush, was mentioned again and again in industry articles of speculation on advanced computer systems. Bush's speculations were to provide some of the basic insights that would lead to Atkinson's development of Hypercard.

One particular article by Bush was constantly cited, an apparent flight of scientific fancy published in the summer of 1945 in the *Atlantic Monthly.* It was not for the consumption of those cloistered in research labs, but in a magazine likely to be found on the verandahs of Virginia estates near Washington, D.C., and on the beaches near the summer cottages of Cape Cod.

This was light summer policy reading for those whose task it was to set the course for a newly powerful America triumphantly emerging from World War II.

Everything Old Is New Again

The summer of 1945 was quite a summer. The miracles of technology had just conquered Hitler and were about to decimate Japan. Radar was now a well-recognized combat tool. Proximity fuses had changed the nature of tactics on air, land, and sea. Radio communications, at best a novelty during the last world war, had become fundamental to modern war and modern life.

There were two secrets that would be decisive in the conduct of the war and inestimably influential in the decades to come. Cracking the atom and cracking the German and Japanese codes were two of the great technical feats of World War II. Both were known to Vannevar Bush as director of the White House Office of Scientific Research. Bush was well prepared to imagine the future and then make it occur.

In the early thirties he had used modern materials and electronics to bring to fruition Babbage's nineteenth century dream of a computer. Bush and his associates dubbed their creation the *differential analyzer*. Immediately prior to the war, he helped develop technology to analyze sound and, by breaking it into component parts, encrypt it.

This very voice encryption technology was used by Roosevelt and Churchill to mask their telephone calls to one another all through the war, and a variant of the technology was successfully applied to the task of cracking Japanese codes. In fact, this helped provide the foundation of modern computer technology.

Bush noted two phenomena as the war drew to a close. There was more information than he or any human being could manage. Information of the greatest significance could easily be missed with potentially appalling results. Bush knew what a near miss the atom bomb had been, and how its achievement was built on a frighteningly large effort, with mind-boggling amounts of data.

Second, he knew that current technology was nearly capable of building machines to manage that kind of volume of information. That seemed to be of the highest importance, and yet the war was soon to end, and development budgets would dwindle. So he wrote an article—kind of an open letter to America's intelligentsia—called "As We May Think," quoted in part in the following discussions.

The Article

> Science has provided the swiftest communication between individuals; it has provided a record of ideas and has enabled man to manipulate and to make extracts from that record so that knowledge evolves and endures throughout the life of a race rather than that of an individual . . .

So read the opening words of Bush's essay. He was certainly aware that the printing press was crumbling under the cascade of information humans now manufactured. With the advent of practical xerography still five years in the future, the problem seemed insoluble.

Information Overload

Four centuries after Gutenberg's press inaugurated a revolution in communication, four decades after motion pictures and radio had amplified the effect, Vannevar Bush recognized that our century created an explosion of information, and no improvement in ways to store and deliver it.

> Professionally our methods of transmitting and reviewing the results of research are generations old and by now are totally inadequate for their purpose. . . . The summation of human experience is being expanded at a prodigious rate, and the means we use for threading through the consequent maze to the momentarily important item is the same as was used in the days of square-rigged ships.

Some years later the academic Derek de Solla Price postulated that 80 to 90 percent of the scientists who ever lived were living at present, and that scientific information was doubling every few years.

As the first atomic bomb blasts were witnessed, Bush's thoughts were not so much on the destructive powers about to be unleashed, but rather on how to get the tide of new information under control. He thought he saw the likely source for the fix.

The Necessary Tools

> The world has arrived at an age of cheap complex devices of great reliability; and something is bound to come of it.

Bush sensed the immanent arrival of a bunch of tools that could be used to manage the intricacies of modern life. He knew of the emerging computer technology, although it was a secret to the public. His article could not reveal details, but he gave the benefit of his own well-informed analysis.

> There will always be plenty of things to compute in the detailed affairs of millions of people doing complicated things. . . . For mature thought there is no mechanical substitute. But creative thought and essentially repetitive thought are very different things. For the latter there are, and may be, powerful mechanical aids.

Here Bush struck at the heart of the matter. Life is perpetually more complex. Computing devices could bring the complexity under manageable control. What Bush may not have seen at the time—because software existed as only the most rudimentary of concepts in 1945—was that computers would become the first nondedicated devices in history.

Toasters are toasters; they make only toast. But computers are stainless steel and silicon chameleons that unceasingly change their capabilities.

What Bush saw clearly was the ability of these forthcoming machines to make all the numbers, words, visions, sounds, and records accessible, in a randomly accessible fashion, and with minimal delay.

The Problem

> Thus far we seem to be worse off than before—for we can enormously extend the record; yet even in its present bulk we can hardly consult it.

As the head of the White House organization responsible for managing the American war effort, Bush was at the peak of a vast hierarchy, recipient of almost unimaginable amounts of new information flow. He had no way of separating wheat from chaff—recognizing and absorbing the valuable data. In other words, he was suffering the modern disease of information overload. Then, it was a rarefied sort of affair. Today, it is epidemic.

> Our ineptitude in getting at the record is largely caused by the artificiality of systems of indexing. When data of any sort are placed in storage, they are filed alphabetically or numerically, and information is found (when it is) by tracing it down from subclass to subclass. It can be in only one place, unless duplicates are used; one has to have rules as to which path will locate it; and the rules are cumbersome. Having found one item, moreover, one has to emerge from the system and reenter on a new path.

Since twelfth century monks began indexing illuminated manuscripts, indexed information has been sorted numerically or alphabetically, then broken into classes and subclasses. Indexing got to be very popular as a method of making texts more useful, a Renaissance example of user-friendliness.

By the end of the eighteenth century, the value of indexing had become widely recognized and the practice well established. Many authors and professional bibliographers took pride in compiling a good index. The first western encyclopedias appeared as a response to information overload. By the end of that century, there were too many books on too many disparate subjects. How was one to gather them all together, extract the juicy parts, and walk away with a reasonable working grasp of what was going on?

No matter how nicely the information was organized, indexed, and printed, it still had to be presented on paper. Inevitably, such approaches suffered from the flaw of linearity—a flaw Bush recognized as fundamental.

> The human mind does not work that way. It operates by association. With one item in its grasp, it snaps instantly to the next that is suggested by the association of thoughts, in accordance with some intricate web of trails carried by the cells of the brain. It has other characteristics, of course; trails that are not frequently followed are prone to fade, items are not fully permanent, memory is transitory. Yet the speed of action, the intricacy of trails, the detail of mental pictures, is awe-inspiring beyond all else in nature.

The same facilities that scientists with whom Bush worked used to accomplish such remarkable feats of information synthesis were the facilities he took as his model for the Memex.

Memex

> Consider a future device for individual use, which is a sort of mechanized private file and library. It needs a name, and, to coin one at random, memex will do. A memex is a device in which an individual stores all his books, records, and communications, and which is mechanized so that it may be consulted with exceeding speed and flexibility.

This core notion was to inspire several generations of computer visionaries and to lead to the development of hypermedia. The first of those so inspired was Doug Englebart.

Augmenting the Human Intellect

Douglas Englebart was trained in the uses of radar. As a result, he was quite familiar with the notion of delivering data in a comprehensible fashion to a screen.

Stationed in the Philippines, he read the article in a Red Cross library, and the idea began its incubation. Soon Englebart embarked on the kind of career thousands of people had looked forward to after the war. Trading on his experience with radar and the GI Bill, at age 25 Englebart pulled down a good job in the area that would one day be known as Silicon Valley.

He decided to look for a goal that would benefit the human race. Then seeds planted by Vannevar Bush began to sprout. Englebart noticed the complexity and urgency of global problems after World War II were surpassing Americans' time-honored tools and methods for solving them. Something new had to be crafted to enable people to work together in groups to solve these increasingly complex problems.

The idea of using computers to augment human intellect for problem solving occurred to Englebart in a flash one morning in 1950 as he commuted to an aeronautical laboratory called Ames, which would later become part of one of the most complex systems of innovation ever devised: NASA.

That day Englebart decided to work on a system for tackling complicated problems. As is often the case with visionaries, the whole picture struck him all at once. But it took him years to translate the searing impressions left on his consciousness that day into reality.

Over the next 30 years, Englebart pioneered a variety of items that we consider fresh innovations today. He imagined and implemented the notion of editing text on a screen. His research group designed and demonstrated the first mouse, a hardware pointing device that relieved computer users of the drudgery of constantly striking arrow keys. He conceived the notion of screen windows, which could conceptually delineate and prioritize the jobs on a computer screen. He built the first practical systems for establishing linkages between different chunks of information held by a computer. He was the first to design and craft hypermedia systems for the computer.

Electronic Information Machines

When I saw the connection between a television-like screen, an information processor and a medium for representing symbols to a person, it all tumbled together in about half an hour. I went

> home and sketched a system in which computers would draw symbols on the screen and I could steer through different information spaces with knobs and levers and look at words and data and graphics in different ways. . . . God! Think of how that would let you cut loose in solving problems.

At mid-century, television was about as rare as CD-ROM players are today. People worked hard to adapt television technology to practical commercial purposes. But television was evolving away from computers at that time. It would be 30 years before the engagement of the two technologies seemed likely, and it is only recently that the marriage has seemed immanent. Just this year, 1989, there has begun to be talk of HyperTV. There have been demonstrations only recently of microcomputers playing back video and randomly accessing video frames. In 1950, Douglas Englebart was an unrecognized prophet.

But like all such ignored prophets in history, his vision was more insistent than his embarrassment at being out of sync with his times. Englebart continued through years of assiduous, detailed work, occasional failures in technology and funding, and continues to work today on systems that bring reality to the vision he so precisely stated in his early years.

HyperTheodore

Ten years after Englebart's epiphany, Theodore Holm Nelson was inserted into the sophisticated and stable campus of Swarthmore. The product of a broken home in the movie business and an early liberal arts major, Ted Nelson forged a lifelong habit of giving everything a try in the name of learning. While still at school he ventured to attend a computer class.

Imagine for a moment, how uninspiring a computer class in 1960 must have been. The machines were big, expensive, and slow. They were run by specialists who would shame today's computer nerds. Even the simplest program required a stack of punched cards, created at a workstation that looked like an overblown typewriter. The keypuncher had to figure out how to put just the right information, in just the right order, on just the right sequence of these cards.

The completed stack of cards was brought to the computer center, where the specialist in charge added the stack in a queue. Then the user would stand by and wait until the stack's turn came for the reader. For the fortunate, the reader would not trash the cards. The computer would chew on the information and as often as not print out the message that struck horror and anguish in the hearts of early programmers:

```
DIAGNOSTIC;
```

which in lay parlance meant, "You screwed up. Either you mistyped one of your punched cards, or worse, your program's logic is flawed. In any case, you are consigned once again to that evil card puncher. Hit the bricks."

Miraculously, Nelson's response to all this was, "Wow!" The bug had bit, and Nelson saw a future few others had ever seen, and no one would ever articulate and define as clearly and entertainingly as he. His lofty academic aspirations (a thorough rewrite of the history of western philosophy or some such) were set aside. He decided to first develop a decent set of tools for academia and research.

Again you see a commonality between the visionaries: dread of the complexity of life, and the hope, the dream that machines can manage the intricacy of it all. Nelson's perception was more advanced than even that. He did not just see the increasing complexity of the world of science and technology, as had Bush and Englebart. He saw something deeper and more awesome. In the seventies he found a light-hearted way of stating the case.

Nelson's words, "Everything is deeply intertwingled," summarize the realization of our time (perhaps of all times) that no thing is not in some way connected to every other thing. Nelson saw that all the great thoughts and discoveries were resting by and large undisturbed. He figured that humanity needed a hearing aid for the messages of the ages. That amplifier of the collective intellect was the computer.

No matter how small and inexpensive the hardware (and Nelson was sure, years before anybody else, that it would get very small and cheap), he knew the secret was in the software. He embarked on a crusade to see to it that the right software got written. The problem was that even he did not have the right words to describe what the right software was like.

So, to our everlasting benefit, he made some up. It seems that he first used the term *Hypertext* in the mid-sixties, applied in a report to a very large computer company, which subsequently rendered the material confidential, locked it up, restrained Nelson from publishing it for the benefit of the rest of the world, and by all appearances made no use of it at all.

For many years Nelson was something of a gadfly, on the periphery of other people's projects, absorbing the best of their ideas, contributing the cream of his own and yet never satisfied enough with their work to stick around. Finally, the pressure of all that stuff in his head burst, and he wrote a book.

The Book

Computer Lib/Dream Machines was not just any book. Nelson happily acknowledges it was mightily influenced by Stewart Brand's *Whole Earth Catalog,* something of a rage in the late sixties and early seventies. Ted Nelson's book was a call to arms for those who fought battles on the plane of the intellect. It provided a Whole Earth-like sampler of the neatest things going on in computerdom at the time, only as introductory material, a way of explaining what computers were all about.

Where *Computer Lib* really took off was in its flights of fancy about what computers could be. Nelson's exercise of freedom extended to the actual layout of the book, which looked something like a cross between *Life* magazine, Da Vinci's notebooks, and an eighth grade class collage. In fact, when the book was licensed for reprint in 1987 by Microsoft Press, replicating the nutty effect of the original turned out to be a typesetter's and editor's nightmare. In the transformation to what was an "acceptable" trade paperback, some of the original loony charm was lost. People who still own a copy of the original mid-seventies version, which Nelson published and of which he sold 50,000 copies himself, treasure it as something rare and worthy. Nelson's razor analysis and vivid insights have no parallel in published works even today.

In the midst of his eccentric vision, however, was the essence of the computer revolution of the future (some of the stuff he imagined does exist today, 15 years after its first appearance in print, but most of it remains to be realized). *Computer Lib* is a melting pot of ideas, concepts, innovative jargon, and fingers pointed at the moon.

In a few words, Nelson suggested the epochal importance of the arrival of the modern personal computer, years before it actually appeared. He predicted that by the early eighties millions of people would have personal computers, and that they would have a dramatic effect on how people carried on their lives. Nobody else was making such predictions at the time, and Nelson was dismissed by most of the serious people who were lucky enough to have any contact with him. A load of nonserious people discovered *Computer Lib,* and in many cases it had a dramatic effect on their thinking and planning.

Nelson's book was meant to be scanned in a random access fashion, 100 words here, another 500 there. Often one would flip the oversize book to get from *Computer Lib,* which was oriented one way, to *Dream Machines,* the other half of the book, which was oriented the other way. In this quirky publication was Nelson's first extensive description of Hypertext and hypermedia.

Hypertext

Nelson said, "Hypertext means nonsequential writing. Ordinary writing is sequential for two reasons. First, it grew out of speech and speech-making, which have to be sequential. Second, books are not convenient to read except in a sequence. But the structures of ideas are not sequential. They tie together in every conceivable way. And when humans write, they always try to tie ideas together in nonsequential ways. The footnote is a break from sequence, but it cannot really be extended."

Nelson recounted that many writers have tried to break away from sequence. Nelson's approach echoed that of Nabokov's *Pale Fire,* of *Tristram Shandy* centuries before, and an odd novel called *Hopscotch,* composed of sections ending with numbers telling you where to branch to. Large books and many textbooks generally use many tricks to get around the problem of indexing and reviewing what has and hasn't been said or done already. However, Nelson grasped that computer storage and screen displays mean that we no longer have to present printed concepts in linear sequence; totally arbitrary structures are possible, and after enough people try them the public will see how desirable they are.

What Nelson had to say made extraordinary sense. If everything was "intertwingled," then Hypertext was the only way to get our mitts on the subject. In the Microsoft Press edition, he expanded, "A Hypertext is a nonsequential piece of writing, only the computer display makes it practical."

Nelson anticipated that computers would one day routinely handle more than simple text, that they would become ways of storing and forwarding graphics, sound and even moving images. Nelson's model was something like a movie studio, filled with artisans of all different shades, colors, and proclivities (intellect and talent-wise, mind you). Of course, none of this meant that careful planning and structured thinking would go away.

Nelson went on to an almost scholarly exposition of what kinds of Hypertext/media there would be: "Basic or chunk style hypertext offers choices, either as note-markers (like asterisks) or labels at the end of a chunk. Whatever you point at then comes to the screen."

This is the definition of Hypertext most commonly followed in the products and ideas bandied about at present. The operative approach is to have explicit footnote or cross-reference style connections—popular jargon for this is the term *links*—between one set of text and another. This approach can be seen in such products as Guide™ from Owl, Hypercard from Apple, and IBM's LinkWay. Buttons are clicked to invoke links that move in one and only one predetermined direction.

Nelson further explained, "Collateral hypertext means compound annotations or parallel text." This concept is quite important. It implies a method of establishing a potentially infinite number of links between one chunk of text and others. Nelson didn't stop with these powerful ideas. He extended the concept of "intertwingledness" on a computer screen even farther—to Stretchtext, a dynamic form of continuous Hypertext.

Here text is truly multidimensional and perfectly available at the user's whim to expand into a larger, more exhaustive treatment of the same material. You can think of such an operation as accessing an abstract of a publication and having its full, indexed version accessible as desired. In fact, this approach has a time-honored tradition in both Sanskrit and Hebrew classical texts, where the basic idea is presented in a simple, terse aphorism, and then the aphorism is broken into its component pieces and expanded upon by subsequent commentators. In Sanskrit, the technique is called Bhashya (literally *illumination*). First it uses the aphorism. Then the commentator would take each word or concept, and expand upon it.

Nelson's concept of Stretchtext harked directly back to time before printing and manuscript, when people relied upon their memories and mental faculties to preserve knowledge. In both instances, the net effect is random access to the information.

Subsequently he expanded on the theme in more compelling and more global fashions, distinguishing among "fresh" (original) Hypertext, "anthological" Hypertext composed from multiple sources, and "grand" Hypertext, a compendium of everything pertinent to a subject.

This is the Ted Nelson dream, a world of ideas and impressions, electronically intertwingled, under the control of people who twiddle with ideas, rather than the folks who twaddle with bits and bytes. His grand vision, which he calls *Xanadu*™, is a world-wide system of hypermedia, when anything can be immediately accessed, where everyone's thoughts can be associated with everyone else's, if they just take the time to pound it into the system, and where none may use anyone else's works without automatically being charged an appropriate computer generated license fee.

At its best, Xanadu would be a world-wide ASCAP/BMI-like system for the protection and distribution of intellectual property. At its worst, one need only conjure up the memories each one of us has of a lost computer file, or an inappropriate computer generated bill that refuses to go away. Every visionary must have an almost unattainable dream, and Nelson's is as high-flown and high-minded as they come.

Ted Nelson may well be the Leonardo Da Vinci of computer software. Nelson, however, is infinitely luckier and infinitely more cursed than Da Vinci. Unlike his Italian soulmate in imagineering, he stands a healthy chance of seeing all his best ideas realized in his lifetime. The curse is that he won't get to do all of the great development himself.

As this is written, the organization that Nelson started to make Xanadu a reality has been acquired by a very successful and rich computer software company called Autodesk®. Ted Nelson himself is not actively involved in Xanadu; rather, he devotes his time to proselytizing his visions of the future and thrashing those who he considers not up to snuff.

Perhaps as the IBM PC brought life to Nelson's notion of the affordable personal computer, LinkWay will get hypermedia for the masses up and running.

Newcomers on the Block

Other imagineers are up and running with variants of Nelson's vision. No less personage than Mitch Kapor, whom we must thank for the blessings of Lotus 1-2-3, has left Lotus and started a company called On Technology. He and his associates seek to develop the operating system of the future, the stated goal of which bears a striking resemblance to Bush's, Englebart's, and particularly Nelson's vision. The spin that Kapor puts on the notion has a particularly business orientation, but Kapor has his mind's eye on the future, as well. In recent public presentations he has been quoted as saying, "The best uses for personal computers haven't been invented yet. To disagree with that is simply a failure of imagination."

That is certainly true, but as the following brief descriptions of recent attempts at both engineering and imagineering will suggest, it is not for lack of trying.

By the early seventies, the stage for the revolution had been set. *Computer Lib/Dream Machines* was meandering through the computer community. The work Van Damm had done at Brown University had filtered into IBM and to a variety of other places from there. Englebart and a group of associates were hard at work at Stanford Research Institute (SRI) bringing demonstrable life to Englebart's visions.

The first tiny evidences of the revolution to come had begun to show up in popular culture in 1973. Stewart Brand, the editor of the *Whole Earth Catalog,* published a fascinating article in *Rolling Stone* about a computer subculture of hackers—folks who did the dry work of computing by day, but carried on computer games by night. Computer crimes began to happen, evidencing the fact that computers were sufficiently well absorbed into western culture to have inspired renegades. Some were terrorists, who would walk into a computer center and pass magnets of magnetic tape spools. Others were chiselers, who might reprogram a bank computer to round off every calculated penny of interest, and transfer the difference to their checking account.

Finding some way of computerizing one's research and analysis was a sure way of achieving tenure for professors—students were rarely allowed access to the big expensive beasts. Off at a relatively small concern in the South San Francisco Bay area, a couple of engineers had fiddled a microcomputer on a chip into existence, although the marketing types didn't quite know who to sell it to. The company was called Intel®.

The Team at PARC

In another portion of what would later be known as Silicon Valley, Xerox set up a well-funded research lab and tasked it with discovering the future early. It was located conveniently close to Stanford

University and was called the Palo Alto Research Center (PARC). The center hired all kinds of brilliant young men and women, gave them a lot of money, and let them loose.

One fellow, Richard Shoup, was fascinated by some work that had been done in Utah in the middle and late sixties by a man named Ivan Sutherland. Sutherland had developed an interactive computer graphics program called Sketchpad, which enables users to draw stick pictures using a digitizing tablet—something like an electronic pad and pen, hooked up to a big computer with a storage tube display. Shoup thought of applying the same idea to a raster display device, using a minicomputer that would be dedicated to that task and that task alone. He did, and it worked marvelously, leaving a lasting impression on the rest of the folks in the lab. Interactive graphics were great.

Another PARC fellow, David Ingalls, was the son of a very famous Sanskrit scholar, Daniel Henry Holmes Ingalls. Influenced by the elegance and power of the structure of the classic language his father had studied throughout his life, Ingalls set out to create a more elegant approach to computer programming. Almost anything would have been better than what was available at the time. Fortran and COBOL were very widely used, and struck all but the most dedicated of computer freaks as alien and difficult. Ingalls sought to make a computer language that was simple enough for a child to use and that endowed software-driven processes and chunks of data with recognizable and rememberable "personalities." The result was a new language called Smalltalk. Everybody liked that, too.

The fellow who is best known of all of the Xerox PARC alumni is Alan Kay. Part of the reason for his fame is the high-profile positions he later held at Atari and then Apple. But the essence of his celebrity revolves around a concept that he and his associates at Xerox PARC developed and tested throughout the mid-seventies: Dynabook.

Dynabook

Dynabook synthesized all the best ideas floating about the computer industry at the time. As idealized, it would be a small, slatelike device with a simple keyboard and a flat, touch-sensitive display. Given that the technology required to achieve such an effect could not be had at any price at the time, the PARC researchers simply assumed that the hardware would show up sooner or later and focused on developing the software. The Dynabook system combined interactive graphics (Superpaint), object oriented programming (Smalltalk), interactive text editing with a mouse (derivative of Englebart's work, as well as others), and hypermedia (Nelson's contributions, although they were not directly acknowledged in any of the PARC Dynabook descriptions). The 1976 Xerox document describing the work gives a good picture of where they wanted to go:

> Although digital computers were originally designed to do arithmetic computation, the ability to simulate the details of any descriptive model means that the computer, viewed as a medium itself, can be all other media if the embedding and viewing methods are sufficiently well provided.
>
> Moreover, this new metamedium is active—it can respond to queries and experiments—so that the messages may involve the learner in a two-way conversation. This property has never been available before except through the medium of an individual teacher. We think the implications are vast and compelling.

The words are academic and a bit redolent of the counterculture jargon of the seventies, but the ideas are both clear and derivative of imagineers who went before.

The systems the PARC innovators built and demonstrated have directly influenced almost everything that has occurred in computerdom in the last five years. The curious lag between the date of their achievements and the first appearance of windowing systems, mice, object oriented programming, user-friendly paint systems, and the rest of it is explained by the fact that Xerox sat on these developments for years. The PARC people were so frustrated that many of them left and looked for employment in places where their ideas would be put to work.

Other Experiments

While PARC was spinning off ideas and people, hypermedia experiments were being carried on in a variety of academic climates.

From the mid-seventies to the mid-eighties, several dozen projects were brought to various states of semicompletion, without ever making it into the open air of wide distribution and use on standard microcomputers.

As the seventies drew to a close, the ideas were flying fast and furious. One no longer needed the corporate indulgence of a Xerox in order to realize one's digital dreams.

Michael Shrayer developed a program called Electric Pencil, which was the first widely received interactive full-screen word processor for microcomputers. To all but a few in Englebart's domain, it was a revelation, and quickly replaced the line-oriented editors that teletype machines had imposed on computerdom.

The appearance of the Apple computer, with its color computer graphics, encouraged quite a bit of experimentation in the areas that Dick Shoup had marked out some years earlier. (However, the machine left some people cold. Michael Shrayer refused to do a version of Electric Pencil for it, and Ted Nelson disdained its early inability to display anything more than UPPERCASE TEXT.)

In the flurry of excitement around microcomputing in the early eighties, amplified by the arrival of spreadsheets, databases, and practical word processing, much of what Ted Nelson had been talking about was temporarily lost. Computers were treated not as a medium of communication, but rather as remarkable new office tools, and in their brief star-crossed consumer variants, playthings.

It was not until Apple had fully established its second generation of computer—the Macintosh—that the notion of intertwingled information came back into style. Then it returned with a vengeance. After tiring of the graphics do-whacks of the early eighties, a variety of academics and R&D types turned to the hypermedia concepts espoused by Bush, Englebart, and Nelson.

Everyone evoked Bush in their reports on hypermedia. Citations of the *As We May Think* article were obligatory. The more timid souls cited Englebart, because he gave the appearance of a restrained, somewhat studious visionary. Only the most courageous of the lot referred to Ted Nelson—loony that he was perceived to be—and then they often gave him short shrift. Deep in their hearts, however, many developers knew he was the one who had set them on fire.

A notable, but by no means exhaustive list of mid-eighties hypermedia projects would include ZOG, a fancy Hypertext system developed at Carnegie-Mellon, and ultimately put into use on board the USS Carl Vinson, one of the nation's first AEGIS cruisers.

Another was Intermedia, a hypermedia system developed at Brown University, which took the unfortunate approach of displaying the interlinkages of different elements with connecting lines of a graphics display. The result looks much like the early telephone wiring schemes that blotted out the sun on New York streets.

Xerox PARC was on the case, as well. The product researchers there developed Notecards™, a package highly regarded by those anointed few who have ever had the good fortune to be allowed access to the Xerox system that runs the software.

Document Examiner™, from a workstation manufacturer by the name of Symbolics, strove to make Hypertext-like linkages in documents a practical reality, as did Neptune™ from Tektronix.

No academic or R&D effort undertaken at the time would ever cast a shadow nearly as long as Apple's Hypercard. The outcome of Bill Atkinson's dark night of the soul was an amalgam of terrific ideas from the past: Hypertalk, the scripting language being a linear descendant of Ingalls' Smalltalk concepts; the integrated paint software owing a debt of gratitude to Dick Shoup; and finally the core concept of linked information, with its roots firmly planted in the rich soil of Ted Nelson's genius. Hypercard was just innovative enough to set the computing world on its ear.

It was so good, in fact, that it passed one of the major tests of great innovation in modern culture. The press, both trade and popular, could simply not understand it. *The New York Times* editorially shrugged its shoulders in its attempt at description, "it's, well . . . Hypercard."

Within a year's time a vast array of add-on hypermedia products were underway. Silicon Beach Software, a company that had made its name by publishing a better version of Apple's MacPaint (the first graphics program for the Mac) called Superpaint™, embarked on the development of Supercard™, a better version of Hypercard. Ashton-Tate published a word processor called Fullwrite Professional™, which boasted features that looked suspiciously like linking tools.

And the race was on in the domain of the IBM PC. A company called Brightbill-Roberts, well known for useful business graphics software, set in motion the development of a product called Hyperpad™. Boasting many of the attractive features of Apple's Hypercard, it sought to resolve the sticky problem of graphics for the manifold types of PC graphics adapters (CGA, Hercules, EGA, VGA, and others) by ignoring the problem altogether. Hyperpad could only manage to handle character-oriented displays, thus leaving no room for anything more than rows and columns of computer characters.

Paul Allen, one of the founders of Microsoft, started a company called Asymetrix, which set in development a powerful system for Multimedia programming within the context of the Microsoft® Windows system. This likely made his former partner Bill Gates happy but promised to frustrate the millions of PC owners whose machines were not powerful enough to properly sustain a Windows-based application.

And finally, in the great American tradition of go-it-alone software development, Larry Kheriaty embarked upon the work that would yield IBM LinkWay. It boasted all of the elements Bush, Englebart, Nelson, and a host of followers had imagined. Object oriented programming, accessibility to normal folks, interactive graphics and text, and the rest of the inventory of features necessary to enable hypermedia on the PC.

INDEX